SPORTS WRITER'S EYE

Also by David Miller

Father of Football (Biography of Matt Busby)
World Cup 1970
World Cup 1974
The Argentina Story 1978
Running Free (with Sebastian Coe)
Cup Magic
The World to Play For (with Trevor Francis)
Sebastian Coe – Coming Back
England's Last Glory
Seoul '88

DAVID MILLER

SPORTS WRITER'S EYE

AN ANTHOLOGY

Macdonald
Queen Anne Press

A *Queen Anne Press* Book

© David Miller 1989

First published in Great Britain in 1989 by
Queen Anne Press, a division of
Macdonald & Co (Publishers) Ltd
66-73 Shoe Lane
London EC4P 4AB

A member of Maxwell Pergamon Publishing Corporation plc

British Library Cataloguing in Publication Data
Miller, David, *1935 Mar 1*
  Sportswriter's eye : an anthology.
  1. Sports
  I. Title
  796

ISBN 0–356–17652–5

Photoset in North Wales by
Derek Doyle & Associates, Mold, Clwyd
Printed and bound in Great Britain by
BPCC Hazell Books Ltd, Aylesbury, Bucks.

CONTENTS

FOREWORD

The world of journalism is a somewhat special one. The world of sport is equally as special. To be endowed with the ability to unite both of them in harmony for over 30 years is rare, and to do so with such talent, humour and love is exceptional.

Having been accompanied by David Miller on several of my extended visits to National Olympic Committees throughout the world, I am well aware of his devotion to our ideals and his knowledge and understanding of the many problems encountered in sport, whether on a national or international basis.

As I am sure all those who peruse this book will realise, the qualities required in order to attain such a level of sports journalism are many indeed. In re-reading all these articles, I found myself sometimes surprised at certain remarks. However, after reflection and having put all the facts in perspective, I must say that David's immediate perception was generally the correct one, and this is not in the least surprising.

It is therefore both an honour and pleasure for me to write this foreword, which gives me the opportunity to express my warmest thanks and appreciation for the excellent service which David Miller has given to the Olympic Movement over recent years.

I wish him every success in his future endeavours which we shall all eagerly await to read.

Juan Antonio Samaranch
President
International Olympic Committee

INTRODUCTION

Journalism and writing have run, or ambled, on either side of my family over parts of two centuries. So too, in recent generations, has a degree of indolence, with a consequent decline of fortunes, so it could be said I was destined for Fleet Street; though arriving there in 1956 was accidental.

My father was, before the Second World War, an actor; mostly in repertory around the country from Exeter to Aberdeen, which is how my mother came to deliver me in Hereford. He was for a while with the Sybil Thorndyke/Lewis Casson company, understudying three parts in the original production of *St Joan*. Illness and financial insecurity diverted him into the hotel business, in which, at a country hotel in the Isle of Wight, he was a facsimile of Basil Fawlty: emotional, irascible, touchingly vain, and cordially disapproving of his guests, his staff and, some of the time, his family. My mother displayed enduring patience with him. In later life my father, I suspect, felt unfulfilled and overshadowed by contemporaries and friends such as Bernard Lee. William Miller, his father, was an actor/manager/musician/writer of the melodramatic tradition of the 19th century, apt to pursue his errant children with the carving knife. He wrote the libretto for Stephen Philpott's opera *Dante and Beatrice*, performed early this century in Manchester and New York by the Carl Rosa Opera Company.

My mother, who in a childhood rage with the preferred older brother had once eaten his stamp collection in vengeance, was endearingly dotty and modestly talented: part-musician, -artist, -linguist, -gardener, wildlife supporter. She was the slightly disorientated child, seeking adult fulfilment, of kind but self-indulgent parents living on the

1

remnants of inherited estate and believing the sun would never set.

Three generations before, her great-grandfathers were what might loosely be termed the first newspaper barons, though a less conspicuous breed than those of this century. Joseph Harrop (1728–1803) had founded, in 1752, the midweek *Manchester Mercury*, oldest of the northern papers and in the Tory interest. His son, James, was deputy postmaster of Manchester when a penny postage was established in 1793, and was removed from office when Fox and the Whigs came to power in 1806. Two years earlier, James had founded the *British Volunteer*, appealing to patriotic enthusiasm during the threatened invasion by Napoleon. The *Volunteer* never had the success of the *Mercury*, and by the 1820s was devoting inordinate space to detailed coverage of public executions: forerunner of today's voyeuristic tabloids.

The *Mercury* represented liberal Toryism of Lancashire. The *Manchester Guardian*, published on Saturday, supported the Whig Reformists, with whom the Liberals had much common ground. James Harrop died in 1823 and his son, John, lacking enthusiasm and initiative, and content to rest on investments, decided to sell. In 1825, the *Guardian* proprietors stepped in, eagerly purchasing Harrop's newspapers. The *Mercury* became, in effect, a Tuesday edition of the *Guardian*, on Manchester's busiest day of business at the exchange, and the *Volunteer*, taking 80 per cent of its readership with it, merged with Saturday's *Guardian*, its name for some years being a secondary part of the title. Thereafter, journalism in the family languished, until a great-uncle, to some social disapproval, made a name for himself at the turn of the century writing in America.

My father's inadvertent contribution to my professional life was his devotion in my youth to my aptitude for games. 'They will never make you your living,' he would insist later. He spent hours teaching me to trap, and to kick with both feet, with a size-three football, which he would carefully inflate, lace and, when necessary, repair; protecting the stitches, as with my cumbersome boots, with liberal applications of

2

dubbin. We spent further hours practising cricket, and in a Hampshire second-hand shop he found me nets for bowling on our 20-yard lawn. During the war, in which he predominantly served as a radar operator on St Alban's Head, he would bicycle and hitch-hike for half a day to see me play in under-11 matches at my preparatory school: an unstated emotional link between us that was in other spheres absent. A benevolent aunt paid the fees for me to attend Charterhouse. An unsurpassable education at this most beautiful of schools, set on a wooded sandstone promontory in Surrey, created for my father, who used to carry his goalposts four miles to play on Hampstead Heath and had left elementary school at 15, an imagined cultural gulf which I was never really able to dispel on his behalf.

The emotional sporting affinity with him deepened when, for two years, I played in the Cambridge side at Wembley, enjoying victories over Oxford teams which included, in the first year, Frank Bough, a stoic centre-half. Ancient Peterhouse, with punting on the Cam along the tranquil, dreamlike Backs, falling in love beneath the willows, dancing to Chris Barber, writing for *Varsity*, the undergraduate newspaper with a 7,000 weekly circulation, and for the Footlights, playing tennis with my senior tutor on perfect lawns, croquet in the Fellows' garden, interminable coffee mornings along King's Parade, and too little study for my Natural Science Tripos, these were a continuation of the Charterhouse idyll.

Switching intention first from medicine, then from teaching chemistry, I found myself in 1956 in need of summer vacation work to pay outstanding bills. A sudden vacancy, compiling the daily cricket scoreboard, occurred at *The Times*, and into it I leaped. Eighteen guineas a week! It was a king's ransom: a trainee schoolmaster then earned £500 a year. Thankfully, the Faculty of Philosophy of Science had taught me to think and the Faculty of Zoology to write reasonably concisely, more so for journalism than would have an Eng. Lit. Tripos. I might never be a Paul Gallico, but hopefully I could spot the wood among the trees.

During that summer, the retirement of O.L. 'Ginger' Owen

3

as rugby correspondent and the promotion of Uel Titley from the desk created a full-time sub editor's vacancy, which John Hennessy, the sports editor, allowed me to fill. There I was, amid the endless Victorian corridors of old Printing House Square, with its coke fires and waitress afternoon tea service on a tray, following in the wake of Bernard Darwin and Beau Vincent. For over three years I handled the esteemed words of such men as Peter Ryde, whose elegance established my love of golf, John Woodcock, a Betjeman among cricket correspondents, gracious Richard Hill on tennis, my then young contemporary Neil Allen on boxing and athletics, the inimitable Geoffrey Green on football.

It was the heritage from these men, in particular the lyricism of Green, who had played for the legendary Corinthians, which established the ineradicable conviction that however great the players, the game was always greater. My own experiences, at Charterhouse and then Cambridge, playing with and being among famous internationals in many sports, had created a breadth of interest. Playing for Pegasus, that echo of the Corinthians, which briefly flourished in the 1950s with a melody that caught public imagination, a pursuit of excellence which carried a feeling of crusade however humble the occasional circumstances, gave one a belief that achievement need not belong only to the winner.

An additional privilege was to experience or come under the influence during my youth of coaches imbued with the spirit of excellence *and* sportsmanship: Tony Wreford-Brown, Bill Nicholson, Arthur Rowe and Joe Mercer in football; George Geary in cricket; Nazrullah Khan in squash; Nigel Gibbs in rugby; Tommy Garnett in hockey; Alan Malcolm in athletics; Wilfred Noyce in climbing.

Impatient to write more than just at weekends, I reluctantly departed in 1959 for the *Daily Telegraph* and an undefined general role, thanks to the kind intervention of E.W. Swanton and Michael Melford. Some forthright comments on the threatened players' strike, over their demand for abolition of the maximum wage (£20), earned me the chance to be, additionally, the soccer correspondent in 1961 of the newly launched *Sunday Telegraph*: City correspondent, Nigel

Lawson. With my wife's ungrudging and constant support, I regularly had to subsidise the impecunious *S.T.* on travelling to see essential overseas football. Though parsimonious, the *Telegraph*s taught me punctuality, and to be able to file from anywhere on anything, instantaneously without writing, and to an exact length, when such was necessary: as with the arrest of Bobby Moore in Bogota in 1970. The *Telegraph*s had all the comfortable predictability, for writers and readers, of Sunday lunch.

An up-market editorial change proposed by Jocelyn Stevens at the *Daily Express* in 1973 brought the opportunity to replace the retiring Desmond Hackett, doyen of popular newspaper sportswriters; and the chance to prove to sceptical colleagues that the popular columns, the world of the 'real' pro, were penetrable by an allegedly pedestrian up-market man. For 10 years I opened the batting for the back page of the *Express* and made, I like to feel, a respectable score. The wicket, however, was getting rough: the *Express*, losing circulation, moved down-market in a panic, and in 1982 I discussed with Norman Fox, during the World Cup in Spain, a return to *The Times*. When he became sports editor, he had the approval of Charles Douglas Home, the late editor, to appoint for the first time a general sports columnist. The last six years have been the busiest and most fulfilling of my time in journalism.

Often I am asked which of the twenty or more sports about which I write is the most exciting. The answer is that they are all different. Nothing can have the slowly mounting drama of a five-day Test Match, occasionally a veritable symphonic poem. No sport imposes the isolation upon a player as does golf, where the duel is less between opponents than between the player and the course and his own ball; so that Lyle's second shot out of a bunker at the last hole of the 1988 US Masters at Augusta was without parallel. No sport demands the bravery of the Alpine downhill, in which Klammer's 1976 gold medal stands supreme.

No sport has me so on edge as a heavyweight title fight, not knowing whether Bruno will last 12 rounds or 12 seconds against Tyson. No game can turn, seemingly so critically, so often as tennis, not merely with each game but on successive points. No game has that synthesis of war, chess and ballet which is football. No game has such a drawn-out crescendo in a single moment of action as the rugby try when run from seventy yards out. Few sports generate the comradeship between competitors as do the modern pentathlon and the decathlon.

Supreme, I think, is the middle-distance track event. There is an almost frightening intensity when the eight or nine starters go to the line for the final of the Olympic 800 or 1,500 metres: knowing that in the next one and a half minutes, or three and a half, runners who have spent four years of lonely training in preparation for this one race have now only to lose concentration for a split second, to lose touch with an opponent for a couple of strides, and their career and maybe their life will be radically changed. This is, in my opinion, the most compact demand on physical, mental and tactical ability in the whole of sport.

None of the past 32 years' pleasure, and unrelenting hard work and inconvenience would have been possible without the exceptional loyalty, energy and tolerance of Marita, my wife. Neither of us would recommend anyone but a confirmed bachelor to become a travelling journalist. The demands are absurd. Journalism destroys marriages wholesale, and too often individuals also. It is as intoxicating, and dangerous, as alcohol, with which it often goes hand in hand. Somehow, we have managed to survive the insensitivity of deadline demands.

A distillation of my views on the role of the sports journalist is contained in the following article, published two years ago by *Olympic Message*:

The vast increase in television coverage of the major sporting events has radically changed the role of the sports journalist working for the written Press. Back in the old pre-television days, which were just ending when I first came into journalism, the first responsibility of the correspondent was to tell the reader what had happened; to give the facts, the result, an impression of the mood of the event. Indeed, the first book to which I ever contributed, as a member of the staff of the *Daily Telegraph*, was titled 'I was There'. What distinguished the sports correspondent was first and foremost the privilege of being present, not to mention being paid for it, at events which were the envy of a million spectators denied the chance by the obstacles of their own work and the distance needed to travel.

Television altered all that. The camera's eye made everybody an armchair spectator. Great sporting occasions, such as the Olympic Games and the World Cup in football, were transmitted instantly to a worldwide audience, so that newspaper readers already knew, from the previous evening, what was the result of the 1,500 metres or the World Cup final. Moreover, they had probably seen the winning goals two or three times, and in terms of the facts had more immediately available information than the journalist on the spot.

This has had two influences upon the sportswriter. Those working for the so-called serious newspapers are obliged to concentrate more upon analysis and interpretation; to write profiles and interviews which will convey the character and motivations of the performer, to keep track of the many forces, political, commercial and geographical, which more and more are exerting a force on prominent sports. Those journalists working for the tabloid papers, which too often carry the tag of 'scandal-sheets', are obliged, often against their better instincts, to look for gossip, criticism of one player by another, and any kind of sensation which will enhance circulation. Though such writers cannot be excused for the damage which they can inflict on individuals and organisations, they are in part the victims of the change imposed upon their operation by the inevitable success of television. They are looking for 'news' which has not already appeared on the small screen, because the reader of tabloid newspapers, which appeal to the less serious section of the population, is less interested in the longer, erudite feature.

Thus 'news' is likely to become the 'quotes' from the losing team manager, or the runner who was tripped, or the boxer who believes the judges were biased; and the *emphasis* is placed upon this 'news'. The newspapers get into an unfortunate area in which they are in part helping to create news. It is possible to run such a 'news' story for three days, without too much difficulty: the first day, the accusation or the rumour; the second day, the denial by the other party; the third day, the reaction of the governing body. A dull week can, I regretfully admit, quite easily be filled by the so-called popular Press. I know, because for 10 years I worked for the *Daily Express*, which had formerly been an outstanding mass circulation daily with a worldwide reputation. It was gradually sucked down, from the late 1960s, into less serious attitudes by the rival pressures of both television and the declining standards of the papers with which it competed. In that period, the *Express* transferred from being a broadsheet to a tabloid, and in my time there I experienced as a senior correspondent the decline in respect from those players and officials with whom it was my duty to remain constantly in touch. The correspondent trying to make legitimate and constructive criticism of sporting affairs finds himself in some difficulty if his newspaper is itself open to criticism for the way in which it is treating sport. This was not wholly nor always true of the *Express*, but the drift in that direction had become detectable, so that it was in a no-man's land somewhere between the *Telegraph* and *The Sun*. In its greatest days, the *Express* had boasted one of the most powerful sportswriting teams in British journalism: Peter O'Sullevan on horse racing, Desmond Hackett on boxing, soccer and athletics, Crawford White on cricket, Ronnie Heager on golf, Frank Rostron on tennis, Pat Marshall on rugby. They told a great story. They were action-men in the front line, rather than essayists. Then along came television and took their story away from them. Their style and their function had become partially redundant.

Yet if television has stolen a time-march on the printed Press in the presentation of sport on the field, there is a development in sport which is entirely the product of the past 20 years or so, and the coverage of which is far better suited to the range of the newspaper correspondent than to television. This is in the area of 'background' surrounding the issues of drugs, politics and commerce which are now, regrettably, so important. It is on account of this that, in Britain, newspapers such as the *Daily Telegraph* and *The Times* have taken to appointing a 'sports news correspondent', with the responsibility to cover specifically those topics which are as likely to be on the front page as the sports page. As a writer, I am rather sad that this has become necessary, because my interest always centres on what is happening on the field rather than in the committee room. Yet it is significant that for the election of the host cities for the Olympic Games of 1992, my newspaper sent *two* correspondents to Lausanne, and not just because a British city, Birmingham, was a candidate. In the past five years with *The Times*, I must have spent a quarter of my time talking to officials and administrators rather than players: about amateurism/professionalism, boycotts, drug abuse, the Korean controversy between north and south, Solidarity support for the Third World, and so on.

One of the duties of the journalist, I believe, is to try to maintain, and to persuade others to maintain, the proper emphasis on sport. This is, most important of all, that it is a game, and is not a matter of life and death. Only when that view is predominant can the real purpose of sport flourish: friendship between peoples under the *pleasurable* challenge of competition. It is essential that however mortified the loser may be, however agonising the moment of failing to win, with all that time and effort of training and preparation seemingly wasted, he or she should be able to congratulate the winner, should be able to feel that a fine experience has been shared. It is a necessary truth of the greatest sporting events that the quality of the winner is established in part by the quality of the loser. It takes a minimum of two to make a game.

Personally, I would like to see the abolition of the national anthem and the use of national flags at Olympic medal ceremonies, because I believe that nationalism is one of the vices at the root of the Games. It would be naive to ignore the fact that the reason for the enthusiasm of many governments to support the sending of their national team to the Games, and for applying to be hosts for the Games, is not exclusively

9

the altruistic promotion of sport and youth. It is that sport provides the cheapest friendly form of national projection.

With all the forces at work on sport from the outside, it is the responsibility of the journalist, as a neutral party, to try to resist the manipulation of sport, if only by exposing those who attempt it. These may be greedy professional players, ambitious administrators, or sponsors who do not understand the nature and the history of the sport upon which they are riding. Sponsors can quickly come to believe that because they are supporting a sport they have somehow acquired the right to control it. The influence of the journalist must be exerted by persistently exposing such manipulation.

It is also a tendency common among administrators to think that they *own* a sport, a view they can take from a starting point of wishing to protect the sport, when in truth they are only the temporary trustees. It is for this reason that there should be a more ready collaboration between officials and Press than there sometimes is; the television and Press are the air which the sporting public breathes, the medium which generates the interest that makes sport the largest social movement of our time. And whereas television goes for the highlights, it is the written Press which daily provides the continuity of information, prediction, speculation and background that feeds our daily conversation.

However, we should beware as journalists of becoming too dependent on either officials or players for 'quotes', for helping us to form our views. It is imperative that, provided they come from a sound foundation, we should have views of our own, should have an independence of opinion and be beholden to no one. We all know the journalist who becomes a tame mouthpiece for a particular official or performer, and whose work then has no professional credibility.

One of the dangers for the journalist, of which I have found it increasingly necessary in recent years to be wary, is the comments made, for quotation, which are deliberately intended to serve the vested interest of the person making the comment. Less and less, I find, are officials speaking in the interest of sport itself, but of some particular policy or course in which they have a personal stake. Of this kind, I think,

10

football team managers are consistently the most subjective, and therefore the most suspect in their comments. Football trainers attempt, through use of the Press, to shape the thinking of the public for their own convenience, to disguise weaknesses in their own team, or to deny that a particular player was unfair. All these are traps in which the journalist can become an unwitting accomplice if he/she is not experienced and, especially, equipped with a good technical knowledge of the sport.

Even in an activity as innocent as sport, it can sometimes take courage to speak the truth, and one of the best examples I can give is of General Vladimir Stoytchev of Bulgaria, famous soldier and fighter for freedom in the last World War, notable former Olympic equestrian competitor and the oldest living member of the International Olympic Committee, from which he recently resigned. The General stated quite emphatically that the boycott of the Los Angeles Olympic Games was wrong, when his own country had been one of those to boycott. Likewise, Anita DeFrantz, one of the newest members of the IOC, had been a vociferous opponent of the boycott of 1980 by President Carter. It is to such people as these that the journalist should turn, to those who are prepared to speak in the interest of sport, rather than political or commercial motives.

In other words, democracy in sport lies as much in the hands of journalists as of those whose job it is to make decisions. It is from the attention, and pressure, of Press comment that such issues as the non-reinstatement of drug offenders will remain in the public eye. In giving this as an example, I am not being specifically critical of the IOC medical commission nor its chairman, Prince de Mérode, whose work in this field is diligent, but am suggesting that the various opinions on a difficult moral issue can be kept in useful circulation. It is, after all, the duty of all commissions, of all governing bodies, to remain open to all sources of informed and relevant opinion. Of course, the journalist concedes that decisions are the right of the elected officers, but it is the responsibility of the journalist to stimulate public discussion. To give another example: the International Ski

Federation has the authority to decide either way, but I believe many people would consider it now consistent for Stenmark of Sweden to be readmitted to the Games, especially in the light of the decision by the IOC, taken unanimously in Istanbul, to admit professional tennis players to Seoul. But again, it is part of our democratic process that the skiing federation should be free, under the Olympic Charter, to make its own decision. It is the duty of the journalist to plead on behalf of all sides: of the individual, and of the organisation. In the perfect world, the journalist should be free of all prejudices, political, racial and also national, whether he/she is from Hong Kong, Nairobi or Quito.

Nationalism is a pitfall for many, even though the Press box should be as impartial as a jury box. Around the world I see many events which are marred by journalists who are no more than travelling supporters with typewriters. In my experience, the French and the Scandinavians are the most neutral in their spontaneous appreciation and applause of the achievements of foreign competitors. For me, the Los Angeles games were marred by the chauvinism of the Americans, many of whom, including their television commentators, were blind to any performer not wearing the Stars and Stripes. At the Press conference for Nawal El Moutawakel from Morocco, the winner of the women's 400 metres hurdles and the first ever African woman gold medallist in track and field, an American journalist complained about the translation of Nawal's answers from English into French and Arabic, as being 'an interruption'.

Television itself is both a servant and a danger to sport's democracy. The attitude taken by television is that because it has paid such huge fees for the broadcasting rights, it can call the tune, and take attitudes to suit its own convenience. I believe this is something which the Press should encourage the sports authorities to resist. There is more chance that the ethics of sport will be protected by the Press than by television. However, in professional tennis and golf, where tournaments are regularly closely tied in to television and sponsors, there is a practice by which favoured journalists are often invited to attend, on subsidised travelling. The risk is that the journalist will then become nothing more than a fellow-traveller, devoid of critical judgement regarding the status of the event. The journalist's critical independence is paramount.

How, then, can the journalist gain these qualities of judgement and independence? Such a question leaves aside the matter of being able to write cogently, colourfully and quickly, to a given length at a given time, sometimes within minutes of the finish of a race or match.

In the first place, it is helpful to have had some experience of competition at a reasonable level, by which I mean a respectable national club standard. It is only this which enables a writer to know, on many occasions, whether a performer is playing well or badly on account of the relative performance of the opposition. This particularly applies, of course, to ball games. To the uninformed, a technically poor match can seem to be brilliantly exciting. It may be, for the spectators, but it is still important to know what is the *level* of performance. It may seem, for instance, that a footballer has missed the chance of a goal from an easy position, yet it may well be that the player has shown brilliant anticipation to get there to be in a position to miss.

Secondly, the journalist has to be under no pressure from his editor or employer to produce a particular kind of story, other than to be accurate. The journalist needs to be free to respond to the moment, to his environment and the mood of the competition. He must not go there with predetermined judgement.

Thirdly, and I suppose this applies to almost any job in the world, it is necessary to gain experience of a variety of conditions, which may well mean the newspaper being able to afford to send the correspondent to foreign events. It is only possible fully to judge tennis players if you have seen them play on all surfaces. And to gain experience takes time, so that it is likely that a sports journalist cannot write with substantial authority and confidence before the age of 40.

Together with experience goes a knowledge of history, and the ability to be able to refer to past milestones, old styles and fashions, former habits and famous personalities. It seemed to me a contradiction when recently a British newspaper dispensed with the services of Danny Blanchflower, the captain of Spurs and Northern Ireland in the late 1950s and early 1960s, a player, and then a writer, of perception. The complaint was that he kept referring to the *past*. That can be overdone, but at the same time it can be a writer's greatest strength.

The last and yet the most important of all qualities, I suppose, is that the journalist must be *fair*. Whether he is or not will probably come from an amalgam of the former qualities I have mentioned. Certainly it is trying to be fair that has always given me the most concern, has caused me sometimes afterwards to lie awake at night. The journalist should not, of course, be afraid of hard work, of long hours, of irregular meals and a hundred inconveniences. In my opinion, however, writing fairly is more important than writing stylishly, though it is nice if one can achieve both. Just as the essence of sport is that it should be played fairly, the fundamental of sportswriting is the same. This means that it is difficult to be close friends with either performers or officials, because occasionally it will be necessary to be critical in order to be fair to someone else, and then a friend can feel betrayed. The journalist must not show partiality. It is, I must admit, much easier to be a supporter and enjoy a wholesome bias!

PART 1

THE TIMES
1956–1959

The Manchester United team whose plane crashed at Munich in 1958 were both my contemporaries and my heroes. The exhilaration of their youth was a thing of beauty; they were like no team I have seen before or since. Their potential lay in the future, and died with them. To watch them play was to be transported with delight.

UNITED YOUTH TRIUMPHANT

The Times, September 1956

MANCHESTER UNITED 2   MANCHESTER CITY 0

Beneath a sunny sky and before 53,000 ardent Lancastrians, Manchester United, League champions, beat Manchester City, FA Cup holders, at Old Trafford on Saturday. Many were pleased; as many were disappointed, for when after half an hour the United players began to display a maturity that belied their age, there was only one possible result.

If, before the daring bright scarlet of United had been hurled against the ethereal blue of City, one had asked anyone seeing his first football match on which team he would lay his stakes, it is a fair guess that United would have caught his eye. Quite simply United looked the better team.

They have everything: a bewildering profusion of talent, but, supremely, a surging irrepressible youth. Such a team of virile Apollos as now stand astride the English football stage will take some beating, and the man who currently moulds their fortune must indeed be happy at what he sees.

City moved with a lost understanding, which was saddening to those who had seen their flowing precision at Wembley last May, but against men like Edwards, Colman, Byrne, and the rest, even the guile of Revie crumbled. Edwards truly is a young giant. He covered all the field in defence, dominating everyone in the air. Some smacking 30-yard passes whistled out to Pegg, and once with a prodigious nod he turned the ball back to Wood from outside the penalty area. Yet for all his size he can stroke the most delicate pass even when going at full tilt. For much of the game he kept a tight grip on Spurdle, leaving Byrne free to watch the roving McAdams, who was playing the role of Johnston.

Thus with Colman harrying the elusive Revie like a terrier and Foulkes forcefully dealing with Dyson and Clark, City offered little penetration. Just once the elegant Barnes, moving forward, found Revie on the edge of the penalty area. Revie pushed the ball back to Dyson on the turn, neatly dragged the return past Jones, saw his drive beat Wood, hit the post and bounce temptingly in the air, but his header was inches wide. Otherwise, Revie was usually getting City out of a hole in defence, while Dyson and Clark seemed too unrobust to enforce any advantage they achieved. Not so the United forwards. The speed of Pegg frequently unhinged Leivers, or left Ewing tackling thin air, while tiny effervescent Berry gave Hannaway a dreadful time, flaunting the ball before his very nose yet never letting him have more than a scent. The directness of these two paved the way for Viollet and Taylor.

After 35 minutes Pegg beat Leivers all ways, and his long, floating centre found Berry almost on the by-line. Berry pirouetted, something that was probably a City defender went thundering by, and his neat back pass was whacked home by Wheelan past a helpless Savage. Otherwise, Savage gave a most competent display, except once when he was caught out of goal like a park attendant in the undignified process of chasing his own hat. When normally in possession he rolled the ball, bowls fashion, with great accuracy to the waiting Barnes or Paul.

In the second half Pegg and Berry continued to tantalise City, and soon Wheelan waltzed through a ruck of groping defenders only to hit the upright. After 25 minutes came a classic movement. Colman found Edwards with a square pass. The latter's exasperating chip went to Pegg, back to Colman, and there was Taylor racing through to pull the ball back; but Berry's shot went nowhere. The second goal followed a quick free kick by Berry. Viollet picked up a long pass, centred, and Wheelan calmly volleyed home. Thereafter, United became contemptuous and only poor finishing on their part saved the face of City.

MANCHESTER UNITED: Wood; Foulkes, Byrne; Colman, Jones, Edwards; Berry, Wheelan, Taylor, Viollet, Pegg.
MANCHESTER CITY: Savage; Leivers, Hannaway; Barnes, Ewing, Paul; Spurdle, McAdams, Revie, Dyson, Clark.

Oh, my Barlow and my Allen of long ago. What days they were, when six goals, as in this FA Cup tie, were common. Here were the embers of the 1954 winners, the embryo of the 1959 winners: and half a dozen managers of the future.

A MATCH TO REMEMBER
The Times, January 1958
WEST BROMWICH ALBION 3   NOTTINGHAM FOREST 3

The largest crowd of the day, 58,100, was amply rewarded at The Hawthorns where Nottingham Forest held West Bromwich to a draw in as fine a match as one could wish to see. A slimy, treacherous surface added to the excitement, making every defensive tackle a thing of doubt. Irretrievable errors were always just around the corner, yet surprisingly few came; both teams chanced their arm, got away with it, and proceeded to play some truly vintage football.

This surely was a match long to be remembered by those who saw it. The first half had hummed along with never a dull moment – swift, artistic sparring, but no decisive blow landed. Tension grew as for 10 minutes in the second half there remained no indication of what, in time, all the huge crowd felt must come. Then Imlach, without warning, sparked the powder, and six goals in 10 minutes sent the packed terraces almost delirious. The middle four fell so fast, three of them Albion's in as many minutes, that the pen could scarce keep apace. Two goals were stamped with the individuality that will keep their memory fresh for many seasons.

All this would seem to deny Forest just praise for their achievement, but on Saturday Albion survived two blows which might have daunted others. In the second minute Allen came out of a tackle limping, to become only an occasional decoy down the wings. The other blow befell Barlow, but of that later. Allen may be a centre-forward of distinction, but Albion's other four forwards continued to play as if nothing had happened. In fact, Allen's wandering midfield role was absorbed by Barlow and Setters at wing-half, Robson and Kevan supplying the central thrust as usual.

It was soon evident that Howe was not going to remain too dignified against the tricky Imlach. When the latter left Setters, Howe, and then Kennedy slithering on their hitherto clean white shorts, Baily's shot from the back pass skimmed the bar. Immediately a searing drive by Kevan was wide at the other end.

Baily, whose shining top and shuffling gait induce a slightly disrespectful affection, was Forest's general, and the hub of some delightful passing during this half. Not only this, there were some spinning, flicked headers judged to an inch; and an unbelievable chip to Imlach over Robson and Setters, where the ball climbed vertically eight feet, ran along an invisible roof and dropped at its destination the other side. It was almost unfair.

Meanwhile, Griffin and Horobin of Albion were proving a

balanced and penetrative pair of wings, creating a host of openings for Robson and Kevan. On good English mud Kevan is a thundering good English inside-forward. Once he got under way it took a wall to stop him, and Forest had not one handy. When Kevan put his head down things were always likely to happen.

So by near misses, a number of close saves by Thomson, and many drawn breaths, the match arrived at the 14th minute of the second half, when Howe missed a tackle on Baily. The ball ran to Imlach, and with Albion vainly thinking him to be offside he coolly beat Sanders. As though 50,000 sergeant majors were breathing down their necks, West Bromwich replied with a thrilling onslaught. Barlow surged down the right, on and on into the penalty area; a tiny flip sideways and Robson drove low into the net. Kevan, imperiously brushing by two men, shot from far out on the left and saw, as he fell, the ball creep inside the right-hand post.

Not content, Horobin, somehow now on the right, wriggled along the by-line and presented Allen with number three. Yet Forest swept through from their third kick off in three minutes, Baily centred from the line, and Wilson had made it 2–3. Now came poor Barlow's sad moment. Imlach, with Sanders out of goal, shot blatantly wide. Barlow instinctively stuck out a hand, tried too late to withdraw it, and Wilson from the spot demanded another encounter on Wednesday.

WEST BROMWICH: Sanders; Howe, Williams; Setters, Kennedy, Barlow; Griffin, Robson, Allen, Kevan, Horobin.
NOTTINGHAM FOREST: Thomson; Whare, Thomas; Morley, McKinlay, Burkitt; Gray, Quigley, Wilson, Baily, Imlach.

Northern Ireland's World Cup adventures in Sweden were a marvellous romance. Peter Doherty's men played as though inspired, yet hardly had the price of the train fare to the next match. Injuries, and the brilliant French, sank them in the quarter-final.

BLANCHFLOWER GUIDES NORTHERN IRELAND HOME

The Times, June 1958

NORTHERN IRELAND 2   CZECHOSLOVAKIA 1

Malmo: In mounting tension and fading light, and with a meagre crowd cheering their every move towards the end, Northern Ireland beat Czechoslovakia in a play-off in group one of the World Cup and are in the quarter-final against France at Norkoepping. The winning goal was scored by McParland in the first half of extra time, and there were wild patriotic Irish scenes on the touchline at the final whistle. Czechoslovakia, having been outplayed for most of the second half, never gave up, but they lacked a general, and the guiding influence of Blanchflower, receiving every ounce of support around him, helped Ireland towards a fine victory.

Not only by their excellent football but by their courage, Ireland deserved to fight again on Thursday. Uprichard, early on, suffered the fate of Gregg with a badly sprained ankle, and later severely damaged his left hand. Peacock, in the second half, twisted a knee, and returned, still doggedly active, to the left wing with Cush at left-half. This leaves Ireland with a tricky injury list, though Gregg may be fit in time.

Czechoslovakia, at the start, looked the better side. They were yards faster in defence, their physique was superior and their heading was at all times domineering. But the lightning dashes of Feurizl, Borovicka and Molnar soon appeared mechanical. All the Czechs were forced into faulty passes and their shooting was far from accurate. Against this Ireland, with their inherent, indefatigable spirit, soon got the measure of things. Keith and McMichael once again were remarkably sure and calm at full-back, and Cunningham was seldom fooled by the wanderings of Feurizl.

Blanchflower, in the first half, could not have improved his performance by one jot. He seemed to be on both sides of the field at once on occasions, and the unerring path of his passes continued to draw admiration. Peacock, too, until his

20

injury, had endless energy, and this, with the exuberance of McIlroy and Cush, turned the scale against the Czechs, who could not find the same depth of reserve, in spite of a flawless performance by Masopust at left-half.

Ireland escaped narrowly at the start when Feurizl's shot sped by a post from Dvorak's square pass. After 14 minutes Czechoslovakia scored when Feurizl and Cunningham went for a high ball in the penalty area, missed, and Zikan nipped in to nod past the handicapped Uprichard. Masopust, in model fashion, made the most of Ireland's early errors with cunning distribution, but a near miss from an indirect free kick gave the Irish heart. A sinuous dribble by McIlroy was only just foiled, and a move including five players ended with Dolejsi fisting out McParland's header. McParland, who has scored all but one of Ireland's goals, equalised almost on half time after three furious shots by Cush had been blocked and the ball went loose.

The second half was mostly Ireland's, but they could not press home their advantage. Bingham headed on to the crossbar, and Zikan at the other end missed one gaping chance. So came extra time. After eight minutes Blanchflower took a free kick which curled to the far post, watched by the Czechs, and McParland calmly did the rest. Bubernik was inexplicably sent off by the referee, and any hope Czechoslovakia had was gone.

NORTHERN IRELAND: Uprichard; Keith, McMichael; Blanchflower, Cunningham, Peacock; Bingham, Cush, Scott, McIlroy, McParland.
CZECHOSLOVAKIA: Dolejsi; Mraz, Novak; Bubernik, Popluhar, Masopust; Dvorak, Molnar, Feurizl, Borovicka, Zikan.

PART 2

DAILY TELEGRAPH
and SUNDAY TELEGRAPH
1959–1973

What would Bobby Robson, England's manager of 1988, give for a team that in nine matches in one season scored 45 goals? Yet then, as now, foundered in the World Cup.

MASTERLY DISPLAY BY FORWARDS
BOOSTS WORLD CUP HOPES
Sunday Telegraph, April 1961
ENGLAND 9   SCOTLAND 3

How to be truthful, but not exaggerate? How to speculate on the future, while keeping the present in perspective? It is almost impossible, after a fabulous afternoon in this sun-strewn stadium. England sauntered, serenely confident, through the first half, reducing Scotland to relative, almost embarrassing incompetence, though all the while Scotland kept their chin up. Then two goals, immediately after half time, gave the game a new face, and with the Scottish forwards darting in and out of an uncertain defence, it seemed, even with the score 4-2, that England were not secure. Then in one of the most rip-roaring sprees imaginable, England proceeded to bang in five goals in 10 minutes.

The highest score in a home international this century speaks for itself. What made Scotland collapse as they did, after being in with a chance, is impossible to say. Not since the Hungarians has Wembley seen such majestic, opportunist and unanswerable attack as shown by all five England forwards, bringing their total to an incredible 32 goals in five matches.

At times it seemed there were 20 white shirts scything their way through the reeling Scottish ranks. Yet they were only five: Douglas, Greaves, Smith, Haynes and Charlton. If only they can recapture the wizardy over the next 14 months, England could once again lead the world. Now for Mexico here on 10 May, and then on to Portugal. It would be so easy, one's pen shaking, uncertain which moments, which superlatives to pull out, not to keep proportions – difficult not to make England a certainty for Chile, let alone Lisbon.

Poor Scotland! They will best remember that quarter of an hour after half time, and stick to this side for their World Cup matches with Eire and Czechoslovakia next month. They cannot now question their need of Law, of Mackay, Wilson and McLeod. It was, I think, fate that they should have been the chopping blocks, not helped by the inexperience of four new caps, and Haffey's erratic goalkeeping. I wonder what Brown, so agile for Spurs and despondent at being ignored once more, would have made of this avalanche? As I expected, too, the full-backs, Caldow and Shearer, buckled in the final reckoning.

Picking up where they left off in November, poised and precise, England in no time had the match in hand. The ball sped from man to man instinctively. Anticipation of each other seemed second nature – as did their successful 4–2–4 formation, so unwisely discarded for the Inter-League match. Haynes was always free of Mackay, by 10 yards or more. Mackay seemed almost content to let him have his head. Yet here also was Greaves, slipping into Haynes' constructive web, playing his part on the assembly line, but up to finish too. Haynes' wandering virtually cut Charlton out of the game on the wing, but always Charlton was searching inside, making himself useful, with many subtle flicks and chips. Smith was helped by the yielding turf partly controlling the ball, while

Douglas was once again the nimble little man we saw against Russia just over two years ago.

With the ubiquitous Law, Mackay was Scotland's attacking inspiration, though they were able to take advantage of the space provided by Flowers playing his withdrawn role. Quinn seemed inadequate, and once again one wonders what Scotland might have done with White there to link with Mackay, as at White Hart Lane.

More than anything, there was the genius of Greaves. He must not be lost to our national team. His composure is uncanny, his feet lick round the ball like a serpent's tongue, he seems to have eyes at the back of his head, and his judgement of half a chance is almost unfailing. McCann could make little of him. So, with Haynes outshining Law as a midfield general, there was really only one answer.

There had been a dramatic start, Springett missing Mackay's cross after only 30 seconds, but Wilson fell and failed to take advantage. After nine minutes, Greaves put Smith away down the wing, and Robson raced up to crash home the pass back from the line. Law then had Flowers worried for a time, but in the 20th minute an incomparable pass from Haynes carved Scotland apart, and Greaves curved in from the left to lob over the advancing Haffey, who might have got there sooner.

With 25 minutes gone, England were at their best, their passes clicking home with the certainty of a cobbler putting in his nails. Soon it was 3-0, Haynes opening the way and Greaves punishing Haffey's error.

Three minutes after the interval Mackay shot in a free kick from the edge of the area, and quickly Wilson headed home McLeod's corner, Springett at fault. But a saucy free kick by Greaves, with Scotland still preparing a wall, gave Douglas the fourth. Now England took control again, and, with 17 minutes to go, Smith began the landslide after Greaves had juggled the opening. Quinn made it 5-3, but two imperious shots by Haynes, a lazy, insolent solo by Greaves, and Smith's second came bubbling up like champagne.

24

ENGLAND: Springett (Sheffield Wed.), Armfield (Blackpool), McNeil (Middlesbrough); Robson (West Bromwich), Swan (Sheffield Wed.), Flowers (Wolves); Douglas (Blackburn), Greaves (Chelsea), Smith (Spurs), Haynes (Fulham), Charlton (Manchester Utd.).
SCOTLAND: Haffey (Celtic); Shearer, Caldow (Rangers); Mackay (Spurs), McNeil (Celtic), McCann (Motherwell); McLeod (Hibs), Law (Manchester C.), St John (Liverpool), Quinn (Motherwell), Wilson (Rangers).

A World Cup qualifying tie in Lisbon, and Jimmy Greaves, a young goalscorer without contemporary equal, is being drawn towards a lucrative career with Milan.

GREAVES AT THE CROSSROADS
Sunday Telegraph, May 1961

Estoril: The Atlantic shimmers beneath an unrelenting sun. Like far-off guns the breakers pound on the golden sands, while prostrate pink and mahogany bodies glisten in the heat and the salt. In the shade of this hotel veranda Jimmy Greaves, soccer's ace marksman, ponders the relative values of life at home and in Italy, if this is not already too late. And ahead of the England team lies a test which will prove indisputably whether or not they have flattered only to deceive.

Tomorrow, in the parched heat of the afternoon, England play the first of their World Cup qualifying ties with Portugal; on Wednesday, a friendly with Italy in Rome; on Saturday, against Austria in Vienna ... three matches in seven days, representing the concentrated effort in unaccustomed surroundings that would be required if they qualify for Chile. By the end of the week, too, Greaves thinks he will know, he tells me, whether the Milan adventure is on or off.

Greaves is an integral, essential part of England's sudden surge back to near-eminence. This shy young man,

25

sometimes misrepresented, just happens to be in the vanguard of a new movement. What he does will influence those who follow. When Greaves signed the option for Milan six months ago, there was a maximum wage in England. Now there isn't, and Chelsea's chairman Joe Mears has suggested terms which might make it worthwhile his remaining at home. The consideration uppermost in Greaves' mind is definitely not solely financial, but the optimum benefit for his young family. Last year he tragically lost one of his two young babies. Now happily another is on the way. With the world at his feet it is hard to know which way to spin.

Because of his renewed uncertainty, Greaves hopes that he is not committed to Milan, just in case … His advisers – he left me to guess who – are sorting it out. But, he says, he won't go unless free to play for England. If the Italians wish to continue to attract our best players, it would seem in their own interests to be as magnanimous as possible in releasing them for all our international matches. World Cup ties alone are not enough. A team must prepare. This is an increasingly international problem which must be resolved.

Meanwhile, our immediate hurdle is Portugal, or more exactly eight of the Benfica Club which plays Barcelona in the European Cup final at Berne on Wednesday week, plus three others. At first sight this would appear to be no problem for an international side which has scored 40 goals in six matches.

When conditions are unfavourable and a team believes they may be prevented from doing their best before they start, it is then that character and personality count. England have three players, at least, who might waver, as happened on the first South American tour in 1959 and in Belgrade the year before. Our 4–2–4 formation is necessarily vulnerable to fatigue. It relies on the midfield mobility of Haynes and Robson, and the incessant fluid thrust of the four forwards. It is not our style to slow things down. Thus, if the attack falters, immediately the defence is overburdened. The rhythm misfired in a 40-minute spell yesterday afternoon against Burnley, who are out here on tour.

My taxi driver from the airport – flashing gold teeth, sunken southern eyes, and a Vauxhall, his great joy, badly needing a rebore – stopped off on the way proudly to show me the stadium. It is one of the most beautiful in the world, a glittering white marble palace open along one side, perfect Cumberland turf and filled with that delicate, sweet-dry Mediterranean air. Two hundred and fifty thousand from Portugal and Spain wanted to see the match. A third of them can get in. The heat bounced up off the terraces and hit me, but the crowd should reduce the heat reflection which the team experienced yesterday; though it finished the under-23 side in Tel Aviv last May.

Portugal also have their worries. What effort will players getting £4,000 each for the European final put into this match, for a paltry £25? 'Team spirit' in this instance could induce the wrong reaction.

The obvious forecast is that England could and should win comfortably, but that the longer they take to score at the start, the harder it will become. If it is still level at half time they might well lose. Unless they do, and barring injuries, I don't expect many changes in Rome and Vienna. The experience is too valuable to the team, but Byrne or Hitchens might get their chance at centre-forward. What I would like almost as much as anything is for Charlton to shake off that dreamy, schoolboyish air and emerge as one of the world's most devastating modern wingers. For this is one of the most exciting positions. He has the potential, though it rarely escapes for more than a few minutes.

For all, not least Walter Winterbottom, these next few are anxious days. A team, a young team, that can put England back at the top is in the making. They know it, they are confident, relaxed. There is an easy discipline. Not for them the inviting local distractions including a sparse four-piece band, dapper in white flannels and I Zingari blazers, idly strumming at a beachside café.

Scotland, with five of their finest ever players – Baxter, Crerand, White, St John and Law – but with their regular wingers injured, lose a qualifying play-off to the eventual World Cup finalists.

SCOTLAND EIGHT MINUTES FROM CHILE
Daily Telegraph, November 1961
SCOTLAND 2   CZECHOSLOVAKIA 4

Brussels: Scotland are out of the World Cup, beaten in a gripping, fluctuating play-off in extra time at the Heysel stadium here this afternoon. Czechoslovakia were immaculate, stroking and pinpointing their passes, always measured and playing within themselves. Yet Scotland twice led, and were within eight minutes of qualifying for the finals in Chile next summer, only for the Czechs to equalise a second time and then masterfully dominate extra time.

Almost certainly the absence of Scotland's regular wingers, Scott and Wilson, cost them the match, for at every crucial period they had not the balance to sustain their attacks, thus overburdening the defence. Hard though Brand and Robertson tried, there was no penetration down the flanks. Even so, in the last seconds of full time Law all but snatched victory with a searing cross-shot that skimmed the angle of the posts with Schreif groping, and in the first minutes of extra time White hit the bar. Scotland fought to the last breath, but on the day just had not the class.

We saw a flawless performance of effortless skill and artistry from the Czech captain, the tiny, dark Masopust, at left-half. Four of Czechoslovakia's best players – Masopust, the left-wing of Jelinek and Kucera, and right half Pluskal – are from Dukla Prague, Spurs' European Cup quarter-final opponents. So, too, were all five of today's reserves, so Spurs will be up against it. Only now and then could Scotland's wing-halves Baxter and Crerand get to grips with the delicate accuracy of the Czech inside-forwards Kucera, the deep-lying

28

Kvasnak, and Scherer, while outside-left Jelinek's speed frequently left Hamilton gasping in the first half. Despite this, I think Scotland at full strength are probably better than England at present. It is cruel luck for them that injury has baulked them, as it did with Wales against Spain.

For half an hour it was rather scrappy, with Czechoslovakia in control in midfield, but finishing poorly. White, drifting into open spaces, kept Scotland's flame flickering, and when Hamilton, trying to clear, headed towards his own goal. Caldow headed off the line, and had again to clear off the line from Scherer. At the other end Popluhar headed away a seemingly certain goal by Law. Then in the 39th minute, St John, beating two men, was knocked for six by Popluhar; Baxter floated over the kick and St John raced in to head home.

Either side of half time Czechoslovakia pressed, Jelinek twice centering low across an open goal with no one there and Scherer blazing a free kick inches over the bar. Then Baxter and Law gave St John a priceless chance to make it 2-0, but he hesitated. Immediately Czechoslovakia threw everything into a furious onslaught which led to their first goal. In the space of two minutes Connachan saved from Kucera and twice from Jelinek. There were three corners in a row and right-back Hledik advanced to head in the third.

Within 40 seconds Scotland were ahead again, St John steering home Brand's free kick. Now it seemed Scotland were there. Grimly they hung on but with eight minutes left Scherer equalised. After White had hit the bar Czechoslovakia stunned their opponents with two goals in four minutes in the first half of extra time, first by outside right Pospichal, cutting in, and then by Kvasnak, from 25 yards.

Only 7,000 watched the game – in a stadium that can hold 70,000.

SCOTLAND: Connachan (Dunfermline); Hamilton (Dundee), Caldow (Rangers); Crerand (Celtic), Ure (Dundee), Baxter; Brand (Rangers), White (Spurs), St John (Liverpool), Law (Torino), Robertson (Dundee).
CZECHOSLOVAKIA: Schreif (Slovan Bratislava); Hledik (Sparta), Tichy (E.R. Bratislava); Pluskal (Dukla), Popluhar (Slovan Bratislava), Masopust (Dukla); Pospichal (Ostrava), Scherer (E.R. Bratislava), Kvasnak (Sparta), Kucera, Jelinek (Dukla).

> Benfica, the European champions, deny Spurs in the most tempestuous European tie I ever saw in Britain.

MAGNIFICENT SPURS GO DOWN FIGHTING
Daily Telegraph, April 1962
TOTTENHAM HOTSPUR 2   BENFICA 1
(Benfica win 4–3 on aggregate)

At the end of a surging drama, which left the nerves trembling, the throat dry, mighty Tottenham Hotspur, the pride of England, bowed out of the European Cup to the magnificent champions, Benfica, at White Hart Lane last night. They went down still fighting, and as few, surely, could have fought. Never, never was there such a match in England, or for that matter anywhere, said some who have followed this great international game round the globe longer than I. And I could well believe them.

Spurs, if any still need be told, had their chances – and what chances – to have won; or at least to have forced a play-off. Yet, like many heroes before them, the slings and arrows over two matches cut too deep into them, left too great a hill to climb. Luck is the greatest ace in football, and it was not dealt to Spurs.

Nor could a soul deny that Benfica were deserved winners.. Their technique, agility, anticipation were a match and more for Spurs; their hearts and lungs as big. The events tumbled over each other, so desperately, so swiftly, that the whole superlative 90 minutes left the mind spinning. In the final reckoning two sad defensive errors in Lisbon and three disputed, disallowed goals by Spurs, one last night, were handicaps that finally consumed them. But, oh, the agony as, with strength sapping, they hurled themselves again and again recklessly into attack over the last pulsating half hour. If only they could have drawn level, one sensed the whole majestic edifice of Benfica's skill would crumble; highly excitable, they might then have floundered.

Bill Nicholson, Spurs manager, put his normal side in the field, on the strength of Saturday's FA Cup victory. Who is to say he was wrong? I think, in retrospect, that had Mackay been in attack his dynamic pace and power would have perhaps changed the tide and brought Benfica to the point of panic.

This was a memorable match, and of all the great players on the field more than any it was Mackay's match. At times it seemed he would willingly have played single-handed. No one ever possessed more energy or resilience, more power to come and come again. No one will ever forget his solo efforts in the last quarter of an hour, bringing Pereira to his knees and, with mere seconds to go, hitting the bar.

As the sun dipped behind the stands, giving way to night, the 65,000 were there, wedged in shoulder to shoulder, half an hour before the start. Right to the start the singing accompanying the band, impromptu, was far greater than anything Wembley has known. And once Benfica were into their stride they made North London realise, deftly, mercilessly, just why they are champions. It was all one could do to keep up with the pace of events on paper: Norman, a nervy pass, letting Germano, the centre-half, clean through the middle, a corner; Greaves, an electrifying burst, bringing a crescendo of noise that not Hampden, nor Old Trafford, nor even White Hart Lane had heard before.

What a forward line is Benfica's! What wingers, Augusto and Simoes. These, and the dusky lithe Eusebio were a menace: Augusto, a great dribbler, extending the dapper Henry. Within minutes from one of these runs, Eusebio, with a raking, defiant swing, sent the ball leaping inches over Brown's bar.

Then, 15 minutes gone, and the first vital blow. Benfica went into a 4-1 lead. Aguas out to Simoes: then the centre-forward went like a greyhound for the return centre, skimming low to the far corner of the goal area, where he slid feet first past Henry to glide the ball in – a lightning, cruel blow. Yet almost immediately Spurs, buoyant, compelled by the dynamic roar, were at the other end and Mackay slashed the ball on to a post via a defender. Benfica's technique was superior, yet Spurs now had it all going for them.

In the 23rd minute, for the third time in the two matches, Spurs had a seemingly fine goal disallowed. One of White's perfect centres was volleyed on by Smith to Greaves, who scored from close in, though tightly marked. The referee gave a goal, but Benfica players dragged him over to an uncertain linesman who had momentarily flagged – no goal. Not outdone or disheartened, Spurs scored, to make it 4-2 seven minutes from half time. White, at the second attempt, chipped into the middle, Smith chested the ball down, and let fly an unstoppable shot.

On the stroke of half time Aguas hit the bar. Such was the impact of this great Portuguese side that while at the start they had been mildly booed, when they reappeared after the interval they were applauded on to the pitch. Within four minutes came the most dramatic turn possible – a penalty for Tottenham. White was fouled by Cruz, and in an overwhelming, awesome hush, Blanchflower, the Spurs captain, prepared to take perhaps the most important kick of his career. Coolly, he sidled up, sent Pereira the wrong way, and put the ball in the corner: 2-1 and 4-3 on aggregate.

It looked like another penalty for Spurs when Germano cupped it away to stop Medwin's header, but the referee waved play on. Growing desperately tired, Tottenham flung themselves again and again into attack, but the vital goal would not come.

SPURS: Brown; Baker, Henry; Blanchflower, Norman, Mackay; Medwin, White, Smith, Greaves, Jones.
BENFICA: Pereira; Joao, Angelo; Cavem, Germano, Cruz; Augusto, Eusebio, Aguas, Coluna, Simoes.

THE MASTERS ARE AS BIG AS THE OCCASION

Sunday Telegraph, May 1962
TOTTENHAM HOTSPUR 3   BURNLEY 1

It was little short of expectation – graceful, gripping, a final to savour. A fountain of skill flowed over the striped olive turf as Tottenham Hotspur and Burnley rose, if not to the summit of their artistry, at least to a pitch which far surpassed anything since 1948. Tottenham, as most expected, won for a variety of reasons – not the least that, being as big as the occasion from the moment they strolled from the tunnel, instead of overpowered by it, they were a goal up in three minutes. Many times before the end they were all but rattled as Burnley, raising their rhythm and pace above Tottenham's, swept down with the precision that had deserted them these last weeks. Yet for all their moments of dramatic, moral ascendancy, Burnley could only peg down the masters once, and then only for a fleeting, bare 30 seconds.

So now Spurs remain in the European stream, to try their hand next season in the Cup Winners' competition. I do not think Burnley can grudge Spurs the distinction, following last year's double, of becoming the only team besides Newcastle in 1951-52 to win the Cup at Wembley in successive years and the first southerners to win four times.

As last year, there was a touch of disappointment because, for all the brilliance midfield, there was not one goal to match all the tactical magic and profusion of technique. The blow to which Burnley finally bowed was a questionable penalty 10 minutes from the end. To Spurs' credit they spent the last half hour with only 10 effective men, Smith hobbling painfully after a jungle charge on Cummings. The writing was appearing on the wall before then, however.

The surprise really was, on the day, not that Tottenham triumphed, but that Burnley so superbly recovered their touch. Even then, without wanting to distort the perspective, none can deny that Burnley, in the unfortunate person of Cummings, contributed to Spurs' first two goals.

Spurs may have fallen short in the European Cup and the league championship because of the pressure of events, but a programme of 57 Cup and League matches in 37 weeks conditions them to thinking clearly in a crisis. The day was cool, Spurs cooler. Such was Spurs' immediate assumption of control that for an awful moment one feared a walk-over. We should have known Adamson, Footballer of the Year, and

McIlroy far better, for by the half hour they had nursed, encouraged and schemed Burnley into a position of sparkling equality.

Several facts earmarked Spurs as winners. Their contracting defence yielded nothing and once they gained possession their patterns out of defence, with Blanchflower consummately wise and shrewd, Mackay brazenly daring and ambitious, were a joy. Moreover, following a patter out of the penalty area, one long pass would then carry them over the halfway line, with Burnley's defence still half on the turn. Burnley, by contrast, were a trifle more deliberate.

Spurs, unusually, had only three forwards synchronising. Whether whole or damaged, Smith, a few headers and his goal apart, was the same ponderous fellow as at Hampden Park recently while Medwin was just not in the same key as the others. Add to this that Greaves, as always, was at times quiet, and it reveals the magnitude of Jones' glorious contribution. Who can blame Juventus for coveting this winger? His mazy runs may often be unproductive but this afternoon he weaved, glided, stopped, spurted, flicking his way past tackle after tackle until it seemed he could run no more.

Who else but little Greaves to strike home that first withering blow? Spurs had just survived a piece of McIlroy wizardry down the left. Brown snapped the ball high down the middle, Smith nodded on and there, as against Manchester United in the semi-final, was pint-sized Greaves streaking away. Cummings and Elder converged; Greaves slowed, fell, recovered, drew the ball back with him, sidled round Miller, who fell flat, and with Blacklaw unsighted, the ball cruised home.

Soon Burnley showed that they meant business after all, Pointer being blocked but Miller thumping the rebound from 23 yards and Brown, bent like a bow in mid-air, punching over. With the crowd hushed and pensive with expectancy, Burnley's shouting conveyed some uneasiness.

Burnley were struggling in midfield, McIlroy repeatedly being robbed as he found the paths of attack cut off, his spearheads smothered by Norman and Henry. In the 24th minute Spurs conjured the most perfect move of the match; from Brown in goal the ball sped through nine passes and as many angles, Smith finally thundering a shot past the post. Yet now, as White began to fade slightly, McIlroy and Adamson imperceptibly took charge. Pointer's mobility was the lever which began to prise Spurs' defence open – this and the controlled, scintillating dribbling of Connelly on the right wing. With half time in sight the tide was running Burnley's way.

In the 30th minute there was momentary fear of another injury as Mackay launched a typical, suicidal tackle on Angus and himself was left writhing on the ground. Gritting his teeth he was soon up again, fit and furious enough to slice the ball away from Robson two minutes later. Just on half time Burnley really throbbed, Spurs reeled. Miller wound up for a pulsating shot at the back of the penalty area, was smothered by Norman in the nick of time with timely anticipation, while from Pointer's flick Robson spun and shot past.

It was still the same afterwards and with five minutes gone Pointer, robbing Mackay, found Harris square. The winger beat Baker on the outside and smacked the ball low in to the goalmouth, where it hit Robson's shins as he ran in and flashed into the net before Brown could move.

With the cheers still dying on northern lips, Spurs were ahead again. From the kick off White floated away on the left, centred low and Cummings allowed Smith to stop the ball, turn laboriously and slam it past Blacklaw. Could Burnley survive such a setback? They could and with attacks firing in rapid succession at each end, it was they – Pointer, Connelly and Robson interchanging and anticipating the intentions of McIlroy and Adamson – who looked about to score. The goal never came.

And so to the penalty. Jones centred from the right. Medwin was tackled, a linesman flagged for a foul on Blacklaw by Smith, Medwin shot the loose ball for the far post where Cummings distinctly jerked his shoulder and right arm to deflect the ball. The referee was head-on to the incident, in no doubt about the decision, and Blanchflower coolly sent Blacklaw one way and the ball the other.

SPURS: Brown; Baker, Henry; Blanchflower, Norman, Mackay; Medwin, White, Smith, Greaves, Jones.
BURNLEY: Blacklaw; Angus, Elder; Adamson, Cummings, Miller; Connelly, McIlroy, Pointer, Robson, Harris.

> Optimism unfounded. England had the players, but not the cohesion and the heart – which Alf Ramsey would find – to fulfil the potential of several great players. In the World Cup quarter-final, Garrincha, Didi and Vava would prove greater.

WORLD CUP FINAL IS WITHIN ENGLAND'S REACH
Sunday Telegraph, June 1962

Santiago: The squall has passed. Last week's degeneration of the World Cup competition was soon halted. The brawling of Italy and Chile gave way to some earnest football and today, England, with much uncertainty behind them, and Brazil, champions towering ahead, stand 90 minutes away from the semi-finals.

The possibility of the seemingly impossible is greater than may be expected. England are better than when they were the only team undefeated by Brazil in 1958, while Brazil, without their Sorcerer, Pelé, are distinctly vulnerable. Of the quarter-finals, this is the match which most catches the imagination, even of Chileans, who themselves meet Russia at Arica. It is the old against the new: as one of this morning's papers says 'virtuosity against virility'.

The name of England abroad, certainly in South America, illogically like that of Arsenal at home, still retains vast respect. Foreigners never believe beforehand that we will be as indecisive as we so often are. They think only of the sort of resolution, mental and physical, with which we suppressed Argentina, never the ineptitude with which we scraped into the last eight against Bulgaria.

The Chilean will struggle with divided loyalty today. He admires Brazil, as we all must for their unruffled assurance, their grandeur, yet secretly he fancies England. As I parked in Rancagua last Saturday before the Argentina match, a Chilean policeman, all smiles, touchingly confided, 'I think *we* are going to win, sir' and when 'we' did, locals cheered to the echo.

English optimism has more than a grain of foundation. Spain, throwing everything into attack under the ignominious shadow of elimination, had Brazil's old guard reeling in one of the most thrilling World Cup matches ever. Full-backs Djalmar Santos, and Nilton Santos, both 30-plus, are slowing down and Spain's wingers, Gento and Collar, repeatedly slipped them. Charlton and Gento are the best outside-lefts in the competition and for this match I would have picked Connelly for his thrust. But I know Winterbottom, for reasons which escape others, has faith in Douglas.

Brazil's rigid 4–2–4 formation gives more opportunity for uninhibited attack than any of the countless contracting defences and their rearguard is the crack in their armour. Yet their faith in their own ability is still awesome. At the height of crisis with Spain, a goal down, they remained unbelievably cool and prised their way out of imminent defeat to a resounding triumph with flawless passing as intricate as the molecular structure of a hydrocarbon.

Perhaps England's ally may ironically be the omnipotent influence of the former manager Feola. Though ill in Sao Paulo it is he that has kept the winning 1958 team intact. In my opinion if the present manager, Moreira, would have the strength of his own convictions and replace D. Santos, Zito, Didi and Vava with Marinho, Zequinha, Mengalvio and Countinho, reserves who would walk into any other team, then England would have little chance.

Since the attack must be our theme it could be argued that Robson should have replaced Moore, but Moore is needed to subdue Amarildo, Pelé's deputy, we hope as effectively as he did Sanfillipo last Saturday. Pelé, who transcends all the normal skills, will not be fit before the final.

An unfortunate attitude existed among our players before they left home – that defeat by Brazil was the ultimate honour. Even yesterday one of the party said: 'Of course, I suppose *you* will be staying until the end.' It would be ridiculous if they were beaten by a preconceived image rather than reality. For there is no doubt at this moment that the final is within their reach. They have survived this far in spite of twice playing badly. They lost by a slip to Hungary, they could win likewise against Brazil.

Greaves has as yet done nothing, Haynes little more. Both, if they were not the players they are, would have been dropped for Hunt and Eastham. So with each successive match there is a chance they may click, and if Brazil could be beaten then so too could Russia or Chile, their prospective semi-final opponents. The ominous rumbles of Russian strength weakened with their 4–4 draw with Colombia.

Gallant Chile, away from Santiago, cannot hold much hope. The cries of the women paper-sellers which ring out until the early hours of the morning sounded more plaintive after Wednesday's defeat by Germany. Chile have an indifferent attack and, but for Italy having two men sent off, would probably not have beaten them. However, it is excellent that Italy should have been eliminated.

One has to admit that the nationalism is somewhat frightening. Team managers are about as safe as Spanish Royalists. Chile's manager, Reira, has built their team over five years, with June 1962 as the sole target. Yet when his side were one down to Switzerland after only six minutes in the opening match, the crowd were instantly ready to damn him to eternity. Crowds with pistols awaited Argentina when they returned in 1958, having failed to qualify, and they had to be secretly rushed away from the far side of the airport. Lorenzo, unopposed czar of the preparations this time, awaits instant dismissal – at best!

The Iron Curtain countries have proved efficient, four of their five qualifying. However, Czechoslovakia's relaxed method, which held Brazil, deserted them against Mexico and England must regret that they are not playing the Czechs, who must be likely to lose to Hungary. At this stage we expect

Hungary to go through and beat Germany or Yugoslavia to reach the final, unless they are physically intimidated by the uncompromising power of Sepp Herberger's Germans.

The most human of moments in this cauldron of skill, wits, and luck was when Hungary's manager, Lajos Baroti, as nice a man as one could meet, caught Winterbottom's arm before their match. 'Good luck,' he said. It took Winterbottom's breath away.

The England team to meet Brazil is: Springett; Armfield, Wilson; Moore, Norman, Flowers; Douglas, Greaves, Peacock, Haynes, Charlton.

The return of Matthews to Stoke City when nearing 50 years of age, adding 30,000 to the gate and inspiring promotion this season to the First Division once more, is a story beyond fiction, never to be repeated. But then, Matthews will never be repeated. Another victory, in a crowded Easter programme, helps add to the legend.

THE MASTER IS STILL MAGICAL
Sunday Telegraph, April 1963
STOKE 1   CARDIFF 0

It was three and a half minutes before he touched the ball. You would have known blindfolded. He may be 48, but expectation and faith have not diminished nor has affection weakened. The pulse still quickens as the legendary feet begin to shuffle forward in that hypnotic tread. Matthews, and Stoke, inched a shade nearer the First Division today. If he had not been playing, and promotion was not at stake, you would have been excused leaving at half time. But for these facts, it was a drab, unmemorable match, littered with fouls and tepid football. Yet it was another step in the phenomenon of a club reborn solely by the laughable £2,500 paid to recapture its own hero out of the distant past.

To be sure, Stoke will not pull up any trees in the First Division if they get there. Their half-back line is not up to it. Yet in an age lacking personalities, their forward line would be an unfailing attraction. Viollet, a bargain at £25,000 at today's prices, scored elegantly after five minutes, and it seemed, with Cardiff's defence pitifully uncertain, that there might be a feast for the 34,000 crowd. But yesterday's goalless draw had blunted the edge, and everything petered out before half time.

When you went to watch the master four or five years ago, it was with misgivings. He and Blackpool were in gentle, obscure decline. Yet now, that many more years past the age when mowing the lawn taxes many men, one is left to marvel at his infectious enthusiasm and liveliness. The spare, almost gaunt frame, aged beyond its years by the disciplined training which alone can have preserved such agility, still has the power to sustain a sprint shoulder to shoulder with men 30 years younger. The lean face and stooping shoulders covered by too much shirt, belie the wiriness of the legs that carry them.

Indeed, most incredible of all, he is now to be seen racing for the through ball. A mere 10 years ago, you pushed the ball to his feet, rather like posting a letter, ran 50 yards to the far post and waited for it to be delivered. It is still being delivered with that same uncanny accuracy which makes it hover in the air, as if on elastic, choosing its own destination. Brave, and insensible, was the linesman who today dared to give him offside when he had outpaced centre-half and left-back.

It was in keeping with the slightly bizarre occasion that Cardiff should have to play a full-back, Edwards, as outside-right – McIntosh, their former amateur international having failed to reappear on the bus after lunch at Shrewsbury. Not a word had been heard even by the time Cardiff started for home again, and one can only imagine that he had panicked at the thought of comparison with his opposite number.

40

Viollet's goal was a gem. McIlroy, who has played better matches, sent the ball with slide-rule precision to the by-line. Ritchie (playing in his first League match in place of Mudie) centred low and Viollet calmly glanced the ball on the volley as John dived across him. For the rest, Clamp and Allen had their names taken by a too-particular Mr Hamer – and, I almost forgot, the master twice headed the ball.

STOKE: O'Neill; Asprey, Allen; Clamp, Stuart, Horritt; Matthews, Viollet, Ritchie, McIlroy, Ratcliffe.
CARDIFF: John; Harrington, Stitfall, Baker, Rankermore, Hole; Edwards, Tapscott, Charles, Durban, Hooper.

In 1964, with more support from my wife than from the *Telegraph*, who paid only for what I wrote, I took the freelance route to the Olympic Games in Tokyo ...

17,000 MILES OF HAM AND EGGS
Sunday Telegraph, August 1964

The Kremlin and the Bolshoi, Siberian pioneering, Japanese shrines and the Olympic Games ... What linked all of these for me was a £160 ticket, Liverpool Street (platform 10) to Tokyo return – £300 less than the normal London-Tokyo tourist return air fare via either India or the Pole. The single journey takes at least four-and-a-half days, but with brief stops in Moscow and Siberia eight days is the shortest reasonable time.

Throughout I encountered no snags apart from one near disastrous error in a train schedule and a brush with Russian Customs on the return half. So long as you are patient but firm you will find Intourist, the Russian travel agency, most co-operative. They meet and transport you at all transit points and it is possible for you to speak English, eat ham and eggs and quench your thirst with tea at all stages of the 17,000 miles.

41

After crossing the North Sea from Harwich, a Russian sleeping-car takes you from the Hook on the 48-hour haul to Moscow via Berlin and Warsaw. Even by 'hard' class it is tolerably comfortable. Sleep was marred by nothing more than the persistent visitations of East German Customs, police, and currency officials. Of the six nations on the trip requiring such formalities, these were the only people never to smile.

The explanation of the speed and cheapness of this route to the Far East is the domestic air hop from Moscow to Khabarovsk in a giant TU-114, Communist air travel being cheaper than rail. At take-off it shudders like some electrocuted dinosaur but it carries its 170 passengers the 4,800 miles non-stop in eight hours.

Inside, it is at first like boarding a refugee boat, and rather frightening. There appear to be twice as many people as seats; everyone brings unlimited hand luggage, including bundles of vegetables, and at any moment you expect to find yourself treading on a couple of geese. The ample, but well-tailored air hostesses – the only Russian women I saw wearing nylons – charge up and down like amiable prep-school matrons, and after 20 minutes or so there is relative order.

In both directions departure is late evening, and on the West-East flight it is an unforgettable experience to see, at 36,000 feet, the dying red glow of today's sunset behind you, while simultaneously ahead is already the thin grey-yellow light of tomorrow's dawn.

I dined and later breakfasted quite appetisingly in company with a Russian woman Master of Sport at shooting, from the distant island of Sakhalin, an airline pilot and a schoolboy from Khabarovsk, and a Japanese mayor. Lusty infants in the arms of hefty bronze-skinned mothers also dined and breakfasted liberally *au naturel*. My Russian companions were fascinated to talk of London and the West.

Khabarovsk, a large, sprawling town, is pitifully drab, as are many of its inhabitants, though they seem well fed and contented enough. Yet it is a hive of activity, bristling with industry, new hospitals and technical training colleges. A big new Intourist hotel is near completion in the inevitable Lenin Square. Being the only Westerner travelling through on that date, I had two delightful interpreters to myself, school-teachers doing part-time work. They spoke almost flawless English, and after a day and a half I had almost convinced them that there was something wrong with the regime which permitted them to see only the *Daily Worker* from Britain.

From Khabarovsk one picks up the Trans-Siberian railway, which puffs its way for another 900 miles to Nakhodka, a tiny port about as big as Newhaven. The train seems in no hurry. The steward regularly brings tea, brewed on the samovar at the end of the corridor. Indefatigable, cheerful women in smart aprons serve breakfast, lunch and dinner without a break. People wander about in pyjamas at all times of the day; you seem to get to know everyone without actually ever necessarily speaking. It is like a seaside hotel on wheels.

The flat, marshy, largely uncultivated waste of land rolls by peppered with isolated little clusters of log cabins linked only by twisting rutted cart tracks. Life is close to the soil here; winter must be hard.

Half-hearing the occasional melancholy hoots from the engine way ahead, you glide through the night along the single track only a few miles from the Red Chinese border. The timing of the whole journey largely depends on the sailing date of the Russian ship *Ordjoni kidze* (4,500 tons) from Nakhodka a few miles north of Vladivostok across the Sea of Japan to Yokohama, which is 30 minutes from Tokyo by one of the incomparable Japanese express trains.

At Nakhodka there is a wait of several hours; you cannot stay overnight as there is no hotel. I wandered up into the town and into the little cinema where the film was just starting. Sitting on wooden chairs, the local maidens were thoroughly enjoying a very scratchy, dubbed but dashing Howard Keel in *Seven Brides for Seven Brothers*.

The voyage, as comfortable and informal as the train, takes two days. Flying fish abound and one sees the occasional dhow, but the ocean is otherwise much the same as anywhere. Anchored in the sweltering heat of Yokohama harbour for laborious immigration formalities, I reflected that what had once loomed as an adventure, across the country which forms one-sixth of the world's surface, had in fact been achieved

43

without a single irritable moment and with little more difficulty than, say, a trip from Plymouth to Aberdeen.

Mount Fuji presents the unique opportunity for the walker
like myself, as opposed to the climber, of reaching a quite high
summit without special skill or danger. It is arduous, certainly,
but quite within the compass of the average fit young person.
For the really earnest Japanese, the aim is to climb by night, so
as to be up the mountain, preferably at the summit, for sunrise.
Every thousand feet or so there are Stations, stone-built cabins,
where you can rest and eat and even sleep for 10 shillings
[50p]. If you are going to be in Tokyo for the Olympic Games
the climb will not be so easy. The Stations are closed from 31
August and the first snow falls in late September.

'A slag heap covered in tin cans' was the first, harsh description of Fuji given me on arriving in Tokyo, quickly followed by
'Climb it once, if you must; only a fool climbs it twice.' At 12,395
feet, Fuji is about the same height as an average Alp, but when
not covered with snow is nothing more, for the last 6,000 feet,
than a cone of loose, filthy volcanic ash. It is only in winter,
when snow-capped, that it is the familiar, beautiful peak.

For the Japanese it is, of course, sacred. At the summit there
is a Shinto shrine. Reverently it is referred to as Fuji-san (Fuji,
Master) and in July and August when free from snow several
thousand pilgrims make their way up. It is they who leave
behind the tin cans and paper, broken glass and apple cores.
This national shrine is also a national disgrace. At any age from
eight to 80, man or woman, they attempt the ascent.

I hurriedly purchased some tennis shoes in Kawaguchi for 5
shillings [25p], a cheap torch and a few snacks, and thus
equipped boarded another bus which, built to carry 40, grinds
painfully up a tortuous road for 90 minutes laden with some 70
climbers in acute discomfort as far as Station Five (about 6,000
feet). Slowly pulling up and away from the belt of firs, there,
suddenly, as if seen from a plane, were the tiny dimly twinkling
lights of Kawaguchi and other towns, while above, Fuji still
stretched immeasurably.

The Stations jut out from the mountainside on man-made
terraces. Prices rise with altitude. The apple which costs six-
pence [2½p] at Station Five is one-and-sixpence [7½p] at the

summit, which is fair enough, and the same applies to the bed and breakfast rate. At every Station the landlord earnestly informs you it is the last at which you may sleep; in fact, you can sleep at them all, including the summit.

At about midnight, after two hours' hard slogging, I turned in at Station Eight. Having fixed a call for four o'clock, I was up in time to see the growing glow of the still-submerged sun. Then came the climax. In less than a minute the whole sun bobbed up above the horizon like a bubble of air escaping from water, and for the first time I could see the foe above clearly: still a seemingly endless stretch of rock and red cinder outlined against a vivid blue sky. And while I had thought during the night that there were perhaps a couple of hundred other climbers, now there were visible a thousand or more, a human chain. I reached the summit by 6.30 and surveyed the crater – 2,000 feet across and last active in the 1870s.

The descent, like most, is far quicker; in the case of Fuji about a quarter the time, because after 1,000 feet you leave the zigzag path and 'dry-ski' in the loose ash for 5,000 feet in almost a straight line. This is quite the dirtiest journey one is likely to make in a lifetime, and the more memorable for me for the fact that I fell and dislocated my shoulder.

Pelé was, in my opinion, the supreme player beyond all others. To the genius of Di Stefano, tactical and technical, Pelé added the physical brio of the Negro. His expectation, and ours, was in 1966 riding upon a cloud. In the event, he was to be criminally cut down.

THE SUPREME ATTACKING
INDIVIDUALIST

Sunday Telegraph, June 1966

The brown eyes are dreamy under heavy lids. Like a lion asleep in the sun, he has that total relaxation that characterises every great Negro athlete. In blue woollen sports shirt and pale grey slacks, a mere five foot eight, you would never guess he possessed the power once to have scored a goal from the half-way line. It is only out on the field that those limbs become poetry in motion.

This is Pelé, pride of Brazil and a budding dollar millionaire at 25. There have been other players who either could run faster, were stronger, possessed such body swerve (though that is doubtful), or could shoot or head as hard. But never have so many qualities been combined in one man. In the Maracana National Stadium in Rio a plaque commemorates the day he dribbled the length of the field through the entire opposition to score a goal. He is the only player ever with the timing and finesse consistently to draw his man and at the last moment pass the ball *between* his opponent's legs. Regularly he deceives them by deliberately kicking the ball against their shins and then sweeping by on the rebound faster than the eye can follow.

When he takes penalty kicks, the speculation is not whether he will score but where he will put the ball. Often the goalkeeper dives in the opposite direction to the ball. Even under pressure, when other players would be doing well to get in a shot, Pelé can feign a first shot and then a split second later put the ball the other way. The left foot is as devastating as the right.

In an era of excessively defensive football, dominated increasingly by tactics, less and less by individuals, Pelé remains the supreme attacking individualist, the greatest crowd-puller the game has known. Over 100,000, the biggest attendance of the year, flooded into the Bernabeu Stadium in Madrid last Tuesday for the friendly match against Atletico FC, and were rewarded by seeing Pelé score three goals and make two others. When he puts his mind to it, he is untouchable.

Yet now, at the peak of his fame, he is already thinking of retirement. After nearly 1,000 games in 10 years, he has had enough, though he would normally expect to have at least two more World Cup competitions – eight more years at the toughest top – ahead of him. I talked at length to Pelé last week in Madrid, where Brazil were completing their preparations for their defence of the World Cup, which begins in Liverpool, against Bulgaria, on 12 July. His startling news came out in the most casual way, without any fuss, for Pelé is the most modest and humble of men, not given to self-dramatisation.

Knowing the strain he has experienced recently, with over 100 matches a season for his club, Santos, and the national team, I asked how long he might stay in the game, expecting no more than a conventional reply. The swiftness of the answer suggested it was something he had thought much about.

'Perhaps, if I'm able, I might stay another two or three years, until I am 28. For me there can be no greater experience than the World Cup in England, the home of the game. Whether we win or not, there can be nothing left to achieve. I have no reason to want to play anywhere else after England. It was a terrible disappointment to me when my club prevented me playing for the Rest of the World in your Centenary match in 1963. My only ambition now is to win, if we can, next month at Wembley.

'Maybe, if I was needed badly, I might play in the World Cup in Mexico in 1970, but I don't think so. I would like soon to play just now and then for an amateur club. I want more time with my family. Playing is not the problem, it is the travelling. I can't remember when I last spent a whole week with my family. My honeymoon in Europe a few months ago was the first holiday I've ever had. The only time I get days off is if I'm injured. Slowly, I will drop out of the game, spending more time on my businesses. Not that money is any problem, but I must still have some occupation.'

This news will come as a revelation to Brazilian football

followers, for as Pelé has risen to fame, so has the national team. When Brazil went to Sweden for the World Cup in 1958 Pelé had played only five international matches. He helped to carry them to victory in the final with a goal of breathtaking brilliance and impudence.

Pelé was born Edson Arantes do Nascimento of humble parents in the small town of Bauru. 'My father was a professional with the Atletico team of Minas Gerais. Until I was 10 I used to play with the other boys barefoot in the streets, often using a bunch of woollen rags for a ball. At 11, I had my first pair of boots, and Valdemar de Brito, the old international and a friend of my father and trainer at the Bauru club, took me along to play for them. I stayed as a junior with the club for four years. I can't remember learning anything special, except that Valdemar impressed on me the importance of being really fit. These days, my weight goes up when I'm in training, and down only when I am not playing, so finely balanced is my fitness. When I was 15, Valdemar took me to join the famous Santos club, which meant I had to leave school and my apprenticeship as a shoemaker.'

Up to then, as far as he was aware, Pelé had done nothing special. When did he first realise that he was a remarkable player? 'I had been with Santos about nine months, and was still 16. They told me I had been chosen to play for Brazil. I thought to myself: "Well, you *must* be good." '

There have, besides Pelé, been three men intimately connected with Brazil's success, and all four came together within 18 months. The others were Dr Hilton Gosling, a professor of orthopaedic surgery at the Santa Casa Hospital in Rio, who became medical adviser and co-selector; Vicente Feola, their short, 17-stone team manager; and Garrincha, the outside-right whose genius is second only to Pelé's. Dr Gosling's role, leading to an entirely new conception of team administration and medical care, has been vital. His principle is that medical knowledge should be used to prevent injury as much as cure it.

'Under his care there have been fewer injuries in the national team between 1958 and 1966 than there were in the two previous years. For example, immediately I became a member of the squad, an impression of my foot was taken. The weight of your foot is distributed through three small areas, the ball, the heel and the outside, and according to the angle at which each player's foot naturally rests, the length of the studs on each part of the boot is varied to maintain this natural position. This avoids small but constant strain being put on ankle and knee ligaments, which can eventually lead to injury under sudden stress.'

Apart from daily medical checks on the players, studying their heart recovery rate after training and matches, there is an exhaustive check on every air, rail or bus schedule, so that the players are subjected to the minimum fatigue. For the World Cup in England, the road journeys from their Cheshire hotel to the grounds at Liverpool and Sunderland have been timed to avoid the rush hour. 'Such small details don't, of course, help you to win matches, but they make sure you don't lose simply because someone is travel sick or tired.'

Neither does Dr Gosling underestimate the period needed to adjust to the four hours' time difference between South America and Europe, which disrupts the body's eating and sleeping rhythm. 'He has shown that only one team in 10 years, coming straight from Europe, have beaten Brazil at home. It takes a week to adjust, just as we need a week when coming to Europe. That is why we *knew* we would beat England in the Little World Cup in 1964.'

Feola, huge, impassive, with a slow, soothing voice as thick as chocolate sauce, is the perfect manager, in the father-figure mould, for excitable Latins. When Brazil played at Wembley in 1956 one of their players ran off with the ball like a sulking schoolboy when a penalty was given against them, and often in the past there had been scenes of temper. With Gosling's help, Feola has turned them into the most disciplined, ruthlessly cool-headed team in the business.

Pelé is genuinely reluctant to admit he is the best player in the world. His problem nowadays is that his instinctive enjoyment of the game prevents him ever shielding himself, or taking it easy.

'Seriously, I don't ever think I or anyone can be the best player in the world, because you cannot excel in every position. I just always feel I must play well in every match. I don't feel I have any special obligation to anyone except myself. People say beforehand that Pelé will win a match, but I don't think this, any more than I think it is my fault if we lose. I just play.

'I still enjoy the game, except when I'm tired. I enjoy it equally with my club or the national team, though the club atmosphere is best and what I would like is to play with the national players in the club team. My marriage has made no difference, except that I now have that much more responsibility.' He married Miss Rosemary dos Reis Cholby, a schoolteacher, at his home in Santos only four months ago.

Because he can win a match with half a minute's wizardry, and because the stakes, in prestige and money, are even higher, Pelé takes a regular battering from defences, who mercilessly chop and kick at those flashing legs and feet. The provocation is immense.

'There was that incident against Argentina two years ago, when I retaliated against an opponent. He had twice spat in my face, and three times kicked me. Several times I warned him. He didn't come to play football, but to prevent me playing. I've been sent off three times, each time the same referee, always for arguing. It was the only way he could become well known: "The referee who sent off Pelé."

'Football today has become far too defensive; it is no longer a show, which is bad for the public. There are many teams who do well not because they are good but because they are negative. I think England, Germany and Hungary are sides who still attack. The last time I saw England was in Rio in 1964. They were then like Brazil are now, they had good players but the machine was not working properly. I'm told it is now. You must have a fine chance, because you are always so strong at home.'

Because there is almost no colour problem in Brazil, where black and white are as one in all but a few walks of life, Pelé has no consciousness of his contribution to the emancipation and status of the Negro, considerable though it has been.

'If you are a star, no one bothers about your colour. All over the world small boys, black, white and yellow, have been called after me. In some sports the Negro has an advantage, but I have never felt superior, or even the need to be. All my progress came naturally – football has been what mattered!'

And football has brought him a fortune. His contract with Santos is now about £1,000 a month, and television and advertising contracts have made him huge sums. He really began to make money after Brazil's 1962 World Cup victory even though he was injured, and he is in partnership with a Santos builder, known to all as Fat Pepe, who manages his affairs.

'I learned a lesson from my father. All his football money, and it was good money, disappeared. I have been careful. I don't have much cash, it is all invested, and I have moved all my family to Santos, buying them a house and business. Money itself hasn't meant so very much to me. I suppose so far I've never had time to spend it. My only luxuries are clothes and records.'

So here he modestly stands, this athletic genius, on the brink of his greatest and last ambition, to win the World Cup in England, for whom the rest of the football world still has so much goodwill, the pity being that many of our small-minded officials take it all for granted.

'You don't realise what this means to us in Brazil. We have more supporters going to England than went across the Andes to Chile. They are even selling their cars to raise the money to be able to say: "I was in England for the World Cup." No other nation would we trust to take our money for tickets in October and not receive the tickets until the next April. Mexico, Germany, nowhere can be the same after England, with its wonderful reputation for both sportsmanship and administration.'

Let us hope that injury does not undermine Pelé again, and that this competition, whether or not Brazil win, will be remembered for his greatness rather than for any mean, underhand tactics of those who must conspire to stop him. The sending off of four players in three preparatory international matches last week was an inauspicious start. Referees will need to be alert and to restrict physical contact or, as the Argentinian manager said on Wednesday, 'We may as well go out with pistols and shoot a few people before we start.'

THE BUTCHERS OF ARGENTINA BEATEN
Sunday Telegraph, July 1966
ENGLAND 1   ARGENTINA 0

England ran out in the brilliant sunshine this afternoon in all-white – an unintentional symbol of purity which would not have been in character in some of their recent matches. Yet Argentina, in blue and white stripes, should instead have been in all-black as the villains of what soon became an absurd spectacle, a farce of a match, not quite as bad as the Italy-Chile affair in 1962 in intensity, but worse in its duration. That England finally emerged in the semi-final of the World Cup for the first time, to play Portugal here on Tuesday, following their third victory in this series and only their sixth ever in the finals, seemed almost an irrelevance after football had been degraded beyond endurance by an Argentine team with cultured feet and kindergarten minds.

Playing against 10 men for nearly an hour, England finally won with the only penetrating finish of the whole afternoon – a deep centre from the left by Peters with 13 minutes to go, headed home with perfect timing by his West Ham colleague Hurst, who was deputising for the injured Greaves. This apart, there was little to cheer on an afternoon which is best forgotten (but which is likely to be considered by the FIFA disciplinary committee tomorrow afternoon). I am sorry that England's achievement was not gained with distinction, but then one has never thought them capable of it.

It was evident almost immediately that Argentina were technically the more accomplished players, and believing that the winners of this match would probably win the competition, I had an uneasy feeling that England had met their Waterloo. It was the Argentines themselves who determined otherwise. The uneasiness soon became disgust as the butchers from Buenos Aires got to work, equally

52

accomplished in every art of the chop, hack, trip and body check. Theirs is the law of the jungle.

With five players, Perfumo, Solari, Rattin, Artime and Mas, all booked, with their captain Rattin sent off for persistent arguing and obstruction of the course of the game following his own wicked foul on Bobby Charlton, with the trainers and manager Lorenzo holding up the game for 10 minutes, and with several of their reserves attacking the referee at the end of the match, Argentina should be refused entry for the next World Cup.

If all they come for is to debase themselves and the game, they had better stay away. One shudders to think what might have happened with a referee of less perception and rigid, inflexible will than Rudolf Kreitlein, of West Germany. His, unquestionably, was the performance of the afternoon, and had he abandoned the match when Rattin refused to leave the field he would have been justified and Argentina must have forfeited it. I am not vindictive, but for the first time ever I was delighted to see a player sent off. Rattin epitomised the rest of his side – a fine player totally without self-control.

What is one left with on the credit side? Very little, for England, even against 10 men, struggled to find a way through. They have a defence, we know, but still no attack. Ball, Hurst and Hunt were lost for an answer for most of the game, and the system which allowed only three strikers is not one to win the crowds even if, as things are going, it still seems to win matches.

England have yet to give a really convincing display and Portugal will be a real test. Once already, earlier this year, Stiles has marked Eusebio out of a match, for Manchester United in the European Cup. This afternoon Stiles was often chasing shadows as he battled to get to grips with the evasive Argentines, who moved backwards as often as forwards and looked content to play for a draw or even the chance of a lucky toss of a coin, until the middle of next week. Against this sort of play England have no answer and there was one dreadful moment, seven minutes before England scored, when Mas had the chance to put Argentina in front. Jack Charlton was caught slow on the turn.

England's best patch was the first five minutes when Bobby Charlton hit a post from a corner kick with a low inswinger and Hurst went close from 25 yards. There was another highlight five minutes after half time when Moore found Wilson in the left-wing position and his centre was hooked viciously by Hurst for the top right-hand corner of the net, only for Roma to make a superb save.

Alf Ramsey insists that England have yet to be given the chance to play their best football. To my mind they had it against France, and failed. The semi-final is rather late to start finding your form. But at least it is something to be there, and Moore, now playing magnificently, Jack Charlton and Wilson give one hope that Portugal will find goals harder to come by than they have so far.

As for Argentina, their appalling mentality is summed up by the player who said afterwards: 'We were hoping to last out for a toss of the coin.'

ENGLAND: Banks; Cohen, Stiles, Charlton J., Wilson; Moore, Charlton R., Hurst; Ball, Hunt, Peters.
ARGENTINA: Roma; Ferreiro, Perfumo, Albrecht, Marzolini; Rattin, Solari, Gonzalez; Artime, Onega, Mas.

KEEPING A PROMISE
Sunday Telegraph, July 1966
ENGLAND 4   WEST GERMANY 2

They had fetched him, three and a half years ago, from quiet Ipswich, a taciturn, shy, deeply reserved man, and calmly leading with his chin, as they say, he had promised to win them the World Cup. There were those who laughed, and some were still laughing when the tournament began. Yet by the finish, with a relentless inflexibility of will, with sterling courage, with efficiency that brought unbounded admiration, his team, England's team, helped to keep that promise.

They did it, Alf Ramsey and England, after just about the worst psychological reverse possible on an unforgettable afternoon. With victory dashed from their grasp, cruelly, only seconds from the final whistle, they came again in extra time, driving weary limbs across the patterned turf beyond the point of exhaustion, and crowned the ultimate achievement with a memorable goal with the last kick of all by Hurst, making him the first player to score a hat-trick in the World Cup final.

We had all often talked of the thoroughness of preparation of the deposed champions, Brazil, but England's glory this day, to be engraved on that glinting, golden trophy, was the result of the most patient, logical, painstaking, almost scientific assault on the trophy there had perhaps ever been – and primarily the work and imagination of one man.

For those close to him through the past three exciting seasons, Ramsey's management had been something for unending admiration, and the unison cry of the 93,000 crowd, 'Ram-sey, Ram-sey' as his side mounted the steps to collect Jules Rimet's statuette from the Queen was the final rewarding vindication for one who had unwaveringly pursued his own, often lonely, convictions.

As the crowd stood in ovation, Greaves looked on wistfully. Injury had cost him his place, and though he recovered, Ramsey had resisted the almost overpowering temptation to change a winning side. This, too, was vindication, his whole aim since 1963 having been to prepare not a team but a squad, so that at any moment he might replace an out of form or injured man without noticeable deterioration in the side. When the time came, the luckless Greaves' omission caused hardly a stir of pessimism.

At the start of the tournament, I had written that if England were to win, it would be with the resolution, physical fitness and cohesion of West Germany in 1954, rather than with the flair of Brazil in the two succeeding competitions. And so it proved, with the added coincidence that it was the Germans themselves, as usual bristling with all these same characteristics in profusion, who were the unlucky and brave victims of England's methodical rather than brilliant football. Before the semi-finals I said that the deciding factor of this World Cup, when all others had cancelled out in the modern proficiency of defensive systems, would be character, and now the character of every England player burned with a

55

flame that warmed all those who saw it. The slightest weakening, mentally or physically, in any position, could have lost this match a hundred times over, but the way in which Ball, undoubtedly the man of the afternoon, Wilson, Stiles, Peters, Bobby Charlton and above all Moore, impelled themselves on, was something one would remember long after the tumult of excitement and the profusion of incidents had faded. Justifiably, Moore was voted the outstanding player of the competition; his sudden, surging return to form on tour beforehand had helped cement the castle at the critical hour.

All assessments of great events should be measured by absolute standards along with the quality of contemporaries, and therefore one has to say that England were not a great team, probably not even at that moment the best team in the world, depending on what you mean by best.

What matters is that they were the best there at Wembley in July, on that sunny, showery afternoon, best when the chips were down in open combat, and that, after all, is what counts – the result, rather than its manner, goes into the record books. Besides, Ramsey had not set about producing the most entertaining but the most successful team. Could he afford to be the one romantic in a world of hard-headed, win-at-all-costs efficiency? Could he favour conventional wingers who promised much and produced little? A manager is ultimately only as good as the players at his disposal; handicapped by a shortage of world-class, instinctive players of the calibre of the South Americans, Italians, Hungarians, or his own Bobby Charlton, and by an over-abundance of average competence, Ramsey had slowly eliminated all those who lacked what he needed for cohesion. What greater demonstration of unity of purpose could there have been than the insistence of the winners, for all the emotion of the moment, that the 11 reserves join them on the lap of honour, and afterwards share equally the £22,000 bonus.

Some complained England were helped by playing all their matches at Wembley, yet certainly in that mood and form they could and would have won anywhere in the country. Besides, under Ramsey, England had had more success abroad than ever before. If nothing else, this World Cup, penetrating almost every home in the land, should have persuaded the doubters, the detractors and the cynics that this is the greatest spectator sport there is, and the final was a fitting climax.

At the start England asserted themselves – Bobby Charlton, exerting a telling influence in midfield, even though closely watched by Beckenbauer, sent Peters streaming through with fine anticipation, into spaces behind the German midfield trio. Suddenly, however, in the 13th minute, England found themselves a goal down for the first time in the competition. It was not an error under pressure, it was unforced. As a centre from the left came over, Wilson stood alone, eyes riveted on the dropping ball. He made to head it down to Moore, but his judgement betrayed him, sending it instead straight to Haller, who whipped in a low skidding shot past an unsighted, helpless Banks.

The strapping Germans and their flag-waving supporters bounced with joy, but within six minutes England were level. Midway inside the German half, on the left, Overath tripped Moore, and even before the referee had finished wagging his finger at Overath, Moore had spotted a gaping hole in the German rearguard. He placed the ball and took the kick almost in one move, a dipping floater that carried 35 yards and was met by Hurst, streaking in from the right, with another graceful, expertly-timed header like that which beat Argentina.

The pattern swung once more in the 10 minutes before half time. The three German strikers, nosing in and out like carnivorous fish, began to create havoc that was only averted after extreme anxiety. In between, Hunt, from a glorious pass by Bobby Charlton, hammered a thundering shot, a difficult one running away to his left, straight at Tilkowski. On the stroke of half time, it was England who were desperately lucky, when a fast dipper by Seeler was tipped over by Banks, arched in mid-air like a stalling buzzard.

Little happened for nearly 25 minutes after half time, the lull punctuated only by 'Oh, oh, what a referee', as Mr Dienst went fussily about his business. Then, with 20 minutes to go,

England's rhythm began to build up again, Bobby Charlton, Ball and Peters stretching the Germans to the extreme of their physical endurance with passes that again and again almost saw Hurst and Hunt clear. With 11 minutes to go, Ball won a corner, put it across, the ball was headed out, and hit back first time by Hurst. It struck a defender, fell free, and Peters swooped to lash it home.

England, sensing victory, played it slow, slow, but Hunt wasted a priceless chance, when it was three red England shirts to one white German on the edge of the penalty area, by misjudging his pass. With a minute left, all was disaster as Jack Charlton was most harshly penalised for 'climbing' over the top of Held. Emmerich blasted the free kick. A German in the penalty area unquestionably pulled the ball down with his hand, and after a tremendous scramble, Weber squeezed the ball home to level the match.

You could see England's spirits sink as the team changed over for extra time but, quickly calmed and reassured by the emotionless Ramsey, they rallied themselves instantly. Ball, still unbelievably dynamic, going like the wind right to the finish, had a shot tipped over, Bobby Charlton hit a post and with 12 minutes gone, England were once more in front as Stiles slipped the ball up the wing to Ball, whose cross was thumped hard by Hurst. The ball hit the bar, bounced down and came out, and after consultation with the Russian linesman, Bakhramov, a goal was given. I had my doubts, doubled after later seeing television, but that surely had to be the winner, for now, socks rolled down, both teams were physically in distress. Again England sought economy with gentle passes, keeping precious possession, wearing the Germans down yet further. Poor Wilson hardly knew where he was after a blow on the head. Slowly the minutes ticked away, agonisingly, until with the referee looking at his watch, Hurst staggered on alone from yet one more of Moore's perceptive passes, to hit the ball into the roof of the net with what little strength he had left, and to make England's victory, like their football, solid and respectable. Whether Ramsey, as silent in victory as defeat, could achieve the impossible and adapt these same characteristics to win in

Mexico in 1970 was a chapter that would unfold over the next four years.

ENGLAND: Banks (Leicester); Cohen (Fulham), Charlton J. (Leeds), Moore (West Ham), Wilson (Everton); Stiles (Manchester Utd), Charlton R. (Manchester Utd), Peters (West Ham); Ball (Blackpool), Hunt (Liverpool), Hurst (West Ham).
WEST GERMANY: Tilkowski; Hoettges, Schulz, Weber, Schnellinger; Beckenbauer, Haller, Overath; Seeler, Held, Emmerich.

MILDEWED BOOTS
Sunday Telegraph, December 1967

On Boxing Day I rescued some rather mildewed boots from the garden shed and socks and shirt from the cupboard under the stairs and joined in one of those annual matches that recalls the primitive origins of football – on the green behind the pub, a wall and the footpath forming the touchlines. The contestants were those regular drinking clients who can still run, or fancy they can, and a team of the local wrestling club who twice weekly train at the back of the same hospitable establishment.

Everything about the match is approximate: the numbers on each side, the duration of play, observance of the laws (especially). The height of the crossbar (non-existent) at any moment is a matter for the discretion of the referee-landlord, and if spectators sense it is lower when the wrestlers are shooting, that is only to offset their advantage in every other department, such as passing to their own side.

Though we led 2-1 at half time, the wrestlers won comfortably in the second half, when their training and ours began to take contrasting effect. Thinking afterwards, in the glow of achievement, having sold a dummy to an opponent – crocked, I think, before the game began – I couldn't help wondering how, as a forward, I would find the contemporary set-up: a full-back always between one's shoulder-blades, forcing one to receive the ball facing one's own goal.

It just isn't a decent life for forwards any more, a point reinforced the next day when the European Footballer of the

Year poll was announced by *France Football*, headed by Florian Albert (Hungary) with Bobby Charlton down to No 2. Where are the new names to catch the imagination? It seems to me the field is narrowing every year, particularly when we get Beckenbauer (West Germany) at No 4 and Gemmell (Scotland) at No 6, both defenders.

Think back over the past decade at the host of forwards there have been in every country in Europe – the Hungarians first of all, the Spaniards, the Yugoslavs with players such as Vukas and Milutinovic and Sekularec, France with Kopa and Fontaine, Germany with Rahn, the Walters, Schaefer and Seeler, and others like Coppens and Van Himst of Belgium, Hamrin and Simonsson of Sweden. The list is endless, but not today. In another 10 years, I wonder, will the player of the year be a full-back?

TRUMAN SISTERS SETTLE ISSUE IN FINAL DOUBLES
Daily Telegraph, June 1968

In time to come it will be recalled amusingly how Christine Janes and her sister Nell Truman won the final set of the decisive doubles in encroaching gloom at Wimbledon on Saturday to take the Wightman Cup of 1968, only Britain's seventh victory in 40 years. Yet the door was really opened 90 minutes beforehand when Virginia Wade notably defeated the French champion, Nancy Richey, in the top singles, 6-4 2-6 6-3, to level the match at 3-all after Britain had surrendered their overnight 2-1 lead. This performance may well be seen in retrospect to have marked the turning point in Miss Wade's hitherto volatile, exciting but erratic career.

After confidently claiming the first set, breaking Miss Richey's service in the 10th game with two stop volleys, Miss Wade was then characteristically thrown out of her stride by a disputed call on her opponent's successful lob in the third game of the second set. By the end of the set Miss Wade was obliged to smile occasionally at her own loss of authority. But she regained command at 3-3 in the final set. It was a new, match-tight, mentally serene Miss Wade who took three games in a row to inflict a rewarding defeat.

Twice previously in the Wightman Cup Miss Wade had served for victory against Miss Richey and failed, and this must now have been on her mind as she served at 3-3. At 0-15 she ran round a lob to hit a winning forehand, and an ace and a drop shot clinched 4-3. In the next critical game two smashes and a forehand pass brought Miss Wade to 40-15, and then in a long rally it was the American who finally hit out. The mouse had beaten the cat, so to speak, at its own game. There was one more momentary crisis. Serving at 15-all, Miss Wade was just wide with an angled stop volley, but two aces brought match point and an achievement that puts a new complexion on her prospects over the next year or two.

In the final doubles those popular sisters epitomised the spirit of so much of British sport – a bizarre mixture of good fortune and calamity, met with equanimity and humour. Winners off the wood, freak half-volleys and steepling lobs were mingled with a succession of winning backhand volleys by Christine and passing shots by Nell, though often they were caught together on the same square foot of the court.

The Americans, Kathy Harter and Stephanie de Fina, who were a scratch pair, won the second set more decisively than they lost the first, so that drama and comedy moved agonisingly towards conclusion side by side.

The luckless Miss de Fina lost her service to love in the opening game of the final set, but then came two errors by Christine, who lost her own service. Miss de Fina next cost America Miss Harter's service with loose drives, but in spite of a double fault, Nell Truman held hers for 3-1. A sizzling backhand return by Nell, an unexpected rose among the cabbages, broke Miss de Fina again, and Christine served for 5-1. At 5-2 Nell served for the Cup – and faltered. On the first point of the next game Miss de Fina served into the wrong court straight at Christine, who dodged and fell flat on the ground. A loud oops and another crash, as Christine again dodged a drive by Miss Harter going out, brought 0-30. Then Miss de Fina smashed out and a backhand by Nell, calmly bisecting the Americans, finally brought the No 1 Court to its feet in acclaim as Britain won the Cup for the first time since 1960.

Britain's lead had vanished at the start of the day, when, in a match containing 18 service breaks, Winnie Shaw had lost to Peaches Bartkowicz 5-7 6-3 4-6, and Mrs Janes had gone down to a transformed Mary Ann Eisel by 6-4 6-3. Miss Shaw's reluctance to hit a backhand down the line and to go for the line with her forehand cost her the chance to beat an erratic opponent, but Mrs Janes, by no means unsound, had little chance against Miss Eisel, who made hardly a single mistake after a catastrophic first day.

Matt Busby's retirement as manager of Manchester United – currently an ailing team – yet remaining general manager, was an ill-judged decision. His successor would be overshadowed. Wilf McGuinness never had a chance ... as my letter predicted.

DEAR MR X

Sunday Telegraph, January 1969

Unenviable Sir,

I think you will have both the best and the worst job in the game, for you are walking into a situation comparable to Arsenal after Chapman – you can hardly hope to do as well, following in the steps of one of the two greatest managers of the century.

You inherit not only an incomparable tradition, but a struggling team in an era when almost all opponents have some joyless antidote to excellence and individualism, the qualities upon which that tradition has been built.

Your job will be made both easier and more difficult

because of the decision, not altogether wise in my opinion, that Sir Matt shall remain as general manager. You will be glad of his unrivalled experience, wisdom and diplomatic counsel, but inevitably you will be sometimes restricted and always overshadowed by his Olympian presence. It will be that much harder to establish the respect and command in your own right which he has enjoyed.

It may well be, whatever your industry and leadership, whatever funds are at your disposal to acquire new players, that Manchester United are about to enter one of their leanest periods since the war. The great players, with the exception of Best, are slowing down, the existing youngsters seem to me to be short of former standards. The type of player you might hope to buy is increasingly rare, and as with Mike England and Allan Clarke, you may fail to get them.

The contemporary changes in tactics and finance have widened the gap between the good and bad clubs but narrowed the margin among the good, to the point where it is almost impossible to be exceptional. Manchester United have always stood for entertainment and adventure, but these elements are being squeezed out of the game, as we saw in Wednesday's frustrating international at Wembley.

In spite of this I hope that with the resources at your disposal you will try to provide entertaining, as well as successful, football whenever possible, and I hope too that you will always be conscious of the good name not only of your illustrious club but of the game itself, eschewing those tactics and attitudes which debase everyone, a cancer which can kill the game.

Manchester United are seen as leaders, not just in England but in the world. Everyone wishes you the best of luck in a job which has taken the leasehold on your soul.

> It should have been a World Cup final between Brazil
> and the holders, but England threw away a two-goal
> lead against West Germany, who then lost an extra-time
> thriller to Italy. Brazil, almost alone in the game,
> refused to contemplate defence.

IT MUST BE BRAZIL – AND A TRIUMPH FOR SKILL
Sunday Telegraph, June 1970

Mexico City: Brazil are as firm favourites to beat Italy in today's World Cup final as England were to defeat West Germany in the quarter-final. As we know to our cost, nothing is certain in football, and I shall be as sad this evening if Brazil fail as I was last week when England suffered a reverse almost more irrational and unjust than the 1950 defeat by the United States in Belo Horizonte. As the football world gathers here for the climax I have yet to meet any player, manager or commentator other than those from Germany and Italy and the most embittered from England, who does not believe that the 1970 final should have been between the champions of the previous two tournaments.

The glittering if brittle emerald in football's functional world of industrial diamonds, Brazil are the logical and rightful successors to England as world champions, a crown they cannot fail to wear with more style and as much dignity. Their exciting, self-conscious talents make their appeal as irresistible as the carnival with which their whole waiting nation is hoping to celebrate not for a night but a week. If football is indeed a synthesis of war, chess and ballet, the ballet of Brazil wins the admiration of every opponent. As the battle continues to rage on and off the field between the merits of entertainment and efficiency, Brazil combine supremely the two facets, a magical exception to the contemporary preoccupation with defence.

64

It is a misconception to think that the championship has suddenly become adventurous; the mentality of every genuinely successful team other than Brazil remains fundamentally cautious and Brazil themselves could not have been more cautious against England. If Brazil win, as they must surely do, they will be the toast of all who admire skill above everything, and simultaneously the first team in the history of the game to achieve greatness in the face of their own defensive frailty.

In a tournament notable for bad goalkeeping Felix is conspicuously vulnerable, while Brito and Piazza, in the centre of defence, are prone to alarming lapses. In midfield Clodoaldo, Gerson and Rivelino would be less than exceptional without the inspired and inspiring trio of geniuses for whom they are the lifeline of supply. Jairzinho, Tostao and Pelé form a warhead of immeasurable possibilities. Jairzinho's astonishing dribbling and shooting, little less formidable than those of the incomparable Garrincha, are fortified by his physical bravery; Pelé's perception and awesome technique at close quarters are undiminished and he is still the master of the unexpected after 12 years of often aggressive intimidation; while Tostao's serene positional sense and refinement of touch, linking the two black pearls, make him a superior weapon to the more direct Vava of 1958-62.

Like a child's rocket with damp touch paper, Brazil sometimes splutter, but once there is ignition the sight is spectacular. To change the metaphor, I do not think that Italy can do an Edward Heath, barring some twist of fate or massive abstention by the Brazil defence allowing Riva, the gunman whose hand has mostly so far got no further than his hip, to sneak a marginal victory. Italy remain psychologically like a man with a bicycle who, although being an excellent rider, feels safer pushing it everywhere on foot following a painful fall – in Italy's case against North Korea.

It is too much to suppose that Italy can find within themselves the adventurous approach which might just turn the tables. Even Italians are pessimistic. Renato Moreno of Tutto Sport of Milan epitomises the feeling: 'It must be Brazil

– I think. Riva is mentally tired and Italy will not alter their defensive tactics. A national team always plays the way its clubs predominantly play – and this is how our clubs play.' Everyone is wondering just what will happen when Italy, as is their way, concede frequent free kicks just outside the penalty area.

At this point I must declare my absolute opposition and rejection of the school of thought which has been lyrical in its praise of the Italy-West Germany semi-final – a marvellous spectacle, certainly, but a technical travesty, similar to the Wales-Scotland game two seasons ago. 'A good match for the people', commented Oduvaldo Cozzi, Brazil's most experienced television commentator, a little dryly. It was this and the other semi-final between Brazil and Uruguay which has consolidated international opinion here that England were logical finalists.

Brazil's manager Zagalo, an ice-cold mind amid all their emotional flames, has stated this opinion emphatically: 'Our most difficult match so far without a doubt was against England. The best defence we have met was England's.' I predict that England will remain the only team against whom Brazil have been restricted to a single goal and I need remind no one of England's superb performance two weeks ago when they deserved at least to draw. As Detmar Kramer, FIFA's German-born official coach, says: 'England's organisation is such that you would always expect them to hold or even beat Brazil.'

Ironically it was in the two matches they lost that England demonstrated why the other finalists had such respect for them. So many irrelevant arguments have been put forward by English commentators since the German defeat, many of them blatantly personal and even spiteful, that perhaps one should spell out the facts as seen by the most professional and experienced and neutral observers here on the spot, as opposed to the armchair manager-critics on both British TV channels who have, for a fat fee, abandoned accepted etiquette in their surgery-by-invitation and some of whose reported comments are beneath contempt: at least Don Revie had the dignity to refuse to join the post-mortem. Well might Ramsey say to Joe Mercer 'Et tu, Joe'. The facts, I feel, are these.

1. England lost to Germany wholly on account of the most improbable and disastrous errors by the unhappy Bonetti. At 10.30 Banks was in the team: by 11 he was in bed. For the want of a nail, as they say, the kingdom was lost. 'The decisive and only reason England lost,' says Jose Wernek of Brazil's most authoritative paper *Journal Do Brazil*, 'was the absence of Banks' – an opinion supported by Ron Greenwood who says 'On the facts of the match this is the only verdict. Even with hindsight the tactics and substitutions remain justifiable.'

2. These substitutions were solely for the purpose of resting players for the semi-final, and had Hurst's header gone in to make it 3-1 the same tactics would have been accepted without dispute.

3. To have attacked and put on a fresh striker instead of Hunter, would have been to enter a lottery like the Italy-Germany affair and besides Ramsey could not have expected a second serious error.

4. The team was as fit as Germany and created as many chances in extra time, but suffered the normal reaction of a side that suddenly finds a game slipping from its grasp. A famous international manager renowned for his preference for attack says of Germany: 'I saw all their matches. They staggered into the quarter-finals, as Helmut Schoen would admit. They only improved from the moment Beckenbauer's goal went in against England.'

5. Ramsey's system was not at fault, but was undermined by individual errors. To be two up with 20 minutes to go was a far greater success than the system's most fierce critics had envisaged. Two British internationals, one Scottish, one Welsh, who watched the match have told me separately, 'I could have cried. I still cannot believe it happened.'

6. Italy and Uruguay reached the semi-final with, on paper, only two strikers and far more negative tactics than England's, yet are acknowledged as the most technically competent other than Brazil and England. Italy's semi-final was falsely exciting. As a British manager says: 'If you had been in charge of either team you would have gone berserk, yet I admit it was great to watch with no responsibility.'

7. Brazil's 'entertaining style' is a red herring: their style is dictated by their individuals, whose talents are such that they could hardly fail to entertain.

8. Even Brazil only got back into the game against Uruguay by a midfield player, Clodoaldo, putting himself in a scoring position with a 40-yard run from a deep position: precisely the same principle on which England built their system.

9. The physical conditions of the heat and altitude have distorted the trends of the championship. The 'spate' of goals have come against either the weak teams or towards the finish of games when teams were tired. The normal element of luck and weariness which 'open' a game in extra time have been at least doubled in Mexico.

10. The criticism of Ramsey which has mounted for the past week is primarily the result of his failure not as a manager but in his human relations with journalists whom he regards as an unnecessary imposition on his time. In Mexico he has reaped the whirlwind. It would be wrong however if it cost him his job – a matter I hope to return to next week.

Finally we come to the question of the Player of the World Cup. It can only be Pelé, an Olympian of this or any era who has given the game a distinction that transcends language, race and nationalism. His claim is outstanding whether judged on this tournament or on his lofty eminence over more than a decade in which, unfortunately, injury has twice prevented him reaching his maximum effectiveness in the World Cups of 1962 and 1966. There is not a player in the world who does not recognise in him a unique talent, and none would begrudge him the honour even should he perform only moderately in this, his second final, in a 12-year span. None will ever forget his electrifying impact on the game in Sweden in 1958 since when his name has been synonymous with everything in the game that is noble and to be emulated.

Some might suggest the footballer of the competition award should go to Jairzinho but he, by comparison, is merely a deadly striker, as is Müller, Germany's phenomenal little jack-in-the-box who makes goalscoring look so simple, and who moves with a deceptive speed which, as with Greaves of old, suggests that he is unmarked, whereas in fact he has slipped his marker in a few, vital split seconds.

Had England survived there would certainly have been claims by Moore and Banks whose stature grew with every appearance. Moore is regarded, almost without rival, as the outstanding defender of the tournament. While the question must be not whether Banks is the best of 1970 but the best of all times? The blow of his loss is matched only by that of Rocha, who played for the first 10 minutes of the tournament only and without whose substantial talents in midfield Uruguay still contrived to reach the semi-final.

The day of extremist Arab terrorism at Munich was the most disillusioning of all my time as a journalist.

OLYMPIC MASSACRE
Daily Telegraph, September 1972

Munich: The extent to which humanity has become immune to tragedy was vividly apparent throughout the day in the Olympic Village where the crisis was viewed, by many competitors, almost as another event in the Games. Who would be the winner?

As the sun beat down, competitors sat around sipping soft drinks and milk and eating yogurt, with transistors blaring, in apparent unconcern for the mounting crisis in Building 23. Three British competitors to whom I spoke as they emerged from the British block said: 'It's too bad, but what's it got to do with us? It's none of our business. We're off to have a sunbathe.' One of them added with a laugh: 'I guess the guys should have taken the money when they were offered it,' referring to the ransom.

Almost none of the competitors I have spoken to, from Australia, America, Kenya, Hong Kong and other countries, has been firmly of the opinion that the Games should be stopped. They all take the view that this is just one more tragedy in a sick world. Anyway, they think, what's it got to do with sport. There is no perceptible interruption to the day's business of training, eating and relaxing for the athletes who have a day free from competition. Cyclists on their racing machines pedal lazily in and out of the groups of cameramen poised round the main square.

Two New Zealanders I spoke to were mainly concerned with the inconvenience of being prohibited from going to their apartment adjacent to Building 23. One of them said: 'Stop the Games? That is ridiculous. It's only a small problem they've got, and they have to see to it whether they stop the Games or not.' An American competitor said: 'I'm through to the finals of the fencing. Don't ask me to be objective.'

My view of the future of the Olympic Games was, with hindsight, unduly pessimistic, even if Munich was followed by three successive boycotts. The moral strength of the Olympics would assert itself: though I still believe that cancellation would have been correct in that terrible September.

MEN DIE BUT SPORT LIVES ON
Sunday Telegraph, September 1972

Munich: The Games will go on – and on. Nothing, it seems,

short of permanent military siege, will deter the ideologists in their pursuit of strength and brotherhood through sport – Black September terrorists, Black Power and IRA demonstrators notwithstanding. The show is back on the road, however sick and discredited, a monster that has become greater than the sum of the people who constitute it. When that hypocritical flame is extinguished tomorrow, the wheels will immediately begin rolling towards Montreal in 1976 and possibly Moscow in 1980. What future abuse lies ahead is anybody's guess. With more sorrow than cynicism, I believe from the evidence of this past tragic week that people are indifferent to disaster, immunised by its worldwide frequency. Competitors may die, but sport burns eternal.

The two reasons given for the continuation of the Games following the grotesque interruption are precisely those which cast grave doubts on the validity of the Games before they began – that the event is so big, administratively and financially, that it cannot be halted, and that the competitors do not wish to waste the years of preparation devoted exclusively to athleticism.

Lord Killanin, president-elect of the International Olympic Committee, a reasonable and liberal man, believes that the momentum of the Olympic movement will remain unchecked. Yet this benign-looking Irish peer, with his deceptively dreamy, pipesmoking exterior, is determined that the gigantism of the Games must be checked, that the almost farcical extravagance of the West Germans in Munich must be discouraged in future.

It is significant that the decision to continue after Tuesday night's massacre was the unanimous decision of the International Olympic Committee – and not, as was suspected, another unilateral, sledgehammer decision by the retiring Avery Brundage, who at times seems determined that the ship shall go down with the captain.

The sequence of events within the IOC on Tuesday evening was that, with two Israelis dead, members decided to hold the memorial ceremony the following morning. Towards midnight, informed by the Federal Government that the hostages were safe, they agreed the Games should continue. At 7.30 they learned the awful truth. The German organising committee considered the possibility of either cancelling the remaining events or curtailing them, but, conscious of the heavy sale of tickets over the closing stages, recommended the continuation. At 9.30 the IOC approved the decision and hurried to the stadium where Brundage made his speech, leaping once more on to his hobby horse of commercialism and racialism (the Rhodesian affair). The speech outraged members of the IOC, let alone the African Confederation, and immediate pressure was put on Brundage to apologise.

Yet this is in a sense beside the point. What mattered was that at a ceremony to mourn 11 murdered athletes, the 78,000 crowd applauded Brundage's insistence that the Games 'must go on'. I was once an athlete aspiring to Olympic participation, and I do not feel I am alone in thinking that reason has departed from these Games.

The cry 'The murders had nothing to do with the Games; they could have happened anywhere' is palpably untrue. If the attack had not by design happened in the Olympic Village, the unfortunate Germans would not have been in such haste to remove the action to the airport. Sixteen hours is brief bargaining time for nine lives. Were the Olympic Village not the size of a small town of 16,000 people it could have been evacuated and sealed, and bargaining could have continued for days.

The indifference of thousands of athletes, continuing to act as if there was nothing abnormal within a few yards of where two of their colleagues lay dead and another nine sat under sentence of death, was itself a factor in hastening that death. With the competitors inside and the public crowding the perimeter fence, indefinite postponement of the deadline was impossible.

The sigh of relief that swept through the Village as the hostages were whirled away overhead in their chariots of doom was the most macabre experience of my life. Before and after their deaths they were no more than statistics, like road accidents.

Yet the Israelis, more than most of those who hardly

noticed their passing, epitomised the true but almost extinct philosophy of the Games, the honour of taking part. They had no chance of winning. For a majority of the others, I am convinced, the Games are not a pursuit of excellence for its own sake, but an over-intensified means of self-fulfilment. 'Don't ask me to be objective, I'm through to the finals,' said an American fencer as time ran out on Tuesday. The motivation of modern athletes is something most of them have not the wish or the intelligence to analyse. David Jenkins, Britain's quarter-miler, admits: 'I don't like to search too closely for my motivation. In 10 years I may look back and think I was a fool. But at the moment my life is geared to running 400 metres. And I enjoy it.'

Within hours of the murders Dr Roger Bannister, chairman of the Sports Council – whose own purity of athletic zeal fired my generation's youth – put out a statement supporting the continuation, claiming that 'competitors should not lose the chance of a lifetime,' with a plug for British sport thrown in. A British team official claimed: 'A theatre does not close if a member of the cast is murdered.' No, but a school play would. A theatre is commercial, and therein lies the moral.

Sir Stanley Rous, president of FIFA, is to propose this autumn that the Olympic football tournament and other team sports, should in future be staged, like the Winter Olympics, in another city or even country, to split the load. 'It is the only way smaller countries could afford to stage Olympic events,' he reasons. Such a move is essential if team sports are not to be eliminated, and Lord Killanin is in favour of limiting all countries in individual sports to one competitor per event, as in boxing and judo. Only such modifications can save the Olympics from extinction.

The Games must be pruned for sanity as well as safety. It will be an awful irony if, in the last week of Avery Brundage's rule, the martyrdom of the Israelis finally brings the Olympic circus to the realisation that it is all the things which that disillusioned old man has pretended it was not – a politically exploited, commercially overgrown, semi-professional event that is wide open to abuse, and even death.

Just imagine the possibilities in Moscow in 1980, if Russian oppression of the Jews remains unaltered. Will Valeri Borzov, double gold medal winner, be safe from being taken as hostage for hostages? Will Sandy Duncan, secretary of the British Olympic Association, be able to say, as he did two days ago, 'At the moment, security here is good'?

By a strange twist, a legal complaint against *Reveille*, for altering my article syndicated from the *Sunday Telegraph*, resulted in my writing for over two years for this weekly popular paper, under a pseudonym. Always straight sport ... as in this interview with the blessed Carwyn.

CARWYN THE RUGBY SHOWS ALF THE WAY
Reveille, February 1973

While British soccer goes backwards, rugby continues to progress. The All Blacks, beaten by the British Lions 18 months ago, are held by Ireland and beaten by gallant Llanelli's technique and spirit. Why the difference? The answer is Carwyn James – the man who has done more for the advance of modern British rugby than anyone in the game.

While soccer coaches are obsessed with defence and caution, Carwyn, a folk-hero in his native Wales and hailed by many as a genius, has achieved the reverse in rugby. It was this lightly-built lecturer in Russian drama at Trinity College, Carmarthen, who coached the Lions to success in New Zealand. It was also his club, Llanelli, which he coached for nine consecutive days before the game, who gained immortality by beating the All Blacks 9-3

The gentle little Carwyn, who inspires almost frightening fervour in the men he coaches, says of the departing All

Blacks: 'They have done nothing new. They have shown us only the old, stereotyped, predictable game. Here in Britain, the game is still evolving, and will continue to improve. I'm very optimistic about the future. All clubs are at last feeling the need for a coach. The game is constantly getting better as a spectator sport.'

After Llanelli's historic victory over the All Blacks, Delme Thomas, Lions forward and Llanelli skipper, said: 'Carwyn is a genius. Everything he told us was right.' Before the Lions tour, Carwyn spent hours in the reading-room at South Africa House in London, studying reports of how the Springboks had beaten New Zealand. Before the British team left he said: 'The New Zealand methods have stood still.' The Lions proved he was right.

Yet here is no ranting, autocratic loud-mouth. He has astonished the New Zealanders, who are used to coaches bawling their heads off. They have almost resented his success because he is not a conventional hard man. Carwyn is the first to tell you: 'I would say unquestionably that the first quality a coach needs is humility. If you set yourself up as God, you can come unstuck pretty soon.' He is critical of the mood which Sir Alf Ramsey has established in the England soccer team. Carwyn played a lot of soccer, and he claims: 'Ramsey has eliminated flair. He has created a pattern in which genius can't blossom. It's deadly dull. You just cannot create a method in which you throw out your most gifted players.'

Born 44 years ago, the son of a miner in the village of Cefneithin, Carwyn went to Gwendraeth Grammar School, became head boy, and was a brilliant fly-half for London Welsh, Devonport Services, the Navy and Wales. He gained only two caps, for it was his misfortune to be a contemporary of the great Cliff Morgan. He believes there are several reasons why Wales crushed England at Cardiff Arms Park – the same day the Irish held New Zealand in Dublin.

'We in Wales were the first to realise the value of coaching, but I believe the great players develop by watching the game and being involved in it from an early age. English rugby tends to be slightly rigid. We saw this at Arms Park when

English forwards would turn their back to opponents to start a ruck instead of driving through, shoulder down, with the ball held on the hip.'

Carwyn admits that England, in an amateur game, have administrative problems. 'It's easier for Wales, because our rugby area stretches from Llanelli to Newport, which is only 60 miles or so. English rugby runs from Cornwall to Northumberland. It is so much harder to get a squad together. Also, England have been slower to accept coaching. It's only this season that Coventry, for instance, have had a coach.'

Carwyn's attention to detail is legendary. He organises all 15 players down to almost the last movement of hand or leg. The Lions won because they refused to be intimidated by the All Blacks' tough men, and Llanelli won because they studied the movements of scrum-half Sid Going to the very last yard. Yet Carwyn is worried at the increasing prominence of coaches like himself and Clive Rowlands.

'We are fast becoming the equivalent of soccer managers – and this is dangerous. It's fine for a professional soccer coach, who is getting paid, to take stick from the press,' he says. 'It's not right, though, that amateurs, who go out there week after week in driving rain for nothing, should be kicked in the teeth. The strain of too much publicity could drive coaches out of the game.'

He sees the danger of professionalism for rugby, but hopes it can be avoided. 'The game has improved partly because we've changed the laws, and partly because, though we spend no more time training than 15 years ago, the time is used to better advantage. With the change in the law to prevent kicking straight into touch from outside the 25-yard line, we've gone through the defensive, psychological blockage. People no longer want to kick.

'When we've altered the lineout, to bring back the two-handed catcher – which I'm optimistic will come – and eliminated the "mark", which I believe gives too much of an advantage to the defending team, the game will progress even more. The problem that is eventually going to hit rugby is when employers stop subsidising the game, which they do now by giving players time off on full pay.'

It cost Carwyn James, and Lions manager Dr Doug Smith, many hundreds of pounds out of their own pockets to lead the successful tour of New Zealand. It would be a pity if rugby drifted towards professionalism and lost the spirit of adventure which has lifted it in the past few years. It would be a pity, too, if soccer did not take a leaf out of rugby's book, and try to change its image to attack, and entertainment.

LONDON SAYS ITS FAREWELL
Sunday Telegraph, April 1973
CHELSEA 1   MANCHESTER UNITED 0

'Who's your favourite footballer in the whole *world*?' The question was addressed by one 10-year-old to another on the steps of the north stand at Stamford Bridge as they waited expectantly for the last appearance of the most widely respected figure in British football. Neither of them would appreciate the fact, but Bobby Charlton, more than anyone except Pelé – at 32, two years his junior – has helped to make the question possible.

The rise of Manchester United, and the spectacular style and achievements of this most famous of those who survived at Munich, added impetus to the new fires of passion for the game generated by the European Cup in 1956 and then the 1958 World Cup, the first to receive saturation world-wide coverage by Press and television. Soccer was before then already a world game for players. Now suddenly there was an awareness by spectators of what the teams and players of other nations had to offer.

In two continents, Pelé and Charlton – and Di Stefano – by their unique abilities created an appetite for the game beyond all prediction. Stanley Matthews had been a legendary figure around the globe, yet comparatively few had seen him for themselves. Pelé and Charlton became more instantly recognisable public figures than the Pope or the US

President. As the commentator in a television documentary on Hungary said in some remote Balkan village the other night: 'They know four words of English here – Bobby Charlton very good.'

Such status in the most remote backwaters is indicative of the man's reputation. Stamford Bridge yesterday was closed 20 minutes before the kick off, not because the match itself mattered nor because Manchester United, now sixth from the indignity of the Second Division – where quite a few people would have been happy to see them go – are a shadow of the team of a few years ago. Best is in limbo, Law is on the free transfer list, where he should have been several seasons back. Charlton outlived them both, and the massed thousands in The Shed were as spontaneous in their applause for Bobby at the presentation ceremony before the start as the fanatical red-and-white horde at the other end.

They came because they recognised in Charlton a player whose contribution to the game has been classic – and colossal. A man whose consistent excellence has been the pleasure of all who followed the game, far beyond Old Trafford. It had mattered not whether you were for or against Manchester United: if you cared for the game you had to be *for* Bobby Charlton. Now, veteran of 17 years of League soccer, he made his farewell to London. It was not a memorable match. Chelsea played most of the football and we saw only the occasional flicker of Bobby's former magic. No one minded.

The bare statistics of his career are impressive enough by themselves: 604 League matches, 108 League goals, 750 first team appearances and 245 goals in all, plus the England record of 106 caps and 49 goals. Yet these contain so much that cannot be written. He has enriched the game wherever he went at a time when increasingly some people, modern tacticians and their henchmen, have made it barren. He has been the unfailing sportsman when sportsmanship has been pushed into the background. He has been generous in an era undermined by meanness of spirit.

Osgood put Chelsea in front in the second half, running the ball the last few yards through a disorganised defence after Baldwin had flicked on a cross from Hollins, who ran with the same prodigious energy as always. There had been some nice touches in the first half from young Brolly on the left flank. Fifteen minutes from the end Stepney made a fine save from Britton, another of Chelsea's bright young hopes for the future. One can only hope that maybe a player such as one of these two or someone from another club will develop into something as splendid as Charlton. The game is badly in need of a replacement.

After the game Charlton said: 'I wanted us to play better for my last game. That was a disappointment. The reception was super. It's nice for a player to be treated like this. I was very touched. I always am by the reaction of a crowd. I was rather embarrassed at all the fuss.'

CHELSEA: Bonetti; Harris, McCreadie; Hollins, Hinton, Droy; Britton, Baldwin, Osgood, Kember, Brolly.
MANCHESTER UTD.: Stepney; Young, Sidebottom; Graham, Holton, Buchan; Morgan, Kidd, Charlton, Macari, Martin. Sub.: Anderson.

Forecasting Cup finals is a mug's game. This is one of the few I got roughly right.

SUNDERLAND CAN WIN IN MIDFIELD
Sunday Telegraph, April 1973

If Bill Shankly will pardon my saying so, Leeds on their day are the most efficient team in England, if efficiency is getting a result. More than that, they are arguably the second best team in Europe. That at least is the opinion of Stefan Kovacs, the man who manages the best team, Ajax. Yet if Leeds lose the FA Cup final next Saturday to Second Division Sunderland, in what would be the most unlikely of all stories, there will be few other than Yorkshiremen who will shed a tear and many will openly rejoice.

79

Why? The regrettable fact is that along the stony road to success Leeds have allowed too many imperfections unnecessarily to mar their repertoire. There has to be some reason why Leeds attract under 35,000 people to European Cup ties. One is tempted to the conclusion that they are a team which can often be admired but for whom there is unlikely to be affection. They have sorely tried the loyalty of even their most ardent friends.

Don Revie, whose devotion to his objective – to make Leeds a great club – is unrivalled over 10 years, whose attention to detail is exhaustive and who is basically a warm and forthright man, has only himself to blame. There has been no need for Leeds to use the gamesmanship and uncompromising 'professionalism' which has forfeited their claim to greatness. They are far too good to have to resort to what at best is unsportsmanlike, at worst invokes the use of a far stronger word. The last time I telephoned Revie, he would not speak to me, apparently because of things I had said about Norman Hunter. That is his prerogative, though I would have hoped he would have been prepared to discuss the issue.

My opinion of Hunter is by no means an isolated one. The pity is that Hunter is a good enough player not to need to do the things he does. The public might be more sympathetic towards Leeds if just occasionally Revie would admit, even partially, that his team are guilty of physical excess and gamesmanship. Yet when Hunter gets his third suspension of the season Revie claims he is 'just a natural ball winner', another euphemism of the modern game. Sir Matt Busby marred his reputation by failing to curb Manchester United's worst excesses and Revie stands accused on the same count. Hunter is by no means the only transgressor.

Sprake developed the foot-up jump to an exaggerated degree. Giles, a superb player, is a notorious, if subtle, tackler. Lorimer's histrionic, instantly evaporating, injuries falsely bring the wrath of referees on opponents and do more damage than even his fearsome shooting. Clarke, the best close-range finisher since Jimmy Greaves, spoils himself by his niggling. Bremner, besides some still provocative tackling, far too persistently questions the referee. The only three players to whom one can give unqualified approval are Cooper, still regrettably recovering from injury, Gray and Madeley.

Let me say that nothing would give me more pleasure than that Leeds should beat Sunderland on Wembley's 50th anniversary by six goals with a masterly display which could be placed among the historic exhibitions of football. People suppose that one is vindictive towards certain clubs or players. Nothing could be further from the truth. All that matters is the quality of the game, which alone will determine its capacity for survival. Leeds are capable of winning by a record margin; but will they?

If they do win I think it will be by three or four goals, but I am increasingly suspicious that Sunderland have an outside chance, if they can get hold of the match in midfield as they did against Arsenal. Bremner is not having a good spell and Giles at 34 will be feeling the strain of a long season. Sunderland's midfield trio of Horswill, Kerr and Porterfield are capable of giving Bremner and Giles less breathing space than they are accustomed to, and if Sunderland once get some encouragement the pace of Tueart and Hughes could trouble even Leeds' defence.

The outcome may well depend on the individual battle between Horswill and Bremner. At Hillsborough in the semifinal against Arsenal Horswill dominated Ball and if he can successfully hustle Bremner we could witness a memorable upset. But if Giles is allowed to spray the ball around in Wembley's open spaces, then I think Clarke, Gray and Lorimer will quickly destroy the Sunderland defence in spite of the impressive development of Watson at centre-half.

What should be remembered is that Sunderland will be probably less overawed by the occasion than might be most outsiders. They have beaten Arsenal and, in front of a 53,000 crowd at Roker, Manchester City. I hope they do not encourage Leeds to make it a clogging match, for they have besides all the romance behind their achievement a marvellous collective spirit. It could be one of the few notable Cup finals – in one of two ways.

STOKOE'S MEN WIN BY SHEER GUTS

Sunday Telegraph, May 1973

LEEDS 0   SUNDERLAND 1

Sunderland won the FA Cup – because Leeds passed it straight to them, and then goalkeeper Jim Montgomery hung on just when Leeds should have snatched it back. That is the inescapable, unpalatable truth which Leeds, possibly the most powerful favourites of all time, must now swallow, choking with disappointment at a result which lets the trophy go to the Second Division for the first time since West Bromwich won in 1931.

Yet Sunderland's sensational achievement also owed so much to their own wonderful resilience, their heart and spirit which can seldom have been rivalled, their will to run when there was no strength left on which to draw. They made history – the most improbably romantic winners in 101 years – because with inflexible determination they made their own luck. This was no fluke but, on the day, a result with which Leeds could not possibly quibble. Much of the football may not have been memorable, but there has not been such tension, nor such excitement, at Wembley since Manchester United won the European Cup.

Of course, there was that controversial moment 10 minutes after half time when Watson, Sunderland's superbly-controlled and commanding centre-half, who will surely one day play for England, made his one serious error in bringing down Bremner. How Mr Burns, the referee, failed to give a penalty, no one, least of all Leeds, can imagine. Maybe Bremner was paying the price of years of influencing referees and Mr Burns involuntarily, sub-consciously, leaned the other way at a vital moment. If that was so, there was a grain of justice in a seemingly unjust decision. That still does not eliminate the argument that Leeds should have led 3-1 at half time, instead of being one down to Porterfield's stunning, ultimately match-winning, volley on the turn. Leeds made their chances. Clarke missed them. In the face of such squandered opportunity, there is small room for complaints against the referee.

Even after that, in the second half, all was not lost for Leeds. Over the last half hour they attacked with 10 men. Repeatedly, Sunderland were on the ropes, hanging on, ducking and weaving their way clear again and again. With 26 minutes to go, Montgomery made two heart-in-mouth, unforgettable saves, assisted by Lorimer's galling, incredible misjudgement a few yards out. That was the death-blow to Leeds, the holders. Time seemed not so much to run out on them after that, but to gallop. They pressed, but in doing so, allowed Sunderland space to counter-attack and nearly score twice more.

The tension for Sunderland's supporters was heightened by the fact that their team scorned even legitimate time wasting, their minds and tactical sense at last overcome by inexperience and the size of the occasion. Forcing deep into the Leeds half, they lost possession unnecessarily, thereby putting their defence immediately under the yoke once more. But they held out.

There have been few more elated winners at the finish, few more dejected losers. It was all some of the Leeds players could do to drive themselves up the steps to collect their medals. And meanwhile the red-and-white Sunderland hordes rejoiced. Deliriously. From the very first deafening roar, when their team turned to wave, before the presentation to the Duke of Kent, the Wearside team drew the strength of a 12th man from the surging wall of noise from the West terraces. 'Haway the Lads,' their crowd cried, as stirring and emotional as ten thousand hunting horns. How their heroes responded!

Right from the start, Sunderland achieved what they set out to do: to cramp Leeds' midfield style, to hustle them and prevent them from building the platform of authority from which to launch the total destruction so widely and confidently forecast. It never happened. For a Second Division side, Sunderland played their share, at times superbly, of what football there was. Never for a moment were they overawed. It was Leeds who faltered. Most conspicuously they did so on the left where Gray never succeeded in destroying Malone, regarded as Sunderland's critical weakness. Kerr came back deep to cut off the inviting channels waiting for Gray, who slowly faded from the scene until he was substituted by Yorath with a quarter of an hour to go. What encouragement the sight of Yorath coming on must have been to Sunderland.

Without the expected penetration from Gray, it was up to Bremner and Giles to crack the Sunderland nut. They could not. Horswill and Porterfield were superb, Horswill marking Giles and not, in fact, Bremner, who was shadowed by Porterfield. Giles, I thought, for all his cool use of the ball from deep positions, too often played square and slowed the game just when Leeds needed pace, so that in the end they had only anxiety, not urgency.

Even allowing for the fact that Clarke should have won the match, Sunderland's defence was still magnificent, compensating for what it lacked in ability to read situations by its recovery power. Up front, the stocky Hughes and darting Tueart were always posing problems for a Leeds rearguard which has lost some of its formidable quality.

There was a spate of fouling by both sides at the start which, for a time, made it look as if the game would deteriorate into one of those all-too-common competitive dog-fights. Leeds were making unaccountable errors, and with 13 minutes gone, Hughes sent a first-time, 25-yard shot curling dangerously over the bar. A minute later Clarke made his first miss. Giles came weaving through and slipped the ball to Reaney, who had come up wide in support. He drove the ball square into the penalty area and Clarke, delaying his shot, was smothered by two defenders simultaneously. The ball broke free, Hunter robbed Halom, beat two men on the left and his hooked centre from the line was deflected into the side netting by Lorimer. Sunderland had had their first couple of escapes.

They replied instantly, Horswill shooting a foot wide from 22 yards. Any suggestion of Sunderland folding had already been banished, but a couple of minutes later they were lucky that Clarke wasted his second chance, presented by Cherry and again snuffed out by Watson.

Another flurry of fouls – Madeley on Guthrie as he came

84

through, Clarke on Hughes, for which he was booked, then Guthrie on Lorimer. Mr Burns missed this last one and immediately there was a flash of steel as Hunter came in and demolished Tueart as reprisal. Leeds are always quick to react – and over-react.

On the half hour Gray had a half chance at the back of the penalty area, but put the ball wide; half a minute later Sunderland were in front. Porterfield, whose elegance, particularly in his turning on his left foot, was an outstanding feature of the game, swept a 30-yard cross-field ball to Kerr on the right. Seeing Harvey off his line, Kerr floated a high chip and Harvey had to back-pedal hard to turn the ball over the bar. Hughes sent over Sunderland's first corner, Halom headed down and Porterfield, with the aplomb of Pelé, caught the ball on his left thigh, swivelled and cracked it into the roof of the net with his right – and reputedly weak – foot.

More fouls. Bremner was spoken to for bringing down Horswill and now, believe it or not, Sunderland were actually on top, with the irony of chants of 'easy' from the ecstatic West end. They should have been silenced a minute before half time when a superb through-ball by Madeley split the Sunderland defence, but Clarke, with the best chance yet, once more allowed Watson the time to come in and stifle it.

Symbolically, in retrospect, as Leeds walked back from the tunnel for the start of the second half, some of them looked up in surprise as the Sunderland team ran past them at a smart trot. *There* was psychological oneupmanship, if you like. Soon, however, a shot by Bremner bounced off Montgomery's chest, but no one was following up to take advantage. Bremner's increasing forays into attack were dangerous for Sunderland – and for Leeds. Soon Horswill came through from midfield and went close, then a rattle of shots by Tueart, Porterfield and Guthrie were blocked, one after the other.

Now came the penalty incident, with Mr Burns waving play on so vigorously that he almost took flight. Leeds were getting ragged in their anxiety, though a fine run by Reaney and a shot taken on the turn by Lorimer, first-time through 180 degrees, was only a yard wide.

Sunderland's resistance was draining away, but now Montgomery's brilliance revived them. He had helped them beat Arsenal in the semi-final with remarkable reaction to a deflected shot when going the wrong way. At Wembley he improved upon it. Lorimer's long centre from the right fell precisely on the stooping head of Clarke beyond the far post. Twisting like a cat in mid-air, Montgomery plunged to his right to turn the ball away. Lorimer moved in and had only to tap the ball inside the right-hand post. Instead, he drove it and Montgomery, lying on the ground, got his right arm to the ball to deflect it up on to the crossbar and away.

On came Yorath, but he could do little. Instead, it was Tueart and Halom who made the late chances, Harvey having to save at full stretch from Halom.

How are the mighty fallen!

LEEDS: Harvey; Reaney, Madeley, Hunter, Cherry; Bremner, Giles, Gray (Yorath); Lorimer, Jones, Clarke.
SUNDERLAND: Montgomery; Malone, Watson, Pitt, Guthrie; Horswill, Kerr, Porterfield; Hughes, Halom, Tueart.

When England lost their World Cup qualifying tie in Poland in the summer of 1973, it was my reluctant opinion that Sir Alf Ramsey had run the useful length of his course as manager. The result, rather than the game, had increasingly become an end in itself. In the event, Ramsey stayed, until after England had been eliminated in the home leg that autumn.

ALF RAMSEY'S ROAD TO SOCCER RUIN
Sunday Telegraph, June 1973

The king, one must proclaim, is wearing no clothes. Incredibly, were we not used by now to his strange, introspective perversity, Sir Alf Ramsey, England's manager, says he was actually 'impressed' by his team's performance when losing 2-0 to Poland in last Wednesday's World Cup qualifying tie. By what score must England lose before the manager shows dismay? His refusal to acknowledge the team's inadequacies, witnessed by millions on television, only underlines the case for putting the destiny of our foremost sport into fresh hands. Ramsey may be deluding himself but certainly not the public.

The significance of this defeat, though admittedly only an amplification of last year's warning signs in the European championship matches against West Germany, is more far-reaching than any since the two crushing defeats by Hungary in 1953-54, in the first of which Ramsey was England's right-back. That signalled the end of his international playing career, and there can be no doubt that, barring some improbable recovery, the defeat in Poland, and his own reaction to it, demands that Ramsey steps down from his 10-year autonomy. It is not so much his team as his principles which are discredited. He would normally be expected to continue until after next year's World Cup finals. Yet the FA, as trustees of the game's welfare, have the prerogative to seek his replacement and appoint a manager with a clearer view of what many regard as the priorities. Ramsey's policies are following a road to ruin.

The fact that England dominated much of the game, spending 35 of 45 minutes in Poland's half of the field, is not justification of Ramsey's selection, as he seeks to suggest, but is, in my opinion, the most damning evidence of all. With such command, England still could not win. The trouble was that they dominated the wrong part of the field. It is of no value to control the middle if, in doing so, there is no penetration. For Ramsey to claim that chances were missed may be true, but they were too infrequent for a country with pretensions to regaining the World Cup they won in 1966.

It is not Ramsey's selection of individuals which is in question but his fundamental approach to the game, undeniably cautious and negative. Consider the facts in Poland. For a match against a formerly second class soccer nation, whose state-subsidised amateurs had been beaten by modest Wales, Ramsey dropped one of the recently most promising forwards, Channon, in order to include an extra defensive midfield player, Storey.

This converted a 4–3–3 formation, quite defensive enough for most people, into 4–4–2, his only two recognised forwards now being Clarke and Chivers. Such is an acceptable tactic only when at least two of the midfield quartet, assisted also by the overlapping of the full-backs, repeatedly break forward to reinforce the attack. Yet three of the quartet, Storey, Ball and Bell, are not goalscorers and the fourth, Peters, recently lamentably out of form, is no longer the exceptional infiltrator he was from 1966 to 1970.

The outcome was twofold. Not only was the team restricted to two striking players – one of them, Chivers, of questionable merit at the highest level – but its forward-moving build-up was stifled. It is impossible to play the ball quickly forward, and to stretch the opposing defence across the width of the field, if there are only two players upfield to receive it. Additionally, with the departure from the scene in 1970 of Bobby Charlton, England lost their only player with any flair for the use of the long ball. As Joe Mercer, general manager of Coventry, has remarked: 'You do not run 40 yards and then give a three-yard pass as we were doing.'

The tactical vision of England's profusion of midfield players was myopic, and only on five occasions did Clarke, Chivers and the full-back Hughes get round behind the defence. Having thus settled, before the match began, for a formation designed to ensure not victory but the avoidance of defeat, Ramsey immediately found himself in the worst possible position: a goal down after only seven minutes and wrongly equipped for a counter-offensive. He maintained this formation – at times England had five players in a line across the middle of the field – through the first half, which was arguably false policy but defensible in view of the fact that England were at least pressing.

Yet the decision not to introduce two, or even one, attacking substitutes when Poland went two up immediately after half time was absurd. England played for the last 44 minutes with ever diminishing assurance and hope while players such as Channon and the adventurous Currie remained on the substitutes' bench. Not that they or others would necessarily have turned the tables. What I and countless thousands watching on TV maintain is that Ramsey is not merely jeopardising the chance of qualifying for the World Cup, important enough in itself, but is, and has for some time, been setting an example to the rest of the country detrimental to the game.

The opinion is not vindictive. It is far more agreeable to be a correspondent of a nation whose team is successful and admired. For three years England's has been neither. The rank and file of England's most ardent followers know this. I travelled to Poland in a chartered plane taking supporters, young and old but united in their loyalty and paying £50 to prove it. They were unanimous afterwards in their condemnation, not of individual performance, but lack of adventure by the manager.

While Ramsey's achievement in 1966 was in creating a superb team spirit – I was among a handful who predicted the victory – one now feels sorry for the players in their devotion to the master's misguided leadership. For seven years I admired Ramsey, but he has obliged his supporters to cross the floor.

Pathetically, I feel, Ramsey has appealed to the public to support his team for the vital return game at Wembley on 17 October which England must now win by two goals or more. This implies doubt in his mind, a suspicion that the team will need support rather than earn it. Does he not realise that England's credibility at Wembley has steadily waned for three years? Ramsey has sadly forfeited almost all the goodwill he built by winning in 1966. Governed by fear rather than imagination, he has relied on functional, safety-first methods, and these are only acceptable to the public when successful. They will only support a losing team, possibly, if it has the merit of entertaining, if its aspirations are the same as theirs. This is not so. Ramsey has persistently used some of the most unattractive, ill-disciplined players in the country.

Jimmy Hill, who is being paid over £20,000 by BBC TV for his supposed expertise, claimed on radio the day before the match that Ramsey would be justified in recalling both Storey and Hunter, who epitomise the over-physical quality of so much contemporary English football, saying, 'It does not matter how England win as long as they do win.' This is the hopelessly false professionalism into which Ramsey and a few other managers have sunk, a belief that the end always justifies the means. Ramsey has preached the virtue of hating defeat above all, overlooking that many still cherish most the quality of victory. Hill took Coventry from the Third Division to the First with administrative rather than tactical flair. It is alarming that, with his professionally authentic background, he should propagate Ramsey's sterile philosophy in such a powerful medium.

Sir Alf has, regrettably, not always behaved like a knight. His wanton rudeness, his aloof, inhospitable attitude to foreigners – as at last Tuesday's formal Press conference – was a grudgingly tolerated eccentricity while he was successful. Now that he is not, it is merely an additional burden for England to carry.

In Poland his philosophy bit the dust. The rest of the football world still look to England for moral leadership. Since Ramsey is seemingly no longer capable of giving it, the FA, whatever the results in Moscow today and Turin on Thursday, should urgently appoint someone who is.

PART 3

DAILY EXPRESS
1973–1982

> Holland, anxious to crush West Germany and settle old scores, forget to concentrate.

DUTCH THROW IT AWAY
Daily Express, June 1974
WEST GERMANY 2   HOLLAND 1

Munich: Holland threw away the World Cup final in the Olympic Stadium here this evening because for 20 minutes they forgot – amazingly for professionals – that being the best team is not enough. You have to prove it. West Germany beat the favourites to take the title for the second time in 20 years because they had the character, the mental tenacity, to refuse to allow Holland to make fools of them after an incredible 65-second opening goal.

While a Dutch victory would have been a triumph for pure skill, there is no denying that Germany's gritty but less-than-polished achievement is the spice of uncertainty which makes football such a fascinating game. We will always remember how little Berti Vogts, nominally Germany's right-back and as hard as a ploughshare, subdued Holland's mainspring Johan Cruyff during that critical first 20 minutes when Germany could have been destroyed. This was when

91

the arrogant strolling Dutch lost the chance maybe of their lifetime – not in the second half when, like England against Poland, they almost overwhelmed the opposition but through anxiety and ill-luck could not get the ball in the net.

Rinus Michels, Holland's manager, should never have allowed, from his position on the bench, his team's crazy attempt to ridicule the Germans after that sensational opening. Their own, instant brilliance probably cost Holland that golden globe.

Holland, with a sleepy, slowly gathering wave of 15 passes, skewered Germany almost before the kick-off blast had died on referee Jack Taylor's whistle. Cruyff, in this vital moment losing his shadowing tank, swept into the penalty area and was fouled two feet inside by Uli Hoeness. Taylor, with nerves of steel, unhesitantly pointed to the penalty spot, a commendable decision against the hosts in a World Cup final. Johan Neeskens scored, and now Germany were laid bare for the killing. Had Holland pressed home their advantage I believe they would have scored another two or three.

Unbelievably, they stood back, savouring a victory which was soon going to be knocked from their hands. For 20 minutes they slow-balled as if taking time off on the beach. The Germans closed ranks, biding their time for a counter-offensive. It came in the 26th minute, with Wim Jansen bringing down Holzenbein for Paul Breitner to score from the penalty spot.

The Germans, responding to the roar of the crowd, to the adrenalin now racing through their own game, swarmed all over the Dutch for the next 20 minutes. Two minutes before half time, Gerd Muller, with that inimitable power and speed of reaction at close quarters in the penalty area, hooked home what was to prove the winner. Yet what a travesty for the Dutch. To a great extent they can only blame themselves – for letting the Germans back into the game and then, in the 37th minute, for a chance squandered by Rep with only Maier to beat which will haunt him and his colleagues for ever.

When Holland steadily built up their command of the second half – after an early header by Bonhof from Hoeness' corner had flashed a foot wide – there seemed time enough for them to repair the damage. Overath, so penetrating for a short time in the first half while Germany held the whip-hand, had faded, Bonhof was being pushed back and could no longer augment the attack. Only the sheer persistence of Hoeness and the astonishing calmness of Breitner kept Germany on a reasonably even keel.

How Holland and their supporters wrung their hands as the chances slipped away. Yet the game, as England know, is about taking your chances, and never was this better shown than by the dynamic little Muller two minutes before half time.

Maier, in his strange, ungainly way, the immaculate Beckenbauer, Hoeness and Muller were the outstanding players in Germany's victory.

HOLLAND: Jongbloed, Suurbier, Haan, Rijsbergen (De Jong 66 min), Krol, Jansen, Van Hanegem, Neeskens, Rep, Cruyff, Rensenbrink (Van de Kerkhof 46 min).
WEST GERMANY: Maier, Vogts, Breitner, Schwarzenbeck, Beckenbauer, Bonhof, Hoeness, Grabowski, Overath, Muller, Holzenbein.

The complexity of the personality of Sir Harold Thompson, a central figure in the dismissal of Ramsey and subsequently the FA chairman, was such that he was never able to maximise his remarkable intellect upon the many problems of the professional game. We, as Pegasus amateurs, had never really understood him.

JUST ONE OF THOSE FABULOUS FLINGS ...
The Guardian, November 1975

Professor Sir Harold Thompson, vice-chairman of the FA, might have been – could yet be? – the most influential and beneficial post-war figure in English soccer other than Sir Stanley Rous. Now 67, a member of the UEFA executive committee, Sir Harold still has potential to exercise his considerable intellect and influence – on player and crowd discipline, on the known corruption of referees in European competition – within the outwardly bourgeois, privately turbulent world of domestic and international soccer administration.

The energy, vision, above all the ideology which Sir Harold possessed, and might have contributed on so much wider a scale, is clearly portrayed in Ken Shearwood's autobiographical history of *Pegasus* (Oxford Illustrated Press, £4.50), the famous Oxford and Cambridge soccer side of the 1950s. Yet equally evident in this nostalgic account of one of the great romantic episodes of English soccer, stretching across a mere 15 years, is that bewildering uncertain aspect of 'Tommy', the web of whose brilliant mind is often so inscrutable. Shearwood recalls in his conclusion on the sad decline of a cherished club unique in history that 'the Cambridge players viewed ... the distant figure of Tommy (at Oxford) with increasing incomprehension.'

This foremost scientist in infra-red spectroscopy, lecturing around the globe in foreign languages, has always been something of an enigma to both his closest friends and critics. Shrewd, eloquent, in his younger days dynamic, his was the creative force which lifted Pegasus from an idea in 1948 to become within three years one of the most esteemed teams in the land: Amateur Cup winners in front of 100,000 spectators at Wembley, the embodiment of the great English traditions of true amateurism and sportsmanship, echoing the Corinthian spirit.

Yet that same intangible aloofness, the impression given of only half-disclosed thoughts, which contributed to the decline of Pegasus, has also restricted Tommy's inexorable rise through the committee ranks of the FA – a complex man too erudite, too intrinsically political, to be the healing influence in the antagonisms between the FA and Football League, to become the unquestioned leader of a sport crying out for his leadership.

The unique quality of Pegasus was that, as a club, it existed only when the whistle went for the kick off. Like the organ grinder's tune, its melody caught the imagination, drew

94

people to it, yet when the handle stopped turning at each final whistle, the club as such was dead until the following Saturday.

As a player of only modest contribution my four seasons with the club, immediately following the second Amateur Cup victory in 1953, were an experience of rare physical and mental intoxication: a collective pursuit of excellence which, however humble and ragged it looked on those less successful, sometimes grotty afternoons in all too earthy surroundings far from Wembley, carried a special feeling of crusade, a responsibility beyond one's self and the club to that intangible concept of the game which for over a century has stirred the minds and imagination of millions.

Those cup final victories over legendary Bishop Auckland and Harwich, inspired by the coaching of Vic Buckingham and the influence of Tottenham's memorable push-and-run years under Arthur Rowe, were the moments of perfection. Thereafter fortunes increasingly waned, following quarter-final appearances in 1954 and 1955, in times of mounting self-doubt and deteriorating loyalty, until playing actually ceased in 1963. Why?

There are many reasons. As Shearwood rightly suggests in his colourful story, the club's initial success was due to the early teams consisting of undergraduates with war service, mature men of 25. By the time the club folded the average age was 20. Shearwood himself, indomitable ex-naval extrovert, part-time Cornish fisherman, granite-hewn centre-half, personified the spirit of the club in its glorious years. He will forgive me if I say that it is ironic that the history of the club, with its reputation for blue-print soccer, should be chronicled by a player renowned for his incongruous virtues – the personification of the maxim that most of the game is played without the ball.

In total contrast was John Tanner, an international centre-forward who played for Huddersfield in the First Division, sensitive introvert, small and slight with wonderful reflexes and tremendous speed who scored goals of which Greaves would have been proud.

But within months of Pegasus reaching the quarter-final at

the first attempt in 1949, a split developed with Corinthian-Casuals, led by Doug Insole, over Pegasus' decision, led by Tommy, to abandon the club's initial one-year rule. This stipulated that players should be eligible during residence and the first year down. Tommy and some of the senior Pegasus players, mostly Oxford, rightly realised that Pegasus would only survive and achieve its objective of raising the prestige of university and school soccer by retaining its better players. Cambridge, where the connection with Casuals was stronger, objected, claiming this would be damaging to Casuals' recruitment from the universities.

In my opinion, having played with both clubs, this was a total illusion. Each could field only 11 men, and the Universities provided sufficient players every year to maintain the stream of supply to both clubs. What I believe was far more damaging was the committee system of selection which tended too much to snatch weekly at straws, picking the player of the moment often for the most tenuous reasons, thereby creating a permanent undercurrent of insecurity among all but a handful of star players, even to the point of generating disloyalty. In this matter, Tommy's vacillation was renowned; there were occasions when players were sitting in their boots at 2.40 only to learn they were not in fact playing.

The real core of decline for Pegasus was not only that it was impossible to play regular fixtures because of individual university requirements, that motivation in any season depended upon Amateur Cup success; but also that from 1954 onwards Cambridge, winning seven of the university matches to Oxford's one over nine years, produced a majority of outstanding players. Yet the seat of power, the club ground (Iffley Road), the whole aura of the club lay with Tommy (at various times secretary, chairman and president), Tanner (treasurer, then secretary) and others at Oxford.

If there was disloyalty, eventually rampant, at Cambridge, there was a failure, perhaps unavoidable, by Tommy to embrace the emotions at Cambridge in the way his charm, logic and willpower did at Oxford. 'I've been thinking ...' Tommy would say and immediately one knew that some new policy decision had taken root behind what Shearwood described as 'that old foxy look'.

In a few words on page 210 Shearwood mentions cryptically, without explanation, that in 1959 Walsh, Scanlan, English, Trimby, Beddows and Pinner left for other clubs. In fact between 1956 and 1962 Pegasus alienated or lost enough international-quality players at Cambridge possibly to have cost them the Amateur Cup at least twice. In 1959–61 Cambridge beat the Amateur Cup finalists, Kingstonian, beat a Spurs reserve side, scored 12 goals to five in three matches against Oxford, and under the coaching of Malcolm Allison, had one of the best teams in the country including Keith Sanderson (later QPR) and Pat Neill (Portsmouth and Wolves). But by now the idealism had yielded to self-interest.

One man who might have held the club together was Jerry Weinstein, sometime assistant secretary, a lawyer with degrees at Oxford, Cambridge and Harvard, a man of exceptional wit and perception, someone capable of rationalising Tommy's dogma. Regrettably, after providing inspiration for several years, he left to take up an appointment in Paris where he later died. The club never subsequently found an administrator with his passion and personality to hold things together when the flame burned low.

Tommy, Tanner, Shearwood, that superb skipper, Denis Saunders, elusive Tony Pawson, expressionless, brilliant Ben Brown in goal: the élite Oxford coterie may have lamented Cambridge's lack of loyalty, but they had enjoyed the last of the wine. And what a vintage!

THERE'S ONE ANSWER – BALL CONTROL
Daily Express, February 1977

Twenty-two years ago, I went on a university soccer tour to Sweden. The supremacy of the Europeans, even minority Scandinavian amateurs, is nothing new to me. We arrived, after 36 hours travelling freight class in what seemed to be the hold of a sluggish steamer, at Gothenburg. Although many of us had last eaten with stability at Liverpool Street station, we beat a Gothenburg university side by five or six goals.

Misguidedly, we thought we were doing our little bit to restore the balance of power. A month or two previously England's professionals, including Byrne, Edwards, Dickenson, Wright, Matthews and Lofthouse, had lost to France and Portugal on tour. Intoxicated with success, temporarily with schnapps (the vodka of Vikings) and with as yet unsubstantiated visions of the land of free love, we headed south to the ancient city of Lund. There, on a golden autumn day beside a pine wood we were clinically slaughtered 7-1.

The match was billed as Sweden v England, though we were merely Cambridge, the opposition a genuine representative side. Yet we included four amateur internationals plus an inside-forward, George Scanlan, who played for Everton in the Central League. We were coached by Bill Nicholson and had spent a fortnight training. For most of the afternoon we were within a foot or two of the ball without actually ever touching it. Last Wednesday at Wembley I felt a lot of sympathy for England against the Dutch.

Those Swedish students – how blond and frail they had looked before the kick off – had the ball on the proverbial piece of elastic, and really took us to the cleaners. They were the scratch side, we the unit. Yet such was their control and the absence of a conventional formation, that we were baffled from the start. By the finish they were literally walking the ball into the net. It was no surprise to me when three years later Sweden startled the world by reaching the World Cup final against Brazil – albeit with an English coach, George Raynor.

Today, the son of one of those Swedish students who does exchange holiday visits with my 15-year-old, can keep a football up in the air on instep, thigh and head from breakfast to lunchtime. And Sweden, still predominantly amateur, and not England competed in the last World Cup finals. The moral is inescapable. While English boys spend from eight to 18 playing matches chasing mini-trophies for the mantelpiece, the Swedes, Dutch, Germans and Brazilians spend the time playing with the ball. We are so busy winning at all levels where it is unimportant that by the time we reach the summit, we lack the most vital ingredient of all – control.

> When Sebastian Coe won the European indoor 800 metres title at the age of 20, it was apparent to those who saw the race in Madrid that here was a runner on the brink of fame.

SEBASTIAN IS SET TO PICK UP TORCH
Daily Express, March 1977

Nice guys always finish last, they say. Sebastian Coe may throw that theory out of the window. The boy – for that is what he still is at 20 – who ran away with the European indoor athletics 800 metres title in San Sebastian, Spain, is about to pick up the torch where Alan Pascoe and Brendan Foster put it down after Montreal.

The stage is ready for a duel which will give athletics the kind of kick it has not had since the days of Roger Bannister, Chris Chataway and Gordon Pirie – between the quiet-spoken Coe and over-confident, extrovert Steve Ovett. Both these gifted, but vastly different young runners are capable of getting close to, if not beating, world record times for 800 or 1,500 metres. Coe reckons he may even ultimately move up to 5,000. Yet they are still three years or so off their peak, which will hopefully coincide with the Moscow Olympics. Their personal rivalry, as yet unfurled, should be as great a spur as any medal.

Ovett, so disappointing in Montreal when he misjudged his tactics from the outside lane of the 800 metres final, has spent the winter, strangely, ploughing through the mud of cross-country runs. Coe, inwardly confident but as modest as

Ovett tends to be brash, has been working at basic speed, with spectacular results, culminating with a sprint of 1 min 46.5 sec, fractionally outside the indoor world record.

There is no question that Ovett has one of the most superb physiques of any middle-distance runner in the world with untold strength. But Coe has shown, by going to the front in San Sebastian after 200 metres and staying there, that his relatively light body conceals enormous reservoirs of power.

It is sad that almost by definition Olympic champions must be odd birds and loners. Coe at the moment appears to be madly normal. We shall wait and see what a summer in the limelight will do for him, but I fancy he is heat-resistant.

The rise and fall and rise of Jimmy Greaves has witnessed fame and frailty hand in hand. His rehabilitation is one of life's happier stories.

GOOD LUCK TOMORROW, JIM …
Daily Express, March 1979

Jimmy Greaves at first drifted and eventually plummeted from being a revered sporting idol into a helpless alcoholic. You and I unconsciously gave him a nudge along the path to a private hell in which he lost his wife, his home, his business, his self-respect. We greedily nourished ourselves off his phenomenal goalscoring feats without a thought of the pressures on him. We devoured that happy-go-lucky little Cockney genius, and to jack himself up, he took to drink. Hitting the drink came to Jimmy from the start as easily as hitting the back of the net, but it was only after 12 incredible seasons, 1957-69 that drinking threatened not just his football but his life.

We all inadvertently helped push him towards the brink …

His great buddies Bobby Smith and Bobby Moore were strong drinkers but stayed the right side of compulsion. The Fleet Street writers, some who only too readily exploited this capacity to be 'entertained', others like myself who misguidedly began to doubt his genius as the game turned defensive in the 1960s. The coaches and managers who took away the game's entertainment in the name of professionalism. Alf Ramsey, whose inevitable decision to retain a winning team for the 1966 World Cup final, and not recall Greaves after injury, was a wound in the heart. Even Bill Nicholson, his manager at Spurs, who gave him two hours to decide on a transfer exchange with Martin Peters from West Ham, only the season after he had scored 27 goals.

Two years later, quitting the game prematurely at 31, Jimmy was soon irretrievably hooked on Guinness and vodka. Now, countless hospital confinements later, he is soberly readjusting in society, divorced but reintegrated with his wife and four children, surviving 24 hours at a time with the precious help of Alcoholics Anonymous. A few days ago, he told me: 'I'm happier now than I've been for many years. I realise now that a turning point on the way down was a lack of fight and character, not to hold on to the game.'

Lest we forget what he achieved here are some reminders: 1956-57, 114 goals as a Chelsea apprentice; 357 goals in 516 First Division matches (average 0.69 per game); 491 goals in all first class matches; 200 League goals before the age of 24.

In his forthcoming book, *This One's on Me* (Arthur Barker £4.95), Greaves has told one of sport's most harrowing tales.

Jimmy loved the game, and we loved the pleasure he gave. Cheers, Jim, good luck tomorrow, and the day after, and thanks for the memories.

Those looking for poetry in sport found it in the gentle Aborigine girl. For her, a game was always a game.

A SILVER LINING

Daily Express, June 1980

Only the thunderclouds are moving better than Evonne Cawley at weeping Wimbledon. If you want to take a break from the angry brigade, what better than the gentle Goolagong girl who still floats on air. The 1971 champion still embodies the essence of Wimbledon nine years and one baby later. Now she pines for another. Baby, not title.

Her backhand was still the purest stroke imaginable yesterday, a feather-fringed razor, as she sweetly demolished fellow-Australian Jenny Walker 6-2 6-2.

Afterwards, with that unaffected modesty which has endeared her to a generation of Wimbledon addicts, she said: 'I'm as keen as ever to win, but I also want more children and maybe we will have a second child next year. I don't want Kelly, my daughter, to get too old before she has a brother or sister. She is now three going on six because she's growing so fast with all the travelling I have to do. It is hard to say whether I will come back again after a second child. It has been done before but I will have to see how it is at the time.'

How it is? Does she mean maternal spread? Surely not, for there is no trimmer mother on or off the courts. There does not look to be a spare ounce, and if anyone accuses her of being 'comfortable' it is only because of that relaxed mood which comes with maturity and the knowledge that life does not end with the handshake across the net.

Little Miss Walker bounced around the court like a happy naive puppy, watched by Mrs Cawley at times as if they were not actually in the same match. They were not. Mrs Cawley was competing less with Miss Walker than with herself. She would nod politely like a judge to junior counsel when one of Miss Walker's better ground strokes left her standing, but really it was not a question of whether but when. Once or twice she faltered, as if playing from memory, but then the timing and the footwork took charge and the reluctant sun owed her a prolonged appearance.

For the last two years she has lost in the semi-finals, to Martina Navratilova and Chris Lloyd. Now she is seeded for a semi-final with Tracy Austin, and says; 'I wouldn't be here if I didn't think I had a chance of winning. When I am timing the ball well, I know I can beat anyone. I am nothing like so tense as I used to be, but every player is getting hard to play. The youngsters seem to be getting a lot more professional.'

No amount of professionalism can ever be a substitute for Mrs Cawley's priceless quality of artistry. Not for the paying spectators.

Nearly half the nation stood still to watch the outcome of the Moscow duel between Ovett and Coe. The second act was even more dramatic than the first.

UNANSWERABLE KICK
Daily Express, August 1980

Revenge for Sebastian Coe was sweet ... and so spectacular. He took the gold in the Olympic 1,500 metres in true Olympic style. Behind him, claiming the bronze was Steve Ovett – the man who had humbled him in the 800. And so Coe proved publicly what he has believed privately for four months – that he *could* outkick Ovett, whatever the pace. He won in 3 min 38.4 sec. But he covered the last 100 metres of a famous victory in a remarkable 12.1 sec, the last 200 in 25.5. It was unanswerable ...

The nice guy shook off his despair, once more a winner. And he provided such a magnificent end to a memorable week for British athletics, with the most prized crown. As East German Jurgen Straub was pushed into second place, and Ovett, the bookies' stone-cold 'cert', into third, Seb silenced the doubters. He stuffed down their throats the belief that he

103

was just a beautifully tuned athlete and not a tactical racer. More than that, he revealed the temperament and the guts to recover in just six days from such a seemingly insurmountable psychological setback in the 800.

Throughout those days he has lived with his bitterness, and resisted colossal pressure from an army of expert well-wishers to strike early – anywhere from 800 to 300 metres from the tape. Now this slim, graceful gladiator goes record hunting again. He will attempt to lower the world best (which he shares on 3:32.1 with Ovett) in Zurich on 13 August. Straub made Ovett's own prediction ring horribly true. Ovett, who had claimed 'a 90 per cent chance' in the 1,500, named the East German, not Coe, as 'the most dangerous opponent'. Now it was Straub's surge down the back straight of the third lap after a slow first 800 in 2 min 49 sec which stretched the field ideally for Coe.

Straub's brave gamble to beat the Brits burned off his compatriot, Andreas Busse, Jose Marajo (France) and the third Briton, Steve Cram, who had been tucked in behind the front three. As Coe went after Straub and Ovett after Coe, it was suddenly a three-man race. Coe's father, Peter, all his training schedules and planning vindicated, said: 'I knew Seb would win once Straub opened it up.'

At the bell it was Straub-Coe-Ovett with Busse, Zdravkovic (Yugoslavia) and Marajo losing touch. As Coe, suddenly for the first time in these Olympics looking the superstar of last season, relentlessly trailed Straub, the strength was being sapped from Ovett's renowned finishing resources. Ovett said: 'I don't bear Seb any grudges. He deserved it. I just could not lift myself after the 800.'

As Coe went past the German 160 yards out, Ovett tried to respond but lightweight Coe, whose frame conceals a colossal stamina at high speed, had gone, never to be caught. As he sprinted for the line Straub came again to rob Ovett of the silver. Coe expressed sympathy for Ovett: 'We've both known now what it is to be losers. We've both sacrificed a lot to be winners.'

Four hours before a victory witnessed around the globe on television, I suggested to Coe that he must face a few moments of mental pain to earn enduring glory. We were sitting under a sunshade beside the deserted training track at the Olympic Village. He smiled and merely said: 'Why not?' I sensed then that more than at any time in the past week, the young student who has won the hearts of the whole spectrum of British sport was ready for his supreme test.

For months I have observed the Himalayan effort and dedication that have gone into this Olympic champion, following him by car on 10-mile runs into head winds over the Derbyshire Peak district behind his Sheffield home. I have seen him run a succession of 800 metres down a lonely measured country road, with only 90-second intervals. I knew the inner steel of the man, the combination of his own quiet but almost brutal self-motivation, his utter faith in the severe and devoted training of his father.

And so I was not surprised when he came back from the dead for his greatest triumph yet. He was relaxed yesterday afternoon in a way he had not been before the 800, when his apprehension had even been detected on TV before the start by his mother Angela, nearly 2,000 miles away in Sheffield.

Ironically, while Seb has always known that his tactics for the 800 had to remain flexible – and in the event, proved disastrous – he had decided weeks ago how to run the 1,500. To do exactly the same as Ovett, the ace racer, has always done: to stay close to the pacemaker, in touch whatever the speed, and strike as late as possible on the final bend. That strategy was based on exceptional sprint repetitions in training, including 150s in 16.4; 600s in 76 and, finally, in Oslo, his spectacular world record 1,000 metres.

He and father Peter were convinced that the later the kick was produced, the more decisive it would be. The problem after the 800 disaster was not to be influenced by that result or swayed by outside advice to go early, but to stick to the plan.

I had walked away from the stadium last Saturday when Seb was glad that the darkness could swallow him up and he fought back tears of anger at his own stupidity. His father's criticisms had been wholly acceptable because, as Peter said after yesterday's triumph: 'I've never lied to my athletes – I've always been the outsider looking on. He's the man who can do it, I'm there to supply him with the right information.'

Those who condemned Peter's criticism last Saturday were not able to see father and son return to the Village arm in arm in the back of a taxi sharing the sorrow which yesterday so perfectly evaporated.

Now, I believe there is no limit to what Sebastian Coe may achieve. In the words of Arch Jelley, John Walker's coach, 'We have seen nowhere near the best of him yet.' Yesterday we saw a new, exciting dimension.

> Too many great champions in the fight game have made one come-back too many. As did the incomparable Ali.

MUGGED IN THE CAR PARK
Daily Express, October 1980

The Americans are accustomed to paying expensively for antiques. The millions they paid at Caesars Palace parking lot was for a dud reproduction of the real, revered original. It was billed as The Last Hurrah, but, heartrendingly, inevitably, all it could ever be was The Last Post.

Muhammad Ali climbed through the ropes last night still a universal idol. He was hustled out an hour later a discredited, dejected, broken old man. Immortal Joe Louis was one of the celebrities, an ailing figure in a wheelchair, stetson and carpet slippers. Ali's trainer, Angelo Dundee, humanely halted the slaughter after 10 rounds to avoid his man requiring the same transport.

As Larry Holmes was declared undisputed world heavyweight champion, the heavenly choir of some Hollywood film score filled the air like a requiem, while searchlights split the night sky illuminating the real winner –

Caesars Palace Hotel. There is something inherently sinister about this city, which some call the true emotional soul of America. A notorious professional gambler, barred from some casinos because of an ability to memorise every card coming off a double deck, had managed to place $25,000, split at different casinos, on Holmes at 17-10 on. 'That was the easiest money I ever made,' he said as the 26,000 crowd, some still only vaguely aware how they had been duped at £250 a ticket by a wholly showbiz promotion, drifted away to drown their sorrows in an estimated $40 million on the tables.

Former champion Floyd Patterson, one of many famous fighters who watched this pitiful, so predictable end of a legend, told me: 'There was only one word for it – sad.' Yet insanely, Ali insists he will fight again. It would be grotesque. You felt almost as sorry for Holmes – reluctant but ruthless destroyer of his former master – as you did for Ali. When the security men surrounded the ring at the finish – as well they might after such a rip-off – there were barely 200 arms raised in the crowd in salute for the champion.

Holmes, smiling for the first time in weeks at his Press conference, dutifully thanked promoter Don King. After all, King owns 25 per cent of the champion, and I suppose his skin, and his bank balance, are thick enough to ride the fans' insults. Yet what had they expected?

'I did what I had to do, and I held back a few times. If I could have knocked him out in the first round I would have done,' claimed Holmes. 'When you fight a friend and brother there is no happiness. Ali fooled everyone again, but not me. I worked with him for four years and I knew his tricks. He hit me a few times, but he never hurt me. For two rounds he took a beating. The referee waited too long to stop it.'

In the old days – perhaps, tragically, even in the recent days before Johnny Owen was punched into a coma – referee Richard Green and Dundee would have allowed it to continue. Now, belatedly, boxing is alert to death in the ring. The Minter fight was swiftly stopped and so was Thursday night's preliminary when former champion Leon Spinks hammered lumbering Colombian Bernardo Mercado, a reincarnation of Primo Carnera.

Then Ali was swept Messiah-like to the stage and the charade began. Dundee fussed around like mother sending daughter to her first long-dress dance. Ali towered above him, winking, feigning grimaces, conducting the 'Ali' chants. King, resplendent in tails with wine-coloured silk lining, just grinned. Holmes leapt into the ring an avenging gladiator, both men clowned at attempts to land punches before the formalities, Ali's corner-man, Budini Brown, spitting ceremoniously towards Holmes. Superbly muscled, Holmes stared down Ali.

At the first bell Holmes whirled in ferociously, jabbing through the taunts of 'C'mon fight, sucker.' There was to be only one sucker inside the ring. Ali backed off, eyes marvellously alive, but body sluggish, swaying and weaving. There was no attempt to fight, only to make Holmes look stupid. Holmes wasn't buying.

Round after round ambled by, all to Holmes, as Ali sat on the ropes mouthing behind his raised forearms. Holmes began to pulp his kidneys, and in the third sent the saliva shooting from Ali's mouth with a right-hander to the temple. If Ali was looking for the ultimate right hook over the top of Holmes' left jab, there was never a chance of landing one. The champion just kept coming like the Space Invader slot machines.

By the fifth, the crowd were howling at Ali to fight. He landed a left, but Holmes ignored it and at the end of the round Ali slumped to his stool already a tired man. He came out wearily for the sixth and was caught by a right and two stinging lefts. The crowd was now booing the static figure, a sound never known before.

The Lip was silent now, and by the seventh it was only a matter of time. A right uppercut rocked Ali in the eighth and back on his stool he was glancing round as if searching for refuge. In the ninth he was cowering, exposed to Holmes' murderous swings , and the 10th brought the end as Holmes ripped through the weakening guard with another uppercut and smashed his head from both sides.

Dundee knew it had to be stopped. Budini, falsely heroic, tried to prevent Dundee from throwing in the towel but Ali's manager, Herbert Muhammad, nodded consent as Dundee summoned the referee. From the ringside somebody hollered at Ali's brother: 'You're going to have to go out to work now.'

GLOWING LIKE A CAMP FIRE
Daily Express, November 1980

At half time high in the grandstand on our side of the ground, someone produced a bugle, and the crisp November air was melancholy with the sound of the last post.

We had all known in our hearts from those first few minutes of thundering hooves stampeding towards the Welsh line that the Centenary celebrations would be an all-black-draped wake. Yet as the destruction continued remorselessly towards a 23-4 New Zealand victory, the melancholy gradually gave way to a feeling of ungrudging admiration, the way the driver of a rusting family saloon sighs enviously at the disappearing exhaust of a Ferrari.

There is no parallel in the whole of sport with the collective level of overwhelming, controlled aggression, laced with skill and sportsmanship, with which this mighty New Zealand team crushed Wales. I have seen great Olympic races, unforgettable soccer cup ties and cliff-hanger Wimbledon finals, but here was something which combined gut-tearing unison of an Olympic rowing eight with the bravado of a Franz Klammer plunging downhill. Some felt it was an anti-climax, but I found it awesome. Here was the frightening beauty of an avalanche – provided you do not happen to be in its path. It remained only to count the toll at the end.

The performance was epitomised by what the knowledge-able tell me is possibly the greatest back row ever seen – Graham Mourie, skipper and tactical mastermind, Murray Mexted, and 'Cowboy' Shaw, a young steer on the warpath who was so unsophisticated that on the tour of Australia he had to be shown how to tie a tie.

'Give generously' yelled the T-shirt teenagers collecting for

109

the Centenary appeal with large buckets from the scurrying thousands ahead of the turnstile before the kick off. I suspected that Wales themselves would.

The only reservation about New Zealand's almost flawless exhibition of power and tactical acumen – apart from the potentially critical absence of a place kicker – was the extent of Wales' mediocrity. Their performance in the cathedral-like splendour of Arms Park – where the singing flowing out of the soul of a nation before the kick off bridged more than just a century of rugby – aptly reflected the most tepid training session mid-week I have ever witnessed in a major sport. If some people in Wales are worried about the survival of true amateurism, they should have been at the training at Bridgend.

The All Blacks under Mourie's direction the following day were, by comparison, as slick as the Royal Military Tattoo. Certainly JPR handled faultlessly, like the great all-round games player he is, and made several memorable last-ditch tackles. Young Rob Ackerman roused the spirit with his courageous running and Gareth Davies at stand-off gave us glimpses of that fantasy in which is anchored the legend of Welsh rugby. But when did you last hear – whisper it – dark suggestions that there were some dragons out there in the scarlet ensign of Celtic honour who were giving less than their all? That is something for the Welsh selectors to resolve before the home championship gets under way.

What I will remember is the sight of one superb team whose spirit glowed like a camp fire, the tactical opportunism of Dave Loveridge, the rampaging bravery of winger Bernie Fraser even with a fractured cheek.

Yet rugby's most precious possession of all, which they must protect with eternal vigilance, is the unquestioning acceptance even in an encounter of such colossal national prestige of the referee's decision. There is no doubt that Nick Allen's psychologically valuable try moments before half time was not legally grounded. Irish referee John West was unsighted, but not a Welshman challenged his decision to allow the enemy the benefit of the doubt.

The crowd, which greeted the teams beforehand with a

drowning roar, attempted to intimidate West vocally, but never invaded the pitch. The inviolability of the referee was perhaps the most lasting treasure of this unforgettable afternoon.

Ian Botham was never a fine captain, always a magnificent all-rounder who *needed* a fine captain. Such as Brearley. The West Indies tour of 1981, marred by the banning of Jackman, was not a happy time for Botham.

BOTHAM JOB ON THE LINE
Daily Express, March 1981

Barbados: England now switch from their crisis off the field, happily resolved, to the less international but equally pressing problem on the field – the captaincy. The cavalier Ian Botham, Guy the Gorilla to his friends, has a week, including the four-day game against Barbados starting tomorrow, to rally a struggling side. That side is in danger of taking another pounding in the surf of West Indies fast bowling in the third Test.

Botham, for all his extrovert show of bonhomie and pedigree as one of our most exciting all-rounders, does not have the team totally behind him. There is still some sympathy for him but fate has decreed that he should lead a modest team against the most formidable side in the world. And his foremost difficulty must be his own form.

Not being the same natural leader as Tony Greig, or master tactician as Mike Brearley, he needs to lead 'up front', as they say, by the magnetism of his own performances. This is at present missing, to the extent that were he not captain his own place might be in question. After attempting unsatisfac-

111

torily to play himself through a period of injury last summer, which some of his colleagues frowned upon, he is now failing to take wickets.

The pressure on him is intensified by Bob Willis' return home and injuries to Chris Old, Graham Dilley and Robin Jackman. There is an undercurrent of resentment in the squad that selection in such a siege situation is thought to be dominated by the captain's opinions, even when they run contrary to and are outnumbered by those of his managers, Alan Smith and Ken Barrington, and vice-captain Geoff Miller. That, of course, was also true of both Greig and Brearley, who exercised considerable influence, but they exhibited more maturity.

There are those players who consider Botham has been learning fast on this trip, but there remains a disconcerting streak of immaturity for a man in such an exposed and vulnerable position. The T-shirts, the obsession with being centre stage at the click of a camera, the sensitivity to criticism, the outward, possibly misleading, emphasis on lightheartedness. These characteristics were compounded when he squandered his wicket in the first Test with the kind of licence given at the peak of success, but not when he and the team are under the whip.

Botham missed a trick badly over the appointment of vice-captain to replace Willis. Now, there is nothing wrong with Geoff Miller, but there is no guarantee, whatever Alec Bedser may say, that if Botham is replaced this summer against the Australians, it will be by Miller. He may also struggle to command a place.

If Botham had been big enough, he should have recognised that Geoff Boycott, our greatest albeit most controversial player, could become a precious ally in adversity. And Boycott, bitterly replaced as captain at different times by both his county and country, though too proud to ask, was aching to be asked. Much has been written about the fact that Boycott was allegedly blackballed as replacement for Willis by the MCC hierarchy back home, and would have been the dressing-room choice out here. Neither, I believe, is strictly true.

112

In the present company Boycott is a giant – in experience, achievement and technique – among the pygmies. But as a man he has that same intellectual aloofness which Enoch Powell has in politics, somehow isolated by his superiority and his own certainty of that superiority. He is a magnificent individual, but undeniably a shade eccentric, a man apart. The players would be divided in a poll on the issue. But Boycott's experience could have been invaluable to the still youthful Botham in a series in which England need to clutch at every straw available rather than at this moment talk of building for the future.

Botham, by all accounts, acknowledges Boycott's seniority on the field by discussing bowling changes, but rarely in such a way as to allow the Yorkshireman the chance to influence him. It might have served England better if both could have swallowed a little of their pride.

HUNTED BY THE TIGER
Daily Express, April 1981

The most precocious boy in sport takes the stage in Bromley High Street, Kent, tonight, bent on deposing one of the most respected world champions. Jahangir Khan, not 18 until December, is, in a word, phenomenal. He threatens a more emphatic domination of his sport than even Borg or Nicklaus have theirs – and conceivably may become the first millionaire of squash.

Australian Geoff Hunt, 14 years at the top internationally, enters the glass-fronted court erected on the Churchill Theatre stage tonight, knowing that he must drain his gaunt frame as never before if he is to resist 'The Sphinx'. That is the nickname given to young Jahangir by veteran Jonah Barrington – who was painstakingly schooled to become a champion by Jahangir's late uncle, that elegant perfectionist, Nasrullah Khan. Nasrullah's son Rahmat, who coaches and manages Jahangir, says: 'Already he is the complete player – all he needs is experience.'

113

Jahangir, whose limbs conceal the spring of a Bengal tiger, is totally expressionless on court. As he systematically destroyed the superlative stroke-player, Qamar Zaman, the No 2 seed in Tuesday's semi-final, Jahangir's only sign of emotion was an imperceptible nod of approval when Zaman hit an outright winner. Or a tiny shake of the head when he himself made an unforced error, or was disallowed a 'let'.

The spice to tonight's Audi British Open final is that Hunt will be attempting to pass the record of seven wins he shares with Jahangir's other uncle – the legendary Hashim, doyen of the Pakistani squash dynasty. Hunt, at twice Jahangir's age, knows that his days are numbered. Only recently he lost 3-2 at Chichester, over 130 gruelling minutes, to the boy who exhibits unbelievable powers of recovery when seemingly outmanoeuvred. Like Barrington, six times British Open winner, Hunt is a partially self-made champion, ruthlessly self-disciplined, as lean and hard as a bowsprit.

But tonight he faces an opponent who not only can run all night but has the feather-touch of Zaman and probably the best defensive backhand the game has seen. Jahangir's father was Roshan, younger brother of Nasrullah, and also an Open champion. Jahangir was taught in Karachi by his own brother, Torsam, 12 years his senior, and at 15 won the World Amateur title as an unseeded qualifier. Tragically, Torsam died a month later, and Roshan entrusted his young son's future to Rahmat, his nephew, with whom Jahangir now lives a stone's throw from the Wembley Squash Centre.

Rahmat says: 'I had to promise my uncle, and Pakistani squash officials, that Jahangir would do best by coming to live in London after Torsam's death. I didn't think it was a gamble, we knew he had the skill, and he's worked tremendously hard to give himself an exceptional physical condition at such an early age.'

For a year, until he turned professional in January 1980, Jahangir attended Mitcham High School to improve his English. Now he devotes himself full-time to the game which can make his fortune, in commercial endorsements more than prize money, over the next 10 years.

Jahangir looks more than 17 with his dark eyes, thick hair

and bristling moustache. But the moment he moves on court he has that elasticity which is the hallmark of youth. He is as exhilarating a spectacle as was the young Bobby Charlton.

Zaman tried everything he knew on Tuesday, but there was no corner he could put the tiny black ball where Jahangir could not reach it. When Zaman tried his drop shots, Jahangir would plunge forward to the front wall and turn a desperate retrieving shot into a devastating lob, for ever forcing Zaman to the back wall and the backhand side wall.

Jahangir, hollow-eyed from his efforts for a short while afterwards, told me: 'I had to keep Qamar at the back of the court, you cannot give him loose balls at the front, even Hunt can't play him there on the front wall. When he had a good spell in the third game, I tried to make the rallies longer to make him tired so that even if I lost the third game I would be sure of the fourth.'

Whatever the old maestro Hunt can produce tonight, I have the feeling that it will be the whiplash boy from Karachi who collects Audi's singularly ugly but prized trophy. And he will go on to win the first of many world titles in the first all-glass court in Toronto in October.

DEFYING DEATH ON THE NILE
Daily Express, May 1981

Cairo: The Nile Marathon is a sort of steeplechase of long-distance swimming – a dodge-the-dead-camel course which makes the English Channel seem like bathing in eau de Cologne. There are still a few challenges left in life – and some of the world's most remarkable men and women had converged on the Nile to explore the boundaries of endurance.

Out of 30-odd starters in Cairo, Mona Aly Resen, an 18-year-old philosophy student from Alexandria, whose ravishing smile is worthy of the lead opposite Omar Sharif, rather than being submerged in oily, putrid waters, beat all but five of the ferocious-looking professional men. Half the

115

competitors in the inaugural 19-mile marathon at Luxor –
ancient city of temples, Thebes – were severely cut by glass in
shallow water when avoiding currents on the return leg of the
two-kilometre course. Britain's young Channel star, doughty
Alison Roberts, from Port Talbot, who had stripped the
underside of a big toe, was cleared to swim only a few minutes
before the start. But, nervous and suffering from severe
sunburn on her back from the first race, she retired after the
first lap with the temperature climbing towards 110 degrees.

The Nile Marathon, this year sponsored by the Air France
hotel group Meridien, began in 1953 and, until a few years
ago, nobody outside Egypt had won it. There were strange
stories of local conditions. Sometimes the race would begin in
the dark, with guide boats, and puzzled Americans returned
home relating how they had been beaten by Egyptians who
they had overtaken at least twice during the night. The first
foreign victory arose out of a disaster when a spectators' boat
capsized: all Egyptian competitors rushed to the aid of those
in the water, while an astute Frenchman kept going to win.

This year it was always certain that the race would be
between three exceptional swimmers – two Americans and an
Argentinian. Claudio Plit, who is built like a wardrobe with
the deepest chest you have ever seen, is the twice
Capri-Naples champion from Buenos Aires who has four
times won the Santa Fe-Coronea 60-kilometres race. He
supports a wife on his prize winning, which last year topped
£10,000, an admittedly modest sum.

Wyoming lawyer Bill Heiss, a contemporary of Mark Spitz
under world-famous Indiana University coach Dr James
Counsilman, had won the Nile Marathon last year and
returned on holiday with his fiancée, hoping that a place in
the first three would help to pay for the trip.

For Doug Northway, a Munich bronze-medallist who set a
world record in Montreal, this would be his first marathon.

For five laps Northway, a lean, smiling opportunist from
Arizona, was stylishly slotted in between Plit and Heiss, but
suddenly, on the sixth lap, the pain overtook him and he
dropped back. By the 10th lap, Plit had opened a 40-yard
lead on Heiss, and that's how it remained to the finish, with

116

Northway slipping back to fifth place behind Egyptians El Messry and El Shazle.

Northway was almost a broken man at the finish, collapsing in the shower and muttering: 'I did it, I did it. I just went out there till I croaked – and how I croaked! It was hell. But by the last two laps I was beginning to enjoy it. Next time I must start training for it properly!'

I asked Heiss which part of the race had been hardest. 'I just hate the whole bloody thing,' he said with a smile, thankful that he had picked up the £1,500 second prize. My lasting thought, however, is … perhaps Brut should sponsor it next year.

TWO SORTS OF FUR-WRAPPED PET
Daily Express, June 1981

There were two sorts of highly expensive, fur-wrapped pet congregated just north of Shepherd's Bush on Saturday night. Each arrived on the back seat of a Rolls or other bespoke carriage costing well into five figures. The commissionaires were equally courteous to both, whether they alighted from quilted couches on four legs or two, and for most of the evening – at least the formal part of it – interest centred on the four-legged variety. That is not to say that, in the long term, the owners of the said carriages would not expend more lavish sums on their two-legged companions, whose charms could be even more compulsive and long lasting than those on four legs, who give their all for around 29 seconds only.

With names such as Studio Shirley, Fifi Laverne, Monalee Be Quick, Perkin's Peach and Shenley Romp being bandied about, it could be confusing knowing precisely who was talking about whom given that accents were predominantly east of Wapping or west of Dunlaoghaire. The climax of this Runyonesque evening arrived when a young lad aptly named Parkdown Jet nipped round White City's floodlit swathe of grass to collect the Spillers Greyhound Derby prize of

£25,000 and an unending prospect of free love which will net his owner around £250 for every tryst. Sean Barnett is clearly a man of acumen. Not only has he comfortably retired from the hotel business, but having bought the 14-month-old blue-grey pup for a mere £300 he last week had the wit to turn down an offer of £50,000.

White City Stadium, where in other times we gathered 50,000 strong to witness the heroic tussle of Kuts and Chataway, is now a rather seedy arena until night arrives to hide the dross and leave only the glamour beneath the lights. Down in the trackside enclosure, beneath the smart seats and the restaurant tables at £23 a chair without wine or cigars, it is a world of vicarious pleasure.

There were fellows there who could hardly afford to put their shirt on the favourite because it was required to block the hole in their jackets. The only man I saw in crocodile skin shoes down where they serve gin and tonic in half pint plastic mugs amid a communal breath of hot dogs, was taking bets, not making them. He had three folds of £10 notes in his mouth and a fat roll in each hand at the time, so that he could not even shout the odds.

At last, as the cigars burned short, came the handlers with their pedigree chums, Parkdown Jet in trap six last in the parade with unusually stiff but arched, power-filled haunches. In last week's semi-final he had cut the 500 metre track record to 29.09 seconds, and showed some reluctance to enter the track, which made me hurry to put a quick pound on Prince Spy.

The Derby roar, as the hare rockets into the straight to release the runners, does not match the Hampden roar, but it has rather more cash riding on it. Barley Field was the early leader, but as they hurtled into the first bend he was not flying and the favourite emerged in the clear. Down the back straight and into the final bend Parkdown Jet held his lead, with Prince Spy second.

As he crossed the line a number of ladies in the posh rows abandoned what was left of any restraint and almost split their expensive seats in demonstrations of satisfaction. For them at least the evening had shown a return on investment.

Down in the centre of the arena there was the touching sight of trainer Ger McKenna unscrewing a glass bottle of water to give the winner a drink, while high in the stand the champagne was flowing.

Part of the appeal of the Boat Race is the public suffering of private pain ...

PAIN IN 16 PAIRS OF EYES
Daily Express, March 1982

At 2.28 on Saturday afternoon, Simon Harris peeled off his outer sweatshirt, glanced across at Oxford's supercharged boat with a frown, and wiped his forehead with the back of his hand. The Cambridge stroke, one of the lightest ever, was about to row a race he is unlikely to forget, nor those privileged to follow the course close enough to observe the pain in 16 pairs of eyes. Could the young engineering student from Maidenhead lead to victory the longest outsiders since Foinavon won the National in 1967? Everything was to Oxford's advantage – weight (10 lb a man), confidence, the bookies' odds of 4-1 on.

In the event, the race proved to be as much about the losers as the victors. To answer Cambridge's thrilling early challenge, Oxford had to produce one of the most ferocious bursts of acceleration approaching Hammersmith for many years. So deep did it burn into Oxford's lungs that Boris Rankov, their history-making five-times winner, would admit afterwards: 'That hurt more than anything in the other four races.'

The story of the 1982 Boat Race – which was Oxford's seventh consecutive win – was that Cambridge, valiantly holding their rhythm and repeatedly attacking in vain over the last two miles, lost by 11 seconds in a time (18 min 32 sec) bettered by only nine winning crews since the war and 11 this century.

Throughout the morning, in midsummer weather, a quarter of a million shirt-sleeved crowd had been gathering along the towpath from Putney to Mortlake. As the two crews taxied on to the stake boats, Harris' father, himself an oarsman, studied his son from one of the following launches. Like all athletes at the ultimate level of training, his son was lean to the point of looking gaunt.

The father knew what his son knew, that the first four minutes to just beyond the mile post would be decisive. Cambridge were as fast, but if Harris, on the Middlesex station, could not stroke them clear to enable cox Gonzo Bernstein to move across to Surrey for the long Hammersmith bend, then they could expect Oxford's power to hit them.

Within a minute Cambridge settled into a long, easy rhythm. The impossible suddenly began to take shape as a realistic chance. As they surged past Craven Cottage football ground, Cambridge inched ahead – a quarter of a length, half a length. A more ruthless cox might have attempted to push Oxford out of the line of the main flood-stream. But Oxford, little inferior to last year's brilliant crew, were held on course by Sue Brown, and at Harrods Repository they counter-attacked according to coach Dan Topolski's pre-race strategy.

They drew level. From the flotilla creaming along in their wake, Harris Senior watched his son try to reply with another burst. It made no impression. As they shot Hammersmith Bridge, you could measure the gap as the sunlight beyond the bridge fell on Oxford with Cambridge still in shadow. Harris Senior murmured something unheard except to himself: an imperceptible sigh of sympathy. The race was over.

MIDDLE CLASS AT PLAY
Daily Express, April 1982

Not the least remarkable thing about the Badminton Horse Trials is that you can spend the whole day without ever seeing a horse. Jostling as if at the January sales, the masses throng the open air bazaar with its aroma of saddle soap, buying the gear of the gentry – hacking jackets in which they will never hack, deerstalkers, though they may never see a deer.

Saturday's crowd of 200,000 in the Duke of Beaufort's front garden dwarfs Wembley or Wimbledon, yet it has to be said that many are exclusively drawn by the voyeurist prospect of seeing riders, especially the occasional unfortunate princess, parted from their horses. Like motor racing or boxing, failure is, to the uninformed, apt to be more dramatic than victory.

Badminton is an institution within which other institutions display their wares like dahlia exhibitors. The Independent Schools Information Service has a stall for those with advanced incomes, while HM Prison Service has a stall to demonstrate arrangements for the less successful. For every two humans present there seems to be one dog, and while you can buy plastic home-disposal units for dog waste, by far the biggest obstacle of the festival is attempting to keep your shoes clean.

In every other respect – the scenery, the sport, the administration, the refreshment facilities, even the public address system – the occasion is a superb celebration of the middle class at play. Although Special Branch with bulging pockets and lizard's eyes mingle among the Royalty-spotter mums with pushchairs, police are generally conspicuous by their absence. The only bad manners to be seen – the dogs apart – are from the tiny minority of tight-lipped riders who treat their horses with as much sensitivity as a car that will not start.

Frankly, you could not blame the horses. Lieutenant Colonel Frank Weldon, past winner and now the director, has designed a course that here and there looks as if it was meant to repel 3,000 Zulus at Rorke's Drift. His cross-country course is a bit like climbing out on the windowsill of a skyscraper. The scene out in the 'country' among the aristocratic oaks at obstacles 15 to 17, the formidable downhill Stockholm fence, the Irish Bank and the unfinished bridge – a point-of-no-return leap over a 12 ft ditch – is one of sheer beauty. Man, beast and nature in harmony.

To watch Lucinda Green or Richard Meade go through almost at a gallop in perfect synchronisation is every bit as awe-inspiring as watching Botham hit a six or Coe break the tape. Meade, on the George Wimpey-sponsored gelding Speculator, which has taken several years of diligent schooling, emphatically denies that the course is too difficult. There were 33 clear rounds.

One of them seemed certain to be the Queen's Stevie B. Mrs Phillips was going a treat, jumping confidently up to halfway. A huge crowd had gathered round the lake, with its awkward descent into the water after the mile gallop from the bridge. There was an undercurrent in the crowd that almost made it a predestined banana skin. Mrs Phillips had not been strong on charm in recent days.

Approaching the jump she slowed, perhaps too much, looking tense. Stevie B caught his back legs and dumped her in the least ceremonious possible Royal launching. The crowd tittered, part embarrassment, part pleasure. The rider, with little fountains coming out of her ears and boot tops, scrambled ashore, smilingly and sympathetically calmed her mount, and departed with considerable dignity. At which a large section of the rubber-neckers went off home to the fish-fingers, thinking that they had seen everything. In truth they had seen only a fraction of this truly exceptional event.

> Winifred Brown was a pioneer of female emancipation who is unlikely to be equalled for versatility.

A WOMAN IN A MILLION
Daily Express, May 1982

It was around midnight as Hughie Green, a young Canadian later to become a British TV presenter, put down his Catalina flying boat on the murky waters of the Menai Straits in the autumn of 1942. It had been a long haul on the regular Transatlantic delivery route from Bermuda and the plane's crew were tired and hungry as they waited for the launch to tow them to a mooring. A crewman opened the bottom hatch to take the towing shackle. Impatiently, Green called out from the flight deck: 'What's the matter with the launchman?' Back called the flight sergeant: 'Nothing, sir, except she's wearing an evening dress and a fox fur!' One of the most accomplished and resourceful women of this century was not going to let the Second World War come between her and the local dance.

Winifred Adams combined the nerve of Sir Francis Chichester as a sailor/navigator with the eye of a Rachael Flint as a double international and county player at four sports. She has packed enough adventures into her 82 years to satisfy a dozen ordinary mortals. She's still going strong, rolling her own cigarettes, swearing at things which annoy her as colourfully as a petty officer, and taking to the high seas 'to prevent myself getting bored'.

Winifred lives on board the gleaming old varnished motor yacht Seaway, with her son Tony, the actor who plays Adam Chance in the television serial *Crossroads*. In a few days they head out of Yarmouth, Isle of Wight, bound for Jersey, where Tony is doing a summer season.

Winifred Brown was the daughter of Sawley Brown, a successful Manchester butcher, who owned a 32-foot cutter built at the same yard as Seaway at Bangor, in North Wales. At one time he held the record from Fleetwood to the Isle of Man and the young Win sailed from the age of 10, the only girl in an all-male crew and berthed in the for'ard sail locker.

At 14 she was expelled from Broughton High School for graffiti in the loo – 'The headmistress can go to hell' – 'and was about to be sent for corrective treatment to a convent in France when the First World War began. She eventually became a VAD nurse in Manchester, meeting the later renowned Vera Brittain, author of *Testament of Youth*. A year after the war, taking off from Blackpool sands, she had her first flight, £5 round the Tower, and remembers a Lancastrian, on holiday in cap and muffler, saying as she climbed aboard: 'Eh, lass, ah'd rather it were thee than me.' By 1924, she was flying solo in her own plane, bought by her father for £500, an Avro Avian.

In between times, she played golf – off four handicap – and tennis for Lancashire; in 1927 she toured Australia with the British hockey team, and represented England at ice hockey – without being able to skate! 'I kept goal. I was six foot tall, and when I knelt down with the pads on, the goal was full. The captain had two people holding on to me so that I didn't fall over during the French national anthem.'

In 1930, she entered the King's Cup air race, at that time a demanding six-leg course right round Britain. Her only ambition was to complete the course; she was refused accommodation at the Aero Club at Hanworth and had to be put up in a pub.

Helping her navigate was Ron Adams, with whom she played mixed doubles for Lancashire. By chance, the weather played into her hands. 'On the Manchester-Newcastle leg the weather closed in, with a lot of low cloud over the Pennines. Fortunately I knew the area well, and was able to cut through the valleys. The others all had to climb above the cloud and came down in Yorkshire, not knowing where the hell they were. There weren't the navigation aids in those days.'

When she landed back at Hanworth, she asked the ground crew chocking the wheels who had won. 'You have!' they said. Overnight was was a celebrity, the first woman to win.

Subsequently Win and her plane appeared on the stage at the Blackpool Palace on the same bill as George Formby and later at the London Coliseum. It was another 51 years before a woman won again. Last year, Josephine O'Donnell took the trophy and invited her famous innovator to join the celebrations in London.

In 1931, for variation, Miss Brown decided to travel 3,000 miles up the Amazon by steamer and then canoe, with the help of four Indian paddlers and an interpreter, as far as Peru – sponsored by the *Daily Express*, to whom she sent back dispatches.

Against father's wishes she had married her co-navigator, and in 1939 they made her most hazardous adventure, sailing Perula, her father's yawl, to Spitzbergen in the Arctic Circle, 600 miles from the North Pole. While they were there Britain declared war and the North Sea was closed. Returning to northern Norway across the convoy routes to Russia, she was told she must leave her boat behind – 'But I bribed them by promising to fly the neutral Norwegian colours, and of course put up the Union Jack as soon as we were out to sea.'

Arriving off the Shetlands in fog, she hailed a passing trawler to inquire the direction of Lerwick, only to be told 'Don't ask me. I've been looking for it for two days.' Inside the harbour, she was once again instructed not to leave because of convoys, 'but we sneaked out again in the fog and returned home to the Menai Straits.'

The World Cup final of 1982 was a nadir of sport, deprived of both Brazil, by their own delightful risk-taking, and of France, by the malign foul of Germany's goalkeeper Schumacher.

SCHOOL OF CYNICISM

Daily Express, July 1982

ITALY 3   WEST GERMANY 1

Madrid: The song which is locked away inside Italian football like a caged bird finally took wing last night. Italy rescued the World Cup final from unanimous condemnation with a flourish of second-half goals from Paolo Rossi, Marco Tardelli and substitute Alex Altobelli.

Yet for an hour both teams had insulted their audience of hundreds of millions. It was the only proper result on two counts – the appalling, unpunished foul by West Germany's goalkeeper Harald Schumacher against heroic France which so coloured the semi-final, and Italy's obvious superiority on the night, and over their last three matches. I am thrilled for the patient, modest and sincere Enzo Bearzot, an indulgent headmaster of a class which fluctuates alarmingly between real flair and outright delinquency.

The crescendo of attack over the last half hour only served to emphasise the disgraceful cynicism of the first hour, in which both teams, as deadpan as undertakers, had been intent only on cremating what should be an enchanting sport. Until the quicksilver Rossi, sustaining his lethal touch, scored his sixth goal in three matches, it seemed we would today be holding a memorial service for the death of sportsmanship, for the passing of a game once graced by Matthews, Pelé and the rest.

There must be a genuine fear that this shop window on the world will be judged to have vindicated the darker side of Italian habits, and will propagate the school of cynicism. In the first 65 minutes there were, by my count, 20 fouls that were bookable, in which the offender had not the slightest intention of playing the ball – yet only Conti, of Italy, and Dremmler, of Germany, had received Brazilian referee Coelho's yellow card. All that is worth recalling of that sterile, shameful first half is the penalty which Cabrini missed in the 25th minute.

Then at last, and mercifully, the spell of despair was broken, and not surprisingly the goal stemmed from one of the profusion of free kicks. Rummenigge brought down Oriali, and while the Italian was still lying there complaining of a broken leg for at least the tenth time in the match, and Germany were busy dredging up a wall, Tardelli swept the ball out to the right where Gentile had found some free space. With the Germans bunched on the wrong side of the pitch, Gentile curled a low cross in behind the defence, Altobelli lunged and missed, and amid panicking defenders Rossi on the far post got the decisive touch.

Now Germany made the same error as had England against Spain, delaying for another 13 minutes the introduction of a substitute to change the pattern. Indeed, Germany continued to play it physical, three of the next four serious fouls being theirs. Then Jupp Derwall withdrew his midfield man Dremmler, sending out the bulky Hamburg striker, Hrubesch, to strengthen the attack. All this did was immediately create the gap for Italy to seal the game on a counter-attack. Rossi sprinted clear on the right, hotly supported by defenders Scirea and Bergomi. After three exchanged passes the ball was switched square across the back of the penalty area to Tardelli who, sidestepping one man, shot an arrow through a cluster of defenders and wide of Schumacher.

As the entertainment rose, so did tempers, and three more were booked. Now Germany were pushing forward recklessly and with nine minutes left were stunned by yet another counter-punch. With Germany hauling themselves back like men at the end of a cross-country run, they arrived in time only as spectators as Altobelli hammered in the third.

Breitner, whose intelligence and energy had been swamped in the early stupidities, now scored a token goal for Germany, who must seriously rethink how they want to play the game. What they have played in Spain has seldom been football, though they, like Italy, have so much skill would they only put it to better use. By the time the King of Spain handed the cup to the veteran Zoff, sport's most public event had just about managed to finish on a respectable note.

ITALY: Zoff; Gentile, Scirea, Collovati, Cabrini; Bergomi, Tardelli, Oriali, Conti; Rossi, Graziani (Altobelli 18).
WEST GERMANY: Schumacher; Kaltz, Stielike, K.H. Forster, Briegel; Dremmler (Hrubesch 63), B. Forster, Breitner; Littbarski, Rummenigge (Muller 70), Fischer.

On a still, humid Mediterranean evening, a milestone is passed in women's sport.

ROSA'S RIGHT TO RUN
Daily Express, September 1982

Athens: Downhill she came for the last five miles, through the pressing funnel of people towards the Parthenon set high against an almost dark, crimson sunset. Rosa Mota of Portugal reached the Temple of Jupiter and wheeled left into the floodlit old 1896 Olympic Stadium. It was a magical moment. On she ran, with one defiant wave of the fist, down the narrow cinder track between the steep marble terraces, the 50,000 expectant faces merging at the rim of the stadium with the night.

It was an unforgettable climax to the first women's championship-winning marathon, with the first three separated by barely a minute following a gripping battle over the last nine miles. As little Rosa crossed the line beneath the illuminated Olympic rings, Laura Fogli of Italy, pre-race favourite, was already in the stadium, Ingrid Kristiansen of Norway only another 150 metres behind.

Seeing the distress on the faces of some of the girls out along the course, the agonised rolling eyes, you could well understand how the original Marathon runner Phaedippides had fallen dead as he delivered his news of 192 Athenian comrades slain by the Persians in 490 BC. Yet these determined women closed the memorable 1982 European championships with a resounding demonstration of their right to run any distance they please alongside the men.

There was a bizarre contrast between the finish and the start at the little village of Marathon, on a scorched, dusty patch of earth. The waiters in the only café spun on their feet, while the priests and local political leaders took up prominent seats by the granite-laid starting line. The grazing goats tried to bolt.

By six miles, Dutch girl Carla Beuskens relaxed and, with a steady gaze, was leading two Russians. At nine miles, Kathy Binns, the blonde Yorkshire lass, was hanging on in eighth place, hair matted with sweat. A mile later, going downhill, 25-year-old Kathy made a brief break to the front, opening up 40 yards. But by 12 miles she was 10th, as the ferocious series of climbs began to 800 feet. She eventually finished in 2 hr 44 min 9 sec for ninth place.

First to fall to the heat of this formidable course was Magda Ilands of Belgium after one hour and 17 minutes. Shortly afterwards Mota had joined the group at the front which was now made up of four. Side by side they ran, snatching at their interval stalls where the drinks were laid out, cold sponges waiting.

By 17 miles at the village of Stavros you would have put your money on Beuskens, now 40 yards clear, eyes down, calm and balanced. But they say you hit the 'wall' at 18 miles. Beuskens must have hit it. By 19 miles Mota had taken over at the front by 10 yards with the Italian and Norwegian in pursuit. The pace quickened as they entered the city outskirts, but they could not close that gap. Steadily it widened, as the cheering reached a crescendo.

PART 4

THE TIMES
1982–

Returning to *The Times* after 23 years, I plead guilty to
youthful misjudgement.

PROFESSIONALS DESTROY CENTURY OF SPORTING TRADITIONS
The Times, January 1983

We were wrong. Those of us who, 20 years or so ago, yearned
for and advocated a brave new world of sport dominated by
professional attitudes have been proved gravely misguided.

Away with amateur fogies, we cried. Down with the dogmas
of our privileged grandfathers; forward with pragmatism and
efficiency. But the professionals blew it. What we got was
rampant expediency. They quickly learned the price of
everything but the value of nothing. Rightly and belatedly
freed from social servility and financial restraint, the pros
have in a few years almost wrecked many of the sporting
traditions and standards fashioned over a century.

That mystic alchemy, sport itself, microcosm of life's big
dipper, has not lost its capacity to inspire the individual, a
Klammer, Coe or Pelé, or to enthrall millions, as
demonstrated by the Melbourne fourth Test or the recent
holiday football attendances.

Yet to have championed as I did in 1960 the abolition of football's maximum wage – that monument to proprietory Victorian injustice which humbled the genius of a Matthews or Mannion with a clerk's wages – today carries the guilt of handing firecrackers to five-year-olds.

To have helped push the All England Club towards leading tennis out of the shamateur world of moral witch hunts which haunted Gonzales and Hoad, into the present era of million-dollar mugging, is to have destroyed simultaneously something of charm and worth.

To have closed for ever the odious separate door for 'Players' at Lord's, only then to have the Long Room overrun by Kerry Packer and a generation of umpire-intimidators is to have created a fire more uncomfortable than the old discredited frying pan.

To have turned golf's dignified, uncluttered calendar of historic championships – when to watch Hogan and later Palmer was to observe Zeus himself – into the interminable, synthetic television world of the Palm Springs-Coca Cola-Mothercare Classic monopoly money is the ultimate in showbiz dilution by dilation.

The last 20 years of sport has seen the establishment of an 11th commandment: no sportsman shall be denied the right to earn his living by any moral consideration implicit in the other 10. As a consequence we have recently experienced the most morally corrupt World Cup yet; the degrading trail of mercenaries to South Africa; the confirmation that two Australian Test players backed themselves mid-match to lose against England at Headingley in 1981; the reinstatement of convicted drug offenders for the 1980 Olympics; continuing carnage on the Grand Prix motor circuit because of inadequate regulations; mismatched boxing bouts unfit for the Reeperbahn; sponsored athletics spectaculars which abuse both athletes and public; Kevin Keegan taking £3,000 a week from the Newcastle public; John McEnroe insulting umpires and opponents almost with impunity.

In any properly ordered sport, such as the Turf, West Germany's goalkeeper would have been suspended from international football for life, if not by FIFA then by his own federation, for his foul in Spain, while Lillee and Marsh would have been banned from Test cricket. I wonder on whom Marsh might have his money this week?

Keegan has pulled a coup in Newcastle as smart as any by O. Henry's doubtful hero Jeff Peters in *The Man Higher Up* upon that 'unlimited asylum for the restless and unwise dollars of his fellow men'.

Of course, the McEnroes of sport will find an echo on the contemporary terraces because they represent the appealing voice of anarchy for disenchanted youth.

Without rigorous though fair discipline, sport becomes meaningless, and it is not to be surprised at if public confidence and interest wanes when the public cannot be certain that what they are paying to watch is *bona fide*. The most elementary mistake so many of the pros have made is to suppose that winning is everything, an idea imported from the Americans along with chewing gum and almost as objectionable. Just as the Etonian is supposed to have replied to the premise that breeding is everything, so winning is fun, but it is not everything. Sport at its pinnacle is foremost about glory, and nowhere does the dictionary definition of that word mention winning, only honourable fame. More often than not it is the quality of the loser which determines the fame of the winner.

It all seemed so simple to us radicals back in the 1950s, the amalgamation of ideology and professionalism, of devoting every effort to winning without denigrating defeat. I grew up in a school where at the time even to wear a tracksuit was considered slightly professional, to warm up was suspect, and to congratulate a goalscorer was reprehensible. I competed at the White City with starting blocks sawn from an old church pew, secured with Meccano. When, as captain of football, I requested the headmaster – an Oxford Blue but a mite too godly for his own good – for permission to take a regular linesman to away matches for greater efficiency, I might as well have asked for a cocktail cabinet in the pavilion.

The master in charge of football, an hereditary idealist, inspired us to run through the proverbial brick wall. But when I first encountered at university the professional mind,

132

in the shape of our coach, Bill Nicholson, and also the absurdity of the England selection committees, amateur and professional, some of whom still did not recognise players by half time, I longed for the merging of the two codes.

Yet the gap was too great. The amateurs had forfeited their right to influence the professional game by turning their back on it 80 years before, simultaneously losing the advantage of mixed competition enjoyed by cricket. The development of the professional game had passed almost exclusively into the hands of tradesmen more often concerned with personal prestige than sporting principles. How many outstanding chairmen of First Division clubs have there been since the war? Perhaps three – Harold Hardman, of Manchester United, Denis Hill-Wood of Arsenal and John Cobbold at Ipswich. They have known how to accept defeat as well as victory, Kipling's two impostors engraved on the entrance hall at Wimbledon.

When I became a journalist I was, like many, convinced that British sport was selling itself short, because amateurishness – as opposed to amateur ethics – still dominated. Walter Winterbottom, in football, and Geoff Dyson, in athletics, internationally respected coaches, were not master of their own domain. When, in April 1962, I overheard Major Wilson Keys, chairman of West Bromwich Albion, say that he would ensure that Johnny Byrne, of West Ham, would not go to the World Cup, for punching a shot over the bar from which the penalty was missed, I felt he was going too far. I know now he was not. We handed the game over to the pros and what did we get? The percentage player and the professional foul.

The moral dilemma was little different from those today confronting Rugby Union over sponsors' boot money, and athletics, where we often do not know who is running to win and who to parade his sponsor's logo. The incorrect solution to either problem could be as dire as it has been for soccer.

> British sport offers something for everyone: if you know
> where to find it.

SELF-SUFFICIENCY AND IMAGINATION
The Times, March 1983

Go into the staff room at five o'clock at Plas y Brenin – two
gallon teapot and sticky buns – and you could be in any
schoolmaster's common room, until you discover that the
unassuming folk around you have adventure pedigrees which
put James Bond in the shade. That fellow over there with a
hole in his wet sock has canoed round Cape Horn, the one in
the scruffy T-shirt has defeated the north face of the Eiger,
and, oh, yes, the one over there in the pebble glasses has skied
down Annapurna. The ordinary citizen can be a part of this
rarified company for as little as £39 for a weekend's climbing
course.

Plas y Brenin, in fact, is a centre of sporting excellence no
less than Wimbledon or Lord's, nestling under the skirt of
Snowdon in the challenging beauty of the Ogwen Valley. It is
here, unobserved by David Coleman, where the air truly is as
cool and clear as the mountain stream and the opponents this
week, next week and for ever are the wind and the swirling
mists, the granite and the ice and snow, where the only
cheering is the chattering waterfall or the mournful cry of the
ewe, that a remarkable team of instructors is assembled by the
Sports Council at their national centre for mountain activities.

Here, in inspirational surroundings, you may learn
everything from merely how not to get lost when out
hill-walking in places where only the hawk is at ease without
an ordnance survey map, to the kind of esoteric technique
which would take you up Everest if your mind did not freeze
first: you may be an inner city schoolgirl, or a middle-aged
executive, but whoever you are, Plas y Brenin will test your
nerve and muscle more than your bank balance.

134

The instructors, unlike some of our contemporary professional sportsmen, have an almost uniform characteristic of modesty. Their vocational enthusiasm persuades them to work mostly a 12-hour six-day week for around £8,000 a year. A relaxed classlessness pervades the whole centre, with its accommodation for 60 students in cosy bunk beds, and robustly filling, punctually served, institutional food.

During the two days I was there, the five courses in progress – an average six students to a course – were classic ice and rock climbing; mountain leader training; mountaincraft and hill-walking; white-water, sea and surf canoeing; and a 10-week outdoor education course, undertaken by a Midlands maths master, two young women (one with a Cambridge science degree) still looking for a fulfilling career, and a refugee from the army. This last course, recognised by the Department of Education and Science, is designed for those intending to become instructors in the Outward Bound tradition, and costs approximately £1,000. Many would say it was cheap for the qualification gained.

Initiative, independence, self-sufficiency, imagination: these are the disciplines emphasised, and are learned, for example, by river passaging in home-made rafts and canoes constructed from inner tubes and logs. And there is the night line: a quarter of a mile of rope up in the pine forest winding through icy streams, over rocks, down steep banks of sodden undergrowth, where the lichens hang like lace. The students must follow the rope hand over fist, totally blindfolded at the dead of night, to sharpen the sense of smell, touch and hearing.

The night I went with them there was cold steady drizzle and it was so dark in the forest that even unblindfolded you could not see a man's face two feet away. The test is so disorientating that when the instructors looped the terminus of the rope back on to itself in a 20-foot circle, the students started retracing the course without knowing they were doing so. After a quick dinner they were due back out again equipped with nothing more than a sleeping bag and a sheet of plastic to bivouac for the night, individually and alone, women included. John Disley, the former deputy chairman of the Sports Council, and on the management committee of the centre, says: 'We're the brand leaders in this field. What we do today, the local education authorities will be doing in a few years' time.'

The next day I went with the canoe group to Anglesey in search of surf, on a glorious day when the colours of sky and mountainside, pines and snow-capped peaks were as intense as a canvas by Goya. Though the waves at Cable Bay were no more than three feet, they were sufficient to test the technique of the men in the care of Terry Storry, who initially learned his mountaineering when cliff and quarry climbing at Exeter University, and was more recently a member of the British expedition which canoed down the Bio Bio river in Chile.

'It's remarkable what that fellow can do,' said a surveyor from Leamington, whose sport is normally limited to flat water canals, and who considered he was getting exceptional value for money from his £130 week, representing what must be a subsidy of at least 50 per cent by the Sports Council. 'Terry can control the canoe backwards, forwards, and sideways in the white-water rapids, seemingly without effort, while we're concentrating on merely staying upright. The instruction here is vastly better than you'll find anywhere else.'

The Sports Council money is not wasted. Though Plas y Brenin last year cost £551,000 to maintain, partially offset by a course income of £263,000, almost everyone who attends is likely to be ploughing back their experience into scout groups, the TA, sea cadets, or private climbing, canoeing, skiing or orienteering clubs. It is an investment in expertise probably much more precise and measurable than, say, the facilities at the Crystal Palace national recreation centre. Alpine courses in climbing and skiing are included in the extensive curriculum.

The climbing spans everything from scrambling without ropes for the more enthusiastic hill-walker, through rock climbing of the Derbyshire Peak, grit-stone type, to the most advanced mastery of vertical ice. There is a climbing training room with 16-foot walls which simulates the half-inch holds

136

which may be all that rests between you and a 600-foot fall. Snowdonia and Scotland may lack the glaciers of the Alps, but the weather conditions can be just as severe, as you are constantly warned.

'We are working to high technical standards,' says Mike Woolridge, one of the many temporary instructors who pass through the centre, some of them working for board and £10 per week. Included in the roll of experts who have contributed to Plas y Brenin's unrivalled reputation is Peter Boardman, killed in an attempt on Everest last year with Joe Tasker.

The quality of the centre is epitomised by its present director, John Barry, a squat, extrovert Irishman who, with Boardman, in 1977 made the first ascent of the south summit of the perilous 23,600-foot Himalayan peak, Gauri Sankar. Last year for recreation, Barry canoed across the Irish Sea – to keep his 68-year-old father company. Then he had to get back to the office, so his father made the return trip alone. Barry's recently published book *Cold Climbs* is an index of horrifying home-based ascents, for which you do not need a passport for the privilege of being scared out of your skin. Barry earns rather less in a week than Kevin Keegan does in five minutes playing football, yet he and his colleagues have decidedly more to offer the young if only they can get to them. The Sports Council is working at it.

Oxford friends accused me of prejudice on this issue, though I suspect they had lost sight of the purpose of Oxbridge sport: indeed of all sport. A fair contest.

OXFORD POWERBOAT POLITICS
The Times, March 1983

Oxford University seem likely to be cheating in the Boat Race on 2 April as surely as if they were powered by an outboard motor. What is alarming is less the effect of this on the outcome of the race, which we all know does not matter unless you are out there in one of the boats, than the fact that nobody at Oxford appears to recognise, let alone admit, that they might be cheating.

The 'motor' in question is a languid, gangling 28-year-old son of a Yugoslav, Boris Rankov, over whose eligibility for the race the ensuing unseemly squabble with Cambridge has reached levels of logical nonsense which exceed the imagination of Lewis Carroll. I hasten to stress that the most dignified act so far in the row – pronounce it how you will – namely Rankov's offer to withdraw, has been rejected by his own Blues committee.

I ought at the outset to declare, if not an allegiance, then an affiliation, having competed for Cambridge several times in other sports, and must also say that, while I have every sympathy for Cambridge on the principle involved, I have no time whatever for their Tweedledum threat to pull out of the race, which can only serve further to lower the tone of the argument and alienate their sponsors and lose public sympathy. They *must* compete. Not to do so would be as futile as the well-intentioned but misguided withdrawal of the British middle-distance runner, Christine Benning, from the Moscow Olympics because of the reinstatement of convicted drug users. The histrionic gesture of withdrawal proves and solves nothing and only lends credibility to the trivial jibe of Oxford's coach, Dan Topolski, that Cambridge are 'looking for an excuse for another defeat'. But I am not concerned with Cambridge.

What is so indefensible about Oxford's position is its obvious expediency, the thin ice of its wholly academic argument and its palpable weakness on both morality and sportsmanship. I feel sure that Charles Wordsworth, nephew of the poet and initiator of the first race in 1829, would agree. The public, quite frankly, neither understand nor care about the subtleties of definition of *in statu pupillari*, which is at the basis of Cambridge's protest, and neither do I. What does matter is that if a great sporting event between those 19th-century fountains of organised amateur sport – rightly evaluated by the BBC as being on a par as a national event with Trooping the Colour, the FA Cup final and the Derby and being one of the most entrenched free social spectacles of modern times – is disfigured by surrender to expediency, what hope is there for the rest? In 1983 do Oxford no longer acknowledge or have a conscience for the concept of *noblesse oblige*?

The facts are that Boris Rankov last year came out of retirement on Topolski's persuasion to establish an individual record fifth consecutive victory. 'I thought I could afford one more term,' Rankov told me. Now he is back looking for a sixth win. Yet he is in his fifth postgraduate year, a junior Fellow on the payroll of St Hugh's College, where he lectures part-time in Roman archaeology while preparing a thesis. In Cambridge terms, in anybody's terms, he is a don, a senior member of the university, no matter by what dexterity of words you try to twist the meaning of 'student'.

He was rowing for Oxford when Simon Harris, the Cambridge president and stroke who rowed a heroic losing race last year and is now being required to fire other people's bullets, was still almost in short pants at school in Maidenhead. Rankov is one of several postgraduates in the Oxford crew containing an assortment of Americans, Canadians and international championship medal winners. Cambridge have a file of unanswered correspondence from Oxford on the eligibility question which finally precipitated, far too late, the recent threat of withdrawal. The technical flaw in Cambridge's stance is that the eligibility agreement was reviewed in 1975 in their favour to admit a 29-year-old, David Sturge, who ultimately was excluded by glandular fever.

Yet any average disinterested bystander, that classic legal

definition of impartiality, would agree that any Oxford v Cambridge contest, or indeed one between any two universities, is for students and that morally – whatever the financial flexibility of our benevolent education authorities which, for all I know, may permit the honest Boris to continue his obscure thesis for another 10 years – Rankov cannot be considered a student. If nothing else, he is depriving a succession of the average three-year-degree students of the opportunity to participate in a unique experience and even in 1983 participation is still, or ought to be, the name of the game. It traduces more than a century of tradition if one must read for a Doctorate of Philosophy to have a chance of a Blue.

Of course, the shape of university life is changing. The intake of women freshers now exceeds 35 per cent and the increase of postgraduates further dilutes student density and the broad base of rowing and other sporting standards. Yet it merely underlines Oxford's attitude of expediency that there are dark rumours, not denied, of touting for foreign postgraduates at international rowing events. The average age of the Oxford crew is 25, of Cambridge 21.

I do not doubt that Ladbrokes, the sponsors who will have contributed £400,000 by 1986, are quietly delighted by the rumpus, given that this year they do not enjoy the public focus of sexual equality on the Tideway. The apocryphal slogans scrawled on the Oxford crew's Transit van last year read: 'This boat is powered by S. Brown's knicker elastic.' For the present, rankling over Rankov will do nicely.

But the issue serves only to diminish Oxbridge sport. You really would suppose that men of intelligence could arrive at a fair and correct solution over a pink gin in the Leander Club. It is about time they started behaving like men instead of students.

A BEAST IN THE FOREST
The Times, March 1983

Making the long, straight walk from Aintree's grandstand

down to Becher's Brook half an hour before the National is like strolling down a runway to the point of no return for the maiden flight of an aeroplane – the definitive moment of beauty or disaster.

In Saturday's spring sunlight, that renowned, frightening fence with its soft green sculptured contours of fir branches camouflaging the unforgiving stakes and telegraph poles beneath, had its own betraying elegance in the lull before the storm. Synonymous with the reputation of this greatest test of man and animal, Becher's awaits like a beast in the forest, huge and awesome. The Brook on the far side is the merest trickle, but the drop, if the horse fails to get length and impetus, is more than two feet greater than the five foot take-off and severest on the inside where the course takes a 20-degree turn. As the crowd gathers outside the rails, and a multitude of photographers on the inside set up their remote-control cameras in the very throat of the Brook, it is difficult to ignore the analogy with Tyburn. Yet here, survival is a fascinating synthesis of skill and courage and luck.

From the broadcast commentary, we know the gladiators are parading before the grandstand, perhaps for the last time in 144 years. Looking back through binoculars the mile or so past the first five fences, towards the start, the heat shimmer rising off the old motor racing track dissolves the jockeys' colours into an indistinguishable kaleidoscope of confetti.

Suddenly they are off and for what seems an age all we can discern is vertical movement as the 41 horses roll down the course like the Severn Bore, past the dozen or more attendant ambulances, several of which now glide into anticipatory action. When I passed the first fence, a lady from St John's was busily folding her red blanket on her faded canvas stretcher much as she might lay out the sandwiches at the church fete. One mentally shivered slightly, but it was reassuring that she and dozens like her were quietly ready for the ferocious pageant they had experienced often before.

At Becher's, I find myself standing next to the duty vet, who has attended the fallen for close-on 40 years. When he was a younger man, he had to shuttle between here and the equally formidable Valentine's. He has had to put down more horses than he can remember, he says, including six in a single race some years ago, but now he considers the jumps in general and Becher's in particular are safer and fairer. 'We don't get horses actually impaled on top, unable to move them, as used to happen.'

First over the Brook, so to speak, on Saturday was a steward in grey pin-stripes, with his entire family in tow; his wife making light of the soft going in spite of the weighty handicap of sparkling stones on her left hand; his teenage daughters chattering like ducklings, oblivious of the earthy jests from the public on the rails and the photographers being fussily rearranged by Daddy. Meanwhile, the St John's ladies decide that perhaps they should have a second red lollipop pole, the signal for summoning an ambulance. When Daddy has got all us media chaps where he wants us, the ducklings decide to rush off instead to Valentine's even though the growing roll of thunder tells us of the advancing field, which has had only five casualties at the first five fences. So awesome is the sound as 144 hooves gallop towards us that one is instinctively tempted, standing a few feet from the precipice, to duck.

And then, with a roaring, crashing, thudding crescendo, flying high above our head, they have come and gone, leaving us in visual turmoil. Four riders are down and as the thunder of hooves recedes towards the canal, a groan goes up on the rails – one of the fallers is Mrs Joy Carrier, the fancied American, who had stood as a nine-year-old where we stand now and likewise been mesmerised by the Niagara of sound and emotion. Today, the dual Maryland Hunt Cup winner is down, her red and blue colours grazed with brown, as King Spruce is balked by Royal Mail. Mr Peter Duggan, thrown from Beech King, lies dazed for a few minutes, seemingly buffeted by a dozen flailing hooves but miraculously not seriously hurt.

It is an extraordinary, emotional, sad contrast – between the moment when a jockey is there galloping amid the maelstrom, high on adrenalin, the body taut, eyes riveted dead ahead, and the next moment when he is suddenly alone and deserted on the sweet-smelling damp turf behind the disappearing field like some crumpled, forgotten chocolate-carton.

If the impact of the first assault on Becher's is frightening in its sheer volume, the second is if anything more dramatic because by now we know the pattern of the race. The first three miles have decimated the charge, and now it is no longer so much a matter of luck as of rhythm, judgement, heart and stamina, by both horse and rider.

Down the long straight they herd towards us once more and we can see the purple and pink of Greasepaint running towards the outside, the light blue and orange of Corbiere on the inside where he has been from the start. Greasepaint clears Becher's fractionally ahead, but Corbiere, neat and compact, lands more cleanly. You sense that Ben de Haan is now riding within himself, on auto-pilot, as it were, and only the strength-sapping ground can take the prize from them, as we watch them go down past so-called Aintree Village against the bizarre backcloth of gasometers, factory chimneys and rearing council blocks – a beautiful picture in an ugly frame, the one immortal and indelible, the other for sale.

The last memory of what must surely not be allowed to be the last National is of Spartan Missile's rider, Hywel Davies, unseated at Becher's second time round, staring forlornly at the fast disappearing buttocks of his mount with his arms raised to the cloudless sky in dismay. Let us hope it was not a symbolic gesture.

DRIVING FORCE OF MORTAL GODS
The Times, May 1983

Monte Carlo: You begin to understand the strange, quasi-religious overtones of motor racing when, immediately after yesterday's first round of timed practice for Sunday's Monaco Grand Prix, the widow of Gilles Villeneuve, killed a year ago in practice at Zolder, is to be seen giving a trackside interview. It is not only those who die who give their life to the sport.

There is something Machiavellian about the beauty of the tight, twisting, two-mile Monte Carlo course nestling in its cosmopolitan bowl beneath cloud-capped Riviera hills, where the exploding noise of gear changes and the screaming top note of the 200 mph turbocharged monsters rebounds like a thunderclap off the harbour walls and the luxurious hotels.

The proximity of ostentatious wealth and mesmerising danger is almost obscene. While the cars hurtle up the hill towards the casino as fast as a jet at take-off, then writhe downhill to the entrance to the tunnel, howl through the chicane and round the harbour rim to the 360-degree bends of the Rascasse corner, all the time pushed to margins of a thousandth of a second, the occupants of the grandiose yachts, gently rocking on their moorings, sip champagne and occasionally stretch their legs.

Of course, the matadors themselves, *les pilotes* as the French call them, are among the wealthiest men in town. As they stroll in flameproof suits from the big mobile homes in the paddock down to the pits they are greeted like gods every stride of the way. World Champion Keke Rosberg flies his own plane, and Villeneuve was said to be the highest paid professional in sport not excluding Borg or the American gridiron footballers. To the outsider it seems to have been an outrageously trivial death at Zolder, going for one last fling for a high place on the starting grid with the sticky-soft practice tyres which increase adhesion and last a mere couple of laps before being thrown away.

Twenty-five drivers and 37 spectators and marshals have lost their lives in 32 years of the championships, and brave men continue to grapple with the multi-million pound jungle of technology which simultaneously races ahead of the game and struggles to keep up with it. A single turbocharged engine can cost £50,000 and one car may have a dozen such engines to keep it in business.

After yesterday's practice, with tomorrow's round still to come, the Cosworth-powered Marlboro McLarens of John Watson and Niki Lauda are outside the 20 qualifiers, because their Michelin practice tyres, designed to accommodate the huge power of the Brabham-BMW and Alfa turbos, were reaching insufficient temperatures, only 40°C instead of 80°C. But the two men are confident that, if it does not rain tomorrow, they can still get on to the grid and then, with hard racing tyres, demonstrate again their tremendous skill on round-the-houses tracks as they did at Long Beach, coming from 22nd and 23rd start positions respectively to finish first and second. The problem here, of course, is that there is almost no room to pass.

The scene in the pits during practice is one of the most bizarre in sport, with a thousand journalists and photographers rubbing shoulders with the mechanics and managers who are working under intense pressure every time a car slides in for attention, adjustment, tyres, advice or even a change of vehicle. Everywhere there are huge piles of liquorice lozenges 10 feet high – the tyres. The expense is mind-boggling. Speech is impossible, the manager communicating with his driver through an intercom plugged into the helmet. Watson, that amiable Irishman driving in his 142nd Grand Prix – the fourth highest total ever – has to get out during the untimed practice while rear springs are changed. The streets have some fearful bumps. Watson stands around eating an unappetising-looking cheese sandwich extracted from crumpled silver paper. He appears to have about as much tension as a holidaymaker in a deckchair.

For Derek Warwick (Candy Toleman) it has been a different sort of day. In the eight a.m. pre-qualifying practice he makes the split by a mere 0.364 sec over Venezuelan Johnny Cecotto. Two turbos failed and with less than 10 minutes to spare Warwick jumped into the car of colleague Bruno Giacomelli and got in the vital lap. It is machines, you see, more than men, in the final reckoning: which is an injustice to the men. In the afternoon Warwick pulls up to 10th to become the leading Briton with an improvement of over five seconds at 1 min 28.017 sec.

The removal of the 'skirts' this season has slowed the cars perhaps six seconds – some two seconds slower than last year plus the probable four-second improvement the cars would otherwise have shown. But it does not stop the turbos dominating the day. The lead changes four times between Alain Prost (Renault Elf) and Rene Arnoux (Ferrari), with their team colleagues, Eddie Cheever and Patrick Tambay –

the man who replaced Villeneuve, and winner at Imola last week – taking third and fourth. Only three Cosworths finish in the top 10 – the TAG Williamses of Rosberg (fifth) and Jacques Laffite (eighth) and Jean-Pierre Jarier's Ligier (ninth).

As Frank Dernie, aerodynamic designer for Williams, said beforehand: 'Monte Carlo is a very difficult circuit indeed to set the car up for. It has some very bad bumps and a lot of slow corners which put good traction and sheer horsepower at a premium. This means that the circuit favours the turbos because they can get off the line smartly and with almost nowhere to pass, there's not much chance of beating them. They can accelerate out of the slow corners and up the hill much better. It's going to be a tremendous problem getting a Cosworth car like ours on to the front row of the grid.'

CONNER, ALONE WITH AMERICA'S SUNKEN PRIDE
The Times, August 1983

Newport, Rhode Island: Around here it is rather as if Mount Everest had been bought by a Japanese camera company. The belated public sportsmanship being exhibited by the slick, socially exclusive New York Yacht Club, as it handed over for the first time in 132 years the coveted America's Cup to ecstatic Australians at a Bellevue Avenue mansion, was in severe contrast to its private, even resentful, anguish.

When Australia II, with its remarkable fin-keel by an untutored designer, Ben Lexcen, came from a minute behind over the final two legs of the seventh and decisive race to win by 41 seconds, the men in peaked caps, blue blazers and white slacks lining the deck of the black-hulled committee boat Black Knight knew they were watching the most treasured bauble in the sporting world dissolve before their eyes. Their *raison d'être* had vanished.

As Alan Bond's wildly rejoicing crew sailed past, the Black

Knight gun which had signalled the finish of the race then fired a four-salvo salute while the members doffed their hats and bowed in acknowledgement to a beautiful, innovative boat and the crew which so nearly failed her. Their fists were no doubt clenched at losing a lead of three races to one, never mind that unbelievable switch on the fifth leg, when Dennis Conner's 57-second advantage evaporated in a mistaken downwind course.

When Conner, the 1980 champion racing in Freedom against Bond's third boat, Australia I, achieved that 3-1 lead, the crackling shortwave radios out on Rhode Island Sound picked up the talk between NYYC Commodores Robert Stone and Bob McCullough, and their helmsman. 'You sailed a terrific race,' said the men from the club. 'Thank you, sir,' replied Conner stiffly that day: Conner the unbeatable, who was in a seemingly impregnable position against the boat he *knew* was faster, but whose crew could not collectively match his vast professional experience. Yet on Monday night, when what the NYYC members had believed to be impossible had actually happened, it was Conner who had to shoulder the burden of America's loss.

As Australia II came late into harbour against the faint remains of a crimson evening sky, the night was a blur of fireworks and rockets and blinking helicopters, the dockside groaning under the weight of thousands of spectators whom Newport may never see again. Television lights flooded the quay, the US syndicate boats Liberty and Freedom formed a guard of honour for Australia II. There on her towing launch, Black Swan, was the red-jacketed Conner, with a fixed, empty good loser's smile gazing up at the myriad of frenzied Australian faces. How different it had been a few hours before as the tanned Conner, looking like Al Jolson with his sun-creamed white lips, had confidently jockeyed his burgundy-coloured boat in the pre-start manoeuvres.

Now it was Conner, unaccompanied by any member of the NYYC, who walked alone through the car park, through the milling streets of hard-luck cries to the Armoury, where he faced the Press, knowing he had blown a winning position. 'I'd like to stay for an hour of questions,' he said when paying tribute to Australia II. But when a mass of camera, television and Press men is witnessing a man with tears swelling his eyes as he says the United States has no cause to be ashamed of their performance, they do not press him with questions. They just let him put on his straw hat, accept a thin cheer, and disappear back into the bedlam outside.

The NYYC might have supported the man who surrendered its heritage, but seemingly did not have the guts. It was left to syndicate chairman Ed du Moulin to appear later and say Conner was still the best helmsman. But the truth was he just did not have the best boat, and after months of relentless pressure, the man who never allowed a mistake had made a monumental one.

Back in New York, where the club was formed in 1844, and settled into its present mansion in 1901, those members not in Newport had been listening to a radio commentary in the bar, with its red leather chairs and portraits of boats and skippers of long ago. The club has no television: it is that kind of club. No one knows what they thought as Liberty's lead disappeared by the start of the final leg.

Richard Thursby, a NYYC member, has said: 'There won't be more than a couple of days' mourning before we start thinking about how to win the damned thing back.' But now it is free to any club and syndicate in the US, never mind the rest of the world, to bid independently. The exclusiveness which the NYYC enjoyed for so long finally turned against it. Never was a US 12-metre permitted to compete against a foreign boat outside the America's Cup; so they never knew, for example, what all the six foreign challengers learnt: that Australia II's tall, slim rudder was also part of her tacking ability, and they copied it.

When Conner finally got into the water against Lexcen's Lightning, as it is known, he was raw to the exceptional qualities which Victory '83 and the others had long since discovered. Ultimately, by the narrowest but for all that colossal margin, the man who gave every command on his boat made the singular error which neutralised the earlier ones by Bertrand. It was the right result.

HEROISM AS HIGH AS THE SEA IS DEEP
The Times, January 1984

Long before one was introduced as a small boy to tales of Macartney, Meredith, Broadribb, C.B. Fry and Captain Webb, and the more modern sporting heroes, Matthews and Bradman, the emotional bedside stories were of men such as Scott and Oates, T.E. Lawrence and Mallory. If the first drama to make me cry was Pigling Bland getting lost over the hills and far away, then the second was Captain Oates walking out from the doomed expeditionary tent into the Antarctic snow saying that he may be gone some time. Altruism could have as much honour as achievement, demonstrated on Everest by one of my schoolmasters, Wilfred Noyce.

The mountains and oceans will always remain a special kind of challenge, and as the American writer, Paul Theroux, has recently observed, the British character is inherently shaped by the surrounding seas. Richard Broadhead is an example of maritime altruism *and* achievement. Yesterday at the Earl's Court Boat Show, that annual indoor anomaly which embraces fantasy and functionalism, the Salcombe adventurer was presented with the Yachtsman of the Year award. The yachting correspondents rightly considered his astonishing rescue of a Frenchman in the Southern ocean during a BOC single-handed round-the-world race last year superior to the Victory '83 crew's pursuit of the America's Cup.

It is worth quoting from *The Ultimate Challenge*, the account by my colleague, Barry Pickthall, of this remarkable race, a passage where Broadhead describes those awesome conditions which Chichester, Rose and Knox-Johnston have conquered, yet which would freeze the mind and muscle of ordinary men. Hand-steering downwind for 12 hours at a time in the Roaring Forties and screaming fifties, with the windspeed indicator permanently locked against its maximum 60 knots, Broadhead would later recount: 'Every 10 minutes or so, the seas [behind] rolled into vertical walls, huge and as high as the mast, and as the bow buried up to the forehatch, I just sat at the wheel holding on for grim death, looking almost vertically down the boat as she started to go over. Then as the wave broke, the bow came up and she surfed off at 30 knots with the whole deck under water. All I could see was the bloody wheel, and the mast and rigging standing up through the surf.'

The romance between life and death is a strangely motivating phenomenon. Guy Bernadin, another Frenchman who came fourth in Class II, would say of his experience of being washed out of the cockpit in ferocious seas from which he miraculously survived: 'It was the greatest moment in my life.' I know a doctor's wife to whom the same thing happened in the North Sea.

What was different about Broadhead's race, in which he finished third over the 27,000-mile, four-leg course behind the Frenchman, Phillippe Jeantot, in the expensively sponsored Credit Agricole and the South African, Bertie Reed, in Altach Voortrekker, was that two-thirds of the way between Australia and Cape Horn he turned back more than 300 miles in Perseverence of Medina, without engine, in the bid to rescue Jacques de Roux from the stricken Skoiern III, thousands of miles from any other assistance. And found him. It was an accomplishment as exceptional as the survival of Bligh and his men set adrift from the Bounty, in conditions considerably more severe; though it would not have been possible without the position-finding assistance of the Argus satellite navigation equipment fitted by BOC to each of the 17 boats, capable of tracing them every few hours to within less than half a mile.

De Roux, a submarine commander, had been 'pitch-poled', stern-over-bow, horrifyingly believing while upside down in darkness that he was going straight to the unfathomable bottom. Skoiern ultimately righted with a mere four inches of air as buoyancy remaining under the deck, and though de Roux pumped out after several hours, a hole in the hull sustained when cutting free the broken mast gave him only hours to remain afloat while permanently pumping. It would take Broadhead maybe three days to get back against the headwind: could de Roux last? An incredible ad hoc combination of satellite information to the race organisers and ham radio operators Rob Koziomkowski in Newport, Rhode Island, and Matt Johnston in Owaka, New Zealand, guided Broadhead to an approximate rendezvous some 50 hours after the SOS alert (the falling mast missed de Roux's deck-mounted Argus disc by inches).

Broadhead is one of those cavalier, freelance roamers whom most of us secretly envy but few could emulate. Leaving Harrow at 16, he followed his whim to the Caribbean and then Australia, for several years as Jack of any trade; then studied farming at Cirencester, and went off in unavailing search of land fortune in Brazil. But childhood Cornish salt was in his blood. He bought a 43-foot boat, sailed to Rio and back as a round-the-world qualifying race, then Antigua and back in search of sponsors. It was one of his several hundred letters of inquiry which aroused BOC – to sponsor the whole race rather than him. Everything was sold in order to enter his former Max Aitken boat nicknamed Perspiration by its unsuccessful Admiral's Cup crew.

Broadhead has the same disarming charm of under-statement as the land speed record breaker, Richard Noble. Discussing the rescue saga, he says it was apparent during radio contact the day before de Roux's SOS 'that he wasn't having much of a time'. You know the kind of situation: 120-foot waves, boat leaking, salt water boils, wet pillow, nobody to help make the tea and toast, in seas which the New Zealander, Dick McBride, calls 'two intersecting lines of moving hills'. Almost lightly, Broadhead relates that he was having to change headsails, without roller reefing, several times an hour to reach de Roux as soon as possible, and was 'a bit tired, feeling the strain a little, when pushing the boat faster than when actually racing.' Well, of course.

When, below deck talking on the radio, he in fact sailed straight past a despairing de Roux, who let off all his flares from a quarter of a mile away with the weather deteriorating again and darkness approaching, Broadhead admits: 'de Roux must have been a bit worried! When I came up, I stood up on the boom, and luckily just spotted his jury sail a mile or so away. If he had been in his life raft, I would never have seen him in those seas.' Jumping between boats, the exhausted Frenchman was fortunate not to break both his legs between the colliding hulls – a reunion as historic as Stanley and Livingstone. An hour later, Skoiern went down. What was it like, in that Antarctic hell hole, before a French frigate took de Roux on board several days later? Broadhead reflects: 'I think it improved his English a bit.' You would expect so. I mean, they had something to talk about.

It would be difficult to argue that what Christopher Dean and Jayne Torvill perfected was *sport*. They created beauty within their mundane environment, and were spellbinding entertainment.

INTO THE REALMS OF ART AND FANTASY
The Times, February 1984

Sarajevo: There is no explanation of artistic genius. Millions of television viewers will be watching two bewitching ice dancers from here tomorrow not just because they are physically almost as perfect as kingfishers in flight, but because the seamless elegance of their movement is the creation of a modest man's mind.

Christopher Dean, who has come off a policeman's beat in Nottingham to achieve stardom in its truest sense, deserves to have carried the British flag yesterday if only in recognition of having lifted his sport into the realm of art. With his enfolding rosebud of a partner he touches the double fantasy of the ordinary person: to be successful *and* beautiful. It is, I suspect, the gracefulness which is admired and will be remembered even more than the Olympic triumph, which it would seem is theirs for the taking. In their final practice in an almost deserted hall last night, they received the spontaneous applause of British competitors from other events, some of whom were witnessing live for the first time the gulf which exists between the Nottingham pair and most of their rivals.

Bobby Thompson, who was born comparatively poor in Salford, longed with a natural instinct to be a ballet dancer, but yielded to his football-following father's unwitting working-class prejudice and accepted the compromise of skating – in the old Derby Street hall. He now coaches not only Wendy Sessions and Stephen Williams, seventh in the recent European championships, but also possibly the closest rivals of Torvill and Dean, the outstanding Judy Blumberg and Michael Seibert from the United States. His opinion of Dean's relatively untrained choreography is one of affectionate astonishment. 'It is incomprehensible,' Thompson says. 'He is to ice dancing what McMillan or Ashton are to ballet. There are people in theatre who might not agree, but I can say it. Jayne and Chris are close friends. When I first saw *Bolero* in private I could not applaud: it overwhelmed me. It makes *Barnum* last year seem naive, yet that was a wonderful theatrical performance. *Bolero* is a statement, it is purity. There is nothing that clutters it.'

Dean had passing advice on choreography from two experts a few years ago: Gideon Avrahami, a Ballet Rambert teacher, and Zoltan Nagy, a Hungarian dancer, who showed him how to embrace dancing technique without being effeminate. In the original set pattern Paso Doble to *Capriccio Espagnole*, we see a matador, the concept of whom concedes nothing in masculinity to those thundering down the bob-run. 'It is sophisticated, not some flamenco travel brochure for the Costa del Sol,' Thompson observes. There are some in the sport who consider the performance as exceptional as *Bolero*.

Could either the Americans, whom I considered were unlucky to be third in last year's world championship in Helsinki, or Natalia Bestemianova and Andre Bukin, of Russia, second then and in Budapest last month, defeat the British pair? Blumberg and Seibert, superb dancers, admit the size of the task. 'Because we start from behind,' Seibert says, 'it is not enough to be equal. We have to be so inescapably better that there is no choice.' They arrived here having just retained the US title, after missing five weeks during which Seibert had had a glandular illness. To regain finesse for the Olympics is in itself an achievement, but Judy, a petite skiing enthusiast says: 'The setback has bonded us. To win, we just have to start at the beginning and be perfect on all three days. The music is the best we have ever had. With *Scheherazade* in the free dance, we have something so different, but this is a great direction for ice dancing, we are trying to do the same thing [as Torvill and Dean].' Seibert, his refined face reminiscent of John Curry's, says: 'It is a classic, original piece that nobody's done before. It's a bitch, physically difficult, but it gives us a great feeling.'

To abandon the conventional American view of ice dance as adaptation of Broadway zip, Blumberg and Seibert have been bold. There has been, too, concern here for several days about tiny signs of tension in Dean, as well as continuing anxiety about the legality of one or two lifts in which Dean's hand rises above shoulder height. Laurence Demmy, the English chairman of the International Skating Union's ice dance committee, who has in the past been accused of being technically pro-Soviet, is adamant that the British pair are authentic. We shall be watching the French and Russian judges.

Thompson, a professional since 19 and one who would not contemplate disloyalty to his own skaters, is sure in his own mind, having observed the steady advance of the sport through different phases. 'Torvill and Dean are on a new plane; I have never encountered such absolute single-mindedness and conviction. I am learning from *them*. Judy and Michael are beautiful skaters, superior to the Russians, but I have to be truthful and say that Chris and Jayne are better. If I wasn't truthful, I couldn't teach.' It is the ultimate fascination of sport that truth in performance does not always prevail.

There have been a handful of adventurous, positive international football managers in the past 30 years: Sebes and Baroti of Hungary, Doherty of Northern Ireland, Kovacs of Rumania, Miljanic of Yugoslavia, Michels of Holland. Hidalgo was maybe the purest of all. 'Chance is beautiful,' he said.

MILD-MANNERED INSPIRATION WHO REFUSES TO COMPROMISE
The Times, February 1984

Paris: 'Good morning. How is your wife? I hope your children are well.' Thus is Michel Hidalgo apt to greet one of his more severe press critics, with the equanimity of Dixon of Dock Green: a placid refusal to be baited, which further antagonises those who claim he lacks character, yet assures him of national popularity. The critics say that he is a tap of permanently lukewarm water; that the only time he ever showed emotion was when Spanish policemen in Valladolid stopped him going on the pitch to protest at Shaikh Fahid's touchline intervention and his five foot seven of indignation nearly started swinging punches.

Hidalgo, France's international football manager for the past two World Cup competitions, epitomises that enviable French concept of sport which holds that it is preferable to finish second with style than first with expediency. Why else did the French for years adore the aspiring Raymond Poulidor in the Tour de France, rather than five-times winner Jacques Anquetil? Such is the national character's yearning for glory rather than mere victory that the wrenching, tumultuous semi-final against West Germany in Seville culminating in agonising defeat on penalties gained the entire team a greater prestige than if they had won and indifferently lost the final.

'To calculate like the Italians is not sport,' Hidalgo said

yesterday, as his squad prepared at Egly outside Paris, for their meeting tomorrow with England at the Parc des Princes. 'That style is impossible for the French nature and spirit. I am impressed with Italy's ability to combine creation with discipline, but what they achieved in the second half of the World Cup final was largely because Conti threw off his obligations to tactical discipline.'

He is an intelligent man, with penetrating, deep blue eyes and neat, sensitive hands, and was an old-fashioned wing-half with Rheims under the management of Albert Batteux, who guided the memorable World Cup side of Kopa and Fontaine in 1958. Never have France won an international or club title. Rheims and St Etienne lost European finals with typical, extravagant flourishes against Real and boring Bayern respectively.

Hidalgo made his name by leading France back to the World Cup finals in 1977, after a gap of 11 years, with the defeat of Bulgaria; and on to Buenos Aires where his side's marvellous performance against Argentina was betrayed only by a Canadian linesman's distant, controversial penalty decision against the luckless Tresor. In 1981, Hidalgo's team qualified for Spain, defeating the Netherlands in Paris with a dare-devil attacking front six: Platini, Giresse, and Genghini in midfield, Rocheteau, Lacombe and Six up front.

The mercurial Platini, who with 17 goals from 21 games, leading Calcio scorer for Juventus together with Zico, and little Giresse will be there tomorrow with Tigana, hoping to reverse the World cup result in Bilbao which flattered Ron Greenwood's prospects two years ago. Hidalgo thinks this may be the best yet of his three four-yearly squads – though after the European championship he will hand over to Henri Michel, the long-serving midfield international from Nantes, who now manages the (professional) Olympic team trying to qualify for Los Angeles.

'In 1978 we had a lot of ability, but not much international experience,' says Hidalgo. 'Then in 1982 we had more experience. Yet in international football, compared with a club team, the side grows progressively all the time as a competition develops. Now we have a marriage of outstanding players and experience: we will find out this summer whether we have a championship team or not.'

He emphatically denies that the European championship is more important than the World Cup, even though France are hosts. 'It may be here on our doorstep, but the teams competing are still only from Europe.'

Many managers pay lip service to the need to protect the quality of the game, but few avoid drifting into contemporary tactical expediency. Hidalgo refuses. When France led 3-1 in extra time against West Germany, they still, like Brazil when they were 2-2 against Italy, continued to attack. He sees his role as far more than winning a match: France have their own character, he argues, and when you can bring the way of life into football, 'that's fantastic'. He has worked patiently over eight and a half years at bringing his players to believe that this is the way they themselves want to play, and has never been pressurised by the public or Press into taking decisions in which he did not believe. 'There are times when the mood is heavy with responsibility, but the coach's job is to reduce the drama, to help the players to realise that it is only a game which will come and go in a couple of days.'

Tomorrow he will probably play with four men in midfield – Fernandez of Paris Saint Germain, Platini, Giresse and Tigana – not for defensiveness, but because he is short of top class strikers; and, besides Platini, he has another midfield goalscorer in Giresse, who has 15 goals this season in 21 matches. Hidalgo does all he can to prevent systems dominating individuals.

'As I grew up in football, I realised we carried a game which had, and had to have, the beauty and virtue and justice of sport. I am against all injustice, even in arranging the draw for tournaments. Chance is beautiful. If the public becomes bored, it will go elsewhere.'

TRACKING DOWN THE DRUG-TAKERS
The Times, March 1984

In 1973, testifying to a United States Senate Committee, Harold Connolly, the 1956 Olympic hammer-throw champion, said that in the American team of 1968 there were athletes who had so many puncture holes from injecting drugs that it was difficult to find a fresh spot to give them a new shot. He added: 'The overwhelming majority of the international athletes I know would do anything, and take anything, short of killing themselves, to improve their athletic performance.'

Connolly admitted to having himself been 'hooked' on anabolic steroids for eight years, after winning his gold medal. At the 1983 conference in Britain of the Central Council of Physical Recreation, Mike Winch, an international shot-putter and member of the International Athletes Club, alleged, without implicating himself, that the medical threat to the health of athletes was now greater than it had ever been. Yet there is only one sport, rowing, in which the international federation has already initiated random drug testing – the only certain means of deterrent.

Random testing is of paramount importance, not only to eliminate cheats for medical as well as sporting 'safety', but to legitimise those athletes, in particular women, who may unfairly come under speculative criticism.

Dr Leroy Perry, a Los Angeles chiropractor who has treated Olympic athletes around the world, is sceptical, for example, about world record breaker Jarmila Kratochvilova of Czechoslovakia, who won both the 400 and 800 metres in Helsinki. He recently told the *Los Angeles Times*: 'I believe her condition now is a physiological impossibility from what she was five years ago, and I don't care how many times she works out. That is not a normal physiological female body. I've treated Olympic female athletes in 34 countries ... but I've never seen a body like that. I can truthfully say that I think there is something chemically different about her physical make-up, and it hasn't come from weight-lifting.'

In 1979 Kratochvilova, who failed to qualify for the European championship final the previous year at 27, had a 51.47 sec best for 400 metres. Five years later, she became the first woman to beat 48 sec. Miroslav Kvac, her coach, attributes the improvement to increased work-load, especially weight-lifting. But Dr Perry insists that while East Germans and other Czechs are using advance treatment with the male hormone, testosterone, Kratochvilova could not have achieved her physical changes in five years by any means other than 'through an act of God'. Random testing would have removed any possibility for such qualified but speculative accusations. Kratochvilova has of course a femininity certificate (issued after chromosome test of hair follicle) and there is the fact that the Western culture of feminine perception, especially American, rejects the more muscular woman acceptable in other societies.

Yet when an American woman coach can say 'It's my honest belief that 75 per cent of women in the American team are not taking drugs,' she is only proving precisely what she is seeking to deny: there will be a high proportion of drug abuse in the Los Angeles Olympics.

However, Prince Alexandre de Mérode, chairman of the IOC medical commission, thinks that the gap between the limits of medical testing knowledge and what the athletes can still use undetected is being reduced. 'We shall be testing for the presence of abnormal quantities of testosterone in both men and women in Los Angeles,' he says.

In experimental tests made in Cologne in 1981 on unidentified samples taken from competitors at the Moscow Olympics, more than 20 per cent were found positive for excess of testosterone – not on the list of proscribed drugs in Moscow – and predominantly among women. The sharp decline of the Soviet Union's achievement in long-distance Nordic events in Sarajevo compared with Lake Placid and East Germany's tiny entry of only three athletes for the European indoor championships at Gothenburg next week, suggest that testing is taking its toll on abuse.

Prince de Mérode succeeded Sir Arthur Porritt as medical chairman in 1967. His lineage goes back across 800 years of Belgian, French and German history, though he is by no means a merely aristocratic window-dressing to the IOC's aura. An ex-parachutist and deep-sea diver with the Belgian forces, a cycling and rowing enthusiast, he disarms sporting audiences by the informality of his manner and dress. What he has above all is that detachment from the forces of self-interest. 'It is essential that the IOC preserves its moral power and its financial independence,' he says. 'We cannot exist without either. Without money, the Olympic movement is nothing. Our position has changed over the past 16 years, and it has to change carefully, but we could not survive on our finances as they were in 1968. I believe that by paying expenses of six athletes and officials of every country to attend Los Angeles, and nearly £3 million for the foreign judges and referees, we are better able to stay free of politics. Of course, the negotiations with a company such as Adidas are delicate, but we must do it.'

While most people would agree with the demand at the Baden-Baden congress in 1981 by the new athletes commission, which includes Sebastian Coe, for a life ban of convicted drug-takers, Prince de Mérode is more cautious, insisting that the work of the medical commission must be towards positive as well as negative attitudes: that athletes must be shown how they can escape from the temptations of drug-aid. 'Cheating will go on to the end of the world,' he admits, 'but our job must be as much to expose the health dangers, of depression, of glandular and cardio-vascular damage, as to ban people. We know that there is blood-doping, the re-injection of the athlete's own fortified blood, which cannot be detected; but do the athletes know that it is only three-tenths effective, and has the risk of accident?'

While he agrees that the reinstatement of positive-proved offenders by the International Amateur Athletics Federation is not good for the image of sport, he is of the same opinion as Professor Arnold Beckett, one of the foremost researchers in the field at Chelsea College testing laboratory, namely that ignorant competitors manipulated by coaches or doctors must not be totally condemned. As Beckett says: 'We don't want to crucify those not responsible – kids who didn't know what they were doing: but it's a difficult and narrow line.'

The prevalence of drug-taking was emphasised by the positive tests, and by widespread sudden withdrawals by athletes before competing at the Pan American Games in Venezuela last autumn. At a recent press conference an American journalist asked Prince de Mérode whether he thought such testing, which had been unexpected by some, was fair. There is general belief among an American public neurotic with suspicion of Russia, that drugs must be taken to stay in the political race. The fact is that American athletes, who have never previously been subjected to domestic testing, are among the world's worst offenders.

It is with his views on restricting the work-load of athletics training that Prince de Mérode is most radical. There is too much competition for the human body to endure, he suggests, and training should be limited by regulation, just as it is in other forms of working employment: a 25-hour week? He argues: 'In sport there is no time limit, but administrators must become interested in this factor. Certainly, it is a type of social regulation. But so is 'saving' money, with the trust funds now allowed under Rule 26. We must think of such things. There cannot be absolute freedom even in the rights of a professional sportsman, any more than there are in medicine, or piloting an aircraft.'

Prince de Mérode follows the thinking of the new definition of the Olympic ideology: that, within the right framework, the rich should not be excluded any more than the poor. 'An instrument of social promotion must be consistent. Everyone is somewhere on the line from absolute amateur to complete professional. We have to evolve. What is important is that we should discover more, physiologically, to assist the athlete to improve, to avoid injury.'

He is emphatic that random testing must ultimately become the standard practice, but does not believe the IOC can control it. There is the question of the reliability of the laboratory – whether it is professionally free of financial or political interference. At present there is no accredited laboratory in Africa or South America; in North America only one (in Montreal) prior to that in Los Angeles for the Games.

'Every competitor should be tested regularly, but the laboratory must be trustworthy, technically and politically. I believe the initiative must come from the international and national federations. Belgium is already random testing for all Olympic sports. It will always be a question of principles versus practicality. How do you know that an unknown who suddenly wins a marathon has been random tested throughout recent years?'

Professor Beckett says that researches are almost ready to test for the use of the human growth hormone and gonadotrophines, though as with other hormonal excess, the advantages are short-lived. The medical commission was receiving the latest research reports in Sarajevo. We can be sure both drugs will be present in Los Angeles.

FIRST LADY OF THE NATIONAL
The Times, March 1984

The saying around the stables it that you are more sensitively cared for as a horse than a human under the eagle eye of Jenny Pitman. And she admits it. The senior lad at one famous stable, reflecting on her unique and spectacular impact upon National Hunt racing, observed knowingly: 'She sure is hard.' The description would not offend Mrs Pitman. A senior handicapper is said almost to have ruptured a blood vessel recently when on the receiving end of her colourful opinion concerning the weight for one of her horses. In her days as a stable girl for her father, one of the hacks came to be known as Sodyer, from her comments on its wilfulness.

Yet this formidable woman, who will send out Corbiere perfectly prepared tomorrow to defend his Grand National title, possesses, beneath an exterior as unflinching as Maxim Gorky's grandmother, the gentle disposition of a nurse. In the words of my colleague, Michael Seely, she is 'a quite outstanding judge of what a horse can do: a traditional realist, which is a rare quality.'

For anyone unfamiliar with the racing world, Mrs Pitman's achievement of becoming the first woman in 144 years to train a National winner and within 12 months take the prized Cheltenham Gold Cup with Burrough Hill Lad, is equivalent to Rachael Flint going out to open against the West Indies with Gatting. In racing, women either muck out the stables or try to look as handsome as the horse in the winner's enclosure.

Tomorrow morning before seven o'clock Jenny Pitman will have watched Corky, as the champion is known, and the jockey, Ben de Haan, have a short workout and will then walk the four and a half mile course to determine just how each ferocious fence should be approached in the prevailing conditions. Just get my horses and riders round safely, she will say to herself, and I'll give up swearing or smoking ... Please God, don't let any of them get hurt. The astonishing thing about the woman who has conquered a man's world is that she is not all Amazon but an emotional mother and, when it happened, a miserably divorced wife; a girl who adored her father and grew up on a Leicestershire farm under his guidance knowing just what she must do to match the boys.

She has just published an autobiography, *Glorious Uncertainty*, which in a sense ought never to have been written. Her joint-author, Sue Gibson, and her publishers should have protected her from baring her soul, from revealing many intimacies of her stricken relationship with the former jockey, Richard Pitman, which would perhaps have been better unsaid. Yet she is so unfalteringly spontaneous and honest that she probably could not help herself, never mind the publishers' expectant rubbing of hands. When I asked her at Cheltenham, just before Burrough Hill Lad fulfilled all her prophecies, whether she was pleased that the truth was out, like Nelson she said she could not tell a lie. 'If I tell the truth, then I always know what I've said. I'm incapable of handling half-truths. No, I'm *not* not glad it's published.'

You wonder, as time will eventually heal, if she will regret some hurtful asides about Richard's relationship with their sons; but he is mature enough still to be predicting fulsomely, as professional commentator, that Corky will win again tomorrow. She herself admits that when, still married, Richard was beaten in the National run-in on Crisp by Red Rum, she was too upset to talk about it for six months. They grew apart, she reflects, largely because he was a successful jockey while she was labouring, anonymously, to become a successful trainer.

Her life, and the book, are fascinating, an amalgam of determination, luck, joy and sorrow. 'I'm just an ordinary person,' she said at Cheltenham among an admiring crowd. 'And I think that's why some people seem to like me. The National victory hasn't changed me. I had no private education, no silver spoon. I'm glad there are people with money and I'm pleased to work for them. But I still don't like parties, or drinking, though I'll occasionally have a brandy if I'm really knackered.'

You can tell the kind of brave/afraid woman she is from the incident in 1982 when Lord Gulliver, a potential National entry, died of a heart attack during a training gallop while ridden by her sister, Mandy. In the grief of the moment the weeping Mandy was told to pull herself together. It was later in private that Jenny's own tears were released.

She rode at 14 months and won her first race at four. There was no gas, electricity or running water in her early childhood days at the farm. Kitchen sink taps, a radio ... these were revelations to come. Working from dawn to dusk, she learnt every wrinkle of equestrian psychology, with working horses which could not be allowed to go lame; which is why she now laughingly agrees that she is gentler with horses than humans 'because the horses don't understand so well'. Those were the days when lunch was a raw turnip in the fields and late at night under a lamp in the stable she would fall asleep in her father's lap after sharing a bowl of bread and milk. Yet this tomboy, who ceremoniously made herself a 'blood brother' with another stable lad, who preferred new wellies for Christmas rather than a doll, was a mean hockey player, a tearaway who scrumped apples daringly, and when she fractured her skull in a fall, refused to cry in front of nurses in hospital.

She hunted as a girl with the Quorn, rode point-to-point at

14, and fell head-over-heels at 18 for the promising young jockey at Bishop's Cleeve stable. 'I loved him so deeply I would have changed places when he was injured.' They married. She changed her religion to Catholicism. Two sons arrived quickly. Lord Cadogan helped them set up their own yard but life was still economically hard. Moreover, 'I didn't understand Richard's riding pressures and he didn't recognise my training progress in point-to-points.' She remembers going to apply for her trainer's licence at the Jockey Club, where the stewards on the other side of the polished table whispered in her presence, which in her country way she thought was rude.

Career and marriage moved in opposite directions until one Christmas when separation and an appendicitis arrived almost the same day. But within four years she was training 28 winners in a season. And then there was Corky. The story of his progress from raw novice, through alarming injury, to champion, is alone worth reading. Mrs Pitman is some lady.

The Princess Royal has emerged over recent years as a woman of perception, not only in her public duties such as for Save the Children, but as a sports administrator: president of the British Olympic Association, and of the International Equestrian Federation, and more recently a member of the International Olympic Committee. Her opinions given here were in an unprepared interview.

HORSE SENSE
The Times, June 1984

Q: You clearly intend to be an active president. In what ways does your Olympic competitive experience assist your duties?
A: Simply from being able to be on good terms with the

competitors, an advantage when meeting and talking to them. Sportsmen and -women tend to get introverted, to believe their own problems are the worst. They fail to realise that there are other sportsmen suffering just as much as they do, that they're all in the same boat. Irrespective of which sport I represented, it's good for them to have their horizons broadened, and also it keeps me in touch with what they think. They're prepared to talk about the things that bother them, and frequently it's not in their own federation's power to do anything about it. I can gather a feeling of their personal worries, yet have a slightly wider view.

The BOA is raising a lot of money this year, and it's a good yardstick. If people are not interested in the Games they don't contribute, and we would have to say to some athletes, sorry, you can't go. It reflects public opinion.

Q: Would you hope to be an Olympic competitor again?
A: The difficulty of equestrian sports is that you're at least 50 per cent dependent on the other half, which is four-legged, and like human athletes they don't grow on trees. I would be very surprised to find another horse that was good enough to enter the Olympics. It's partly a matter of luck, though of course money can shorten the odds a bit. If you can buy, you can wait a bit longer and the chances of getting the right animal are greater, but the better it goes the more you have to pay. If you have the luck to buy as a four-year-old, it's cheaper.

Q: What do you most remember from the 1976 Games as being different from other competitions, as being emotional, pleasing or difficult?
A: The sheer size is most noticeably different. At other international competitions you will probably know most people in your own sport. The advantage of the Olympics is not only meeting foreign competitors but different sports from within your own country, where normally there isn't the chance. There is much more of an atmosphere, largely because of the large attendance. It was a pity that the equestrian events were outside Montreal, simply because a lot of the benefits are from the opportunity to mix.

The pressures are greater, and because it's a four-year-cycle, the chances of going again are probably remote in most sports. There's great satisfaction from being there and from finishing the competition, especially the endurance events, quite aside from winning medals. There is that *rarity* value. All the people taking part know the effort required to get to the top, and to achieve it for a particular time is that much more demanding. You really only have one chance in most sports, and even in the less physically demanding sports you have to pace yourself between Olympics, and very few are able to do that.

Q: Do the Games still have anything of the original ethical force of taking part and youthful communion?
A: Funnily enough, yes. Because 90 per cent of the people taking part are not really going there with a chance of winning a medal, there are a heck of a lot of sports where it's very open. Because countries not normally at international competition come to the Olympics, nobody knows quite how good they are, and pressures have different effects on even established stars. The rarity value inspires real amateurs to produce performances on the day, which professionals can find difficult as time goes by. A professional may have his eye much more on the future, thinking he may be best but that there's always another day, another pay packet, which this is not. There will always be the scope for the person with the ambition to go to the Olympics and win a medal and say 'that's that'. They're not necessarily interested in a sporting life beyond, they have a short term precise goal of getting it right on the day, and if they time it right they can still be better than any professional.

That will always be the true Olympics, and I think the *taking part* by numerous countries who come yet do not turn up elsewhere, is why they come. It's not a question of winning medals but the satisfaction of having produced your personal best on the day.

Q: Was it agreeable or were you in any way resentful of being side by side with professionals?
A: I was happy enough, my expectations were rather different, and it was a bonus, it was for a limited period. In addition to

those who want to be professional, there are many who gain in their careers on the side, if successful, as teachers or coaches, and why not? Many are temperamentally unsuited to stay in competitive professional sport, which is a hard game! There are always new people coming up. Can the Olympics embrace both amateur and professional? I think it would be very difficult to have an Olympics with any division. Should there be an age limit, say, or should medal winners be excluded from subsequent participation? It would be difficult to work effectively.

They say there's no such thing as an Olympic amateur. That's partially correct, because I think everybody has to be a professional with a small 'p' in their attitude to get to that level, and to have the freedom to do the training which is necessary. Sponsorship does make it easier. I hope I would not have been regarded as a professional in my approach. I was thorough in keeping up my standards. More than that I don't think I was professional, I did do other things at the same time.

Q: What is the value of the Games in a professional era?
A: They have a huge value in potential to professionals and those who want to make a career in sport, and a medal will enormously enhance their earning ability. Whether that's right or wrong I'm not sure, certainly it would be wrong to have a direct reward for winning. Obviously in the old days there was no scope for earning money and it was forbidden, but nowadays with greater leisure-time activities this is one of the world's growing industries, where sport is available to more and more people, and a proportion of those want to do very well. I wouldn't argue that this is not a perfectly reasonable ambition.

Q: How much does the national cry for success matter to true sport?
A: I might be unfair to say the media has carried a degree of responsibility for this. I don't think the sports federations do. The medal table affair is totally contrary to IOC principles, a wind-up for non-participants, and it has virtually no effect on many of the competitors. Team sports and individual sports

have a different effect on people: it inspires some and completely flattens others. Put a Union Jack on a competitor's pocket and send them out, and they perform a street above their normal level, but put a basic individual in a team sport where scores count collectively, and suddenly they're looking over their shoulder.

Q: Is that not a fascinating aspect of the Games?
A: Yes and no. My own feeling is that all team sports should be thrown out of the Games, because of their effect on a wide scale, not just on individuals. For the media and people back home it's so much easier to generate emotion for a team activity than it is for most individual sports. Of course there is emotional pressure on some star individuals, but these events do not affect the public the way the team events do. I think the team ethic is a pity, it produces too much nationalism. The Olympics were meant to be a test of individual brilliance. It would simplify the present problems, especially size, to slim it down to that basic principle. It is said that some team sports would die without the Olympics, but I don't think that's true.

It would be better if the team ethic were removed from the opening ceremony, for instance, to have all the flags of competing nations but not the en bloc marching. The feeling would still be there. And besides team sports, we should look at those which are not measured by absolute terms but by arbitrary judgement: dressage, skating, gymnastics. We need a clearer definition of what a sport is. Sculling is an Olympic sport, but what about an eight? In sailing, is a pair a team?

Q: Should the limited amount of sponsorship funds be aimed at the likely medal winners or more down the scale at grassroots facilities?
A: It's not an either or question, there has to be a balance. There has to be a degree of sponsorship for those who are likely to be successful. If you gave the same amount to everyone, one or two would still get to the top, but would the others benefit from the help? You can say people should get to the top by their own initiative, but that's not being wholly realistic if you want them to be as good as they *can* be. If they need more help, it should be available.

Equally, it's completely wrong to keep all the sponsorship for those who have made it and not give to the bottom. Curiously enough, the funny old system of this country, letting each sport work it out for themselves, does work. There are some sponsors prepared to put in money lower down and get little visible return, as well as those wanting to sponsor the top end, both doing a super job. It's easy to look around and see how America or Eastern Europe do it, but I feel the British are quite well suited to the strange mixture we have. Those who say we should do more have the scope to do so. But it's cyclical, sports come and go, and there's nothing wrong with that. At the end of the day, medals don't matter.

Q: Do the British still have a balanced view of sport or have we become too concerned with winning?
A: Perhaps there's an element at the top which may be preoccupied with winning, but perhaps that's because they are more *able* to win. I wouldn't think, even looking around at the youngsters in equestrianism who seem hell bent on winning at the wrong time in their lives, that it's much different from any time in the past. It's the sheer weight of numbers which makes it more obvious. To say there has been an all-round lowering of standards of sportsmanship is exaggerated. In most sports they are highly competitive on the field but friendly enough off it. It depends on your age and upbringing: people may either say sportsmen are badly mannered, or that they're highly motivated and it's a forgivable part of the buildup. But there's no excuse for outright bad manners.

Q: Did you experience examples as a competitor?
A: I used to find that lodging objections, which is the thing to do now, was often highly unnecessary and time wasting. Quite extraordinary! People would say you might win it, even though it ought not to make any difference to the result. Why make it? I suppose I'm old fashioned!

Q: How much will the Games be devalued by the current boycott?
A: Well, I didn't go to Moscow. Do you think the boycott devalued those Games, were they any less of an occasion? Some

170

leading competitors who were absent might not have got there anyway, they might have had an off day, have pulled something before they got there. If people still remember it as an excellent sporting occasion, with personal best performances and Olympic records, then it is more of a loss for those who don't turn up, especially those who have got no choice and had a genuine chance of a medal. I think boycotts are self-defeating. There will be certain sports and categories which will suffer more from the loss of competitive edge. But the competitors who get there fit and sound will do their best whether the boycotting nations are there or not.

Q: What steps are available to the IOC to avoid future boycotts, considering that this is the third consecutively?
A: They've all been different, and I wonder if the Games have now got it out of their system! It would be naive to think that removing team sports would remove the nationalistic element, it would in some countries but not others. There will probably always be somebody who would want a boycott. I think they all want the Games to collapse there and then, but so far they haven't. If the Games can prove they can rise above these things and carry on, and still be there four years later for people to come to whatever they may feel, the Games can survive.

Certainly they have got to change if they want to keep up standards. The IOC must stick by some principles. If principles do become a thing of the past, then the Games will fold. As with other sporting bodies, there may be a swing of votes for the interests of Africa and Asia, and whatever people may think about keeping the Games in one place, competitors like them to move about. The best competitors may not notice, they've travelled so much, but lower down the scale those who simply appreciate taking part also appreciate seeing different countries.

It would be difficult to pick any country with a lily-white record totally free of political interests or whatever boycotts are likely to be about. There are advantages in spreading the Games. They did much for Japan and Mexico. If they could stop being quite such a burden, there is a lot to be said for

171

taking them around the world. Individual countries put in a tremendous effort, as Sarajevo did, and it gives them facilities for an international future.

Q: What were your impressions of Sarajevo, as an official?
A: It was new to me, I hadn't been to a Winter Olympics. They were fortunate with the size of the Village, and the number of people who could get to know each other. I was able to see how hard our chefs d'equipe work, the paperwork, the arguments over facilities, of which the competitors see nothing. There's so much to be done on their behalf, transport, food and so on, and it went very well. It may be different in Los Angeles? The Yugoslavs tried very hard, and the Games went well. What was so nice about it was that if there was a moment of chaos, no one minded.

Q: Should there be more equality of events for women?
A: I'm not sure I'm qualified to speak, having grown up in a sport with genuine equal competing opportunity, certainly in this country, for a long time. There are obviously going to be sports which women do in less numbers than men, irrespective of whether they're capable. Maybe one may have to say yes to any sport, although it might not get many competitors. If you have some sports where women are not as fast or strong as men and have separate events, maybe you have to provide this for all sports. I'm surprised at some women's determination in these directions, but that's because I don't want to be a 10,000 metres runner, and find it difficult to be totally objective.

Q: Your father, Prince Philip, has held international sporting posts. Would you ever consider being elected to the IOC?
A: A difficult one. When my father took on the FEI (Fédération Equestre Internationale) it was still very much a time of the amateurs, of trying to help – which is why they now complain some people are too old. But somebody had to do it. It takes a lot of time, more than the professionals are prepared to admit, to organise it so that they can earn a livelihood. Many sports are run by people who don't get paid

172

for it, and it's jolly generous of them. If professionals had to take a cut out of their earnings to pay for it, they might take a different outlook on life. Things have changed a lot in the years since my father has been in the FEI, as they have in the IOC, they're under more political pressure than in the past.

If I was asked by the IOC, the answer might be yes, but I'm not sure what I could contribute, whether I'd be an advantage or a disadvantage. Members of the Royal Family tend to be politically neutral, and are quite good at it. In essence, it might be an advantage for the IOC. But equally it would be naive to think that in this age, while everyone would like to keep politics out of sport, that it is possible to do so entirely. We're not in control of all the pressures that exist around us. It's a pity, because sport is one of the few things capable of drawing us together from all over the world, every colour, creed and political persuasion. When they get to the Games, they find they all have the same problems, the same goals. There are few other areas where that's possible.

> On the same pitch with the immortal Di Stefano ... a little late, maybe.

PERFECTION WITHOUT A GLANCE
The Times, June 1984

Paris: In an hour's play of eight-a-side I doubt if he ever looked once in the direction he was passing, yet never missed his man throughout the game. At 57, Alfredo di Stefano is still the master of the short ball. He is here for the finals of the European championship to watch his long-ago adopted country, Spain, take on the fancied French here this evening, and the way things are among older players he was having a get-together with such men as Just Fontaine and Eusebio, and what could have been more appropriate on a sunny afternoon at the Stade BP than to get the ball out.

It was more than 20 years ago that I first met him, an austere figure sitting on a wall outside his hotel in Porthcawl, looking across the Bristol Channel with his private thoughts before a World Cup qualifying tie against Wales. He scored a brilliant goal at Ninian Park, but he was destined to be the greatest player never to grace the final with either Argentina or Spain. The next year in Chile, he was injured before Spain's first match.

He has just ended his contract as manager of Real Madrid and is wondering what may turn up. It is unthinkable that he should ever be out of the game and, inevitably, now he was the focal point of the knockabout between an international team, more or less, and a side of former German internationals, including Heinz Hoetges, capped 62 times.

In all those wonderful years with Real Madrid, his detached air somehow set him above and apart from the others, as though he were operating in his own rarified plane. He would turn away from the ball if hit, not with a grimace but with slight disdain, and it was the same yesterday: you still do not give him a bad pass without receiving a frown, and unfortunately I gave him a few. His displeasure was nothing compared with the roasting he gave a Brazilian colleague, while all I received was the occasional *Defense, Ingles!* if I did not chase back when he thought I should have. It was a rare ambition fulfilled, if a shade late in life, to be on the same stretch of grass and calling for the return ball, which he would slip with that flick of an ankle that still deceives.

His opinion of the football – the serious stuff, that is – these last couple of weeks is slightly dismissive. 'Most of them are thinking only of winning,' he reflects. His favourite side, apart from France, is Portugal. 'They play with the ball,' he says with a shrug, as if he finds all this running about without it a trifle tedious.

GLORY AT LAST

The Times, June 1984
FRANCE 2 SPAIN 0

Paris: The name of France had long been morally engraved on the European championship trophy in 1984, but in the Parc des Princes last night Spain attempted to scratch it out in a smash-and-grab raid. None can regret that the Frenchmen resisted them, if not with the same élan which has characterised their most eloquent and elegant performances then at least with an unshakeable belief in the virtue of attack. As France went up to collect the cup, Spain's players were casting dark oaths and gestures at the Czechoslovak referee, Christov, who had stamped on their excesses in the first half and early in the second gave the questionable free kick which helped to bring Platini his ninth and arguably most critical goal of the tournament. As they had against Denmark, Spain demonstrated that they could simultaneously play concerted, intelligent football and kick lumps out of the opposition without compunction; had they concentrated on the former, they might well have stolen France's hour of glory legitimately.

Instead, the name of Michel Hidalgo echoed around the stadium in wave after wave of emotional relief as French football celebrated the reward it has so long deserved. In two World Cups and now here in his own country, the quiet, modest Hidalgo has encouraged artistry, romance and honour in the game. He will be among a handful of international managers down the years – Sebes and later Baroti of Hungary, Feola of Brazil, Herberger of West Germany, Michels of Holland – remembered as men of integrity and imagination.

Only an injury-time goal by Bellone, a galloping flourish of a counter-attack as Spain flung themselves forward against 10 anxious men, gave the score a late, unarguable security: five desperate minutes earlier, Leroux had been sent off for his second foul, following an earlier booking. It was the ebony Tigana, with his long crossfield pass, who made that second goal, and it would not be difficult to claim that he was the most significant figure in France's five victories, even allowing for Platini's flurry of usually superbly-taken goals. Tigana's was always the courage on hand when France, and Platini, faltered.

The way in which Spain instantly began to lunge the boot at any Frenchman suggested that George Courtney, the English referee, may not have been far removed from justification with his many bookings in the second semi-final. Christov now booked Gallego and Carrasco inside the first half hour, and there might have been others; in this period Spain had physically and tactically closed the game. With 11 men behind the ball when defending, they were also more accurate and penetrating on the counter-attack. Platini was muted, Giresse stifled by quick marking, and for a long while Tigana, finding little response, could not place a pass correctly. In contrast, Alberto, Santillana and Señor often posed threats for the French.

Spain had Gallego replacing the suspended Maceda as sweeper, and still had five in midfield, which helped account for their early superiority. Hidalgo, it seemed, might have used another midfield player – Genghini, who replaced Lacombe 10 minutes from the end – rather than retain four defenders; the heavy-footed Leroux was spare and often moving ineffectually upfield.

The intense whistling from the crowd after Spain's bookings did nothing to aid France, who might well have gone one down a few minutes later. Battiston had to head off the line from Santillana when protecting the right-hand post at a corner. The first goal came from a combination of improbable circumstances. Salva Garcia was ruled to have pulled Lacombe's shirt just outside the area, though it looked as if he fell unaided. Spain lined up their wall, Platini bent the kick round the right-hand side, and Arconada in goal, a hero in the victory over Germany, dived to grasp the ball, only to allow it to squeeze under him a foot over the line: a rare error.

With an hour gone, Tigana at last started to dictate. He nearly made a goal for Giresse, then himself lobbed wide.

Santillana headed over by a foot at the other end. The game was still not won, and Platini narrowly failed to settle it with a brilliant header. Spain continued to search for the goal to bring about extra time. Who knows, they could even have won the trophy on penalties, with only a single victory in the first round.

FRANCE: J. Bats (Auxerre); J-F. Domergue (Toulouse), M. Bossis (Nantes), Y. Leroux (Monaco), P. Battiston (Bordeaux) (sub: M. Amoros, Monaco); L. Fernandez (Paris St Germain), M. Platini (Juventus), A. Giresse (Bordeaux), J. Tigana (Bordeaux), B. Lacombe (Bordeaux) (sub: B. Genghini, Monaco), B. Bellone (Monaco).
SPAIN: L. Arconada (Real Sociendad); S. Urquiaga (Athletic Bilbao), J. Camacho (Real Madrid), J. Señor (Real Zaragoza), V. Muñoz (Barcelona), C. Santillana (Real Madrid), R. Gallego (Real Madrid), F. Carrasco (Barcelona), S. Garcia (Real Zaragoza), J. Alberto (Barcelona), F. Lopez (Seville). Subs: R. Fernandez (Valencia), M. Sarabia (Bilbao).

A DREAM FINALLY COMES TRUE
The Times, July 1984

Mission Viejo: To be in the wide open spaces of Saddleback Valley, beneath the 6,000-foot peaks of the Santa Ana mountain range of the Cleveland Forest National Park, was to realise that the Olympic Games are so much more than just athletics and swimming, which tend to hog the limelight. The sort of crowds you see on the Tour de France, some 20,000, crammed the roads and banks. Only this was something different.

As the veteran cyclist Connie Carpenter-Phinney and the youthful Rebecca Twigg sprinted down the last hill and up the final gradient at Mission Viejo, bursting clear of three rivals, separated by the width of a tyre in a desperately enthralling climax to the women's 49-mile individual road race, a British housewife, aged 64, stood quietly under the canopy of the little main stand and tried to smile rather than cry with happiness.

It was a poignant moment of irony as Valery Fyssoev, of the Soviet Union, president of the Federation of International Amateur Cycling, had to step forward in his official tangerine

177

blazer and congratulate the first American medal winners in cycling since 1912, while on the hill above him a sheet hung out of a bedroom window with the taunting slogan: 'Don't Russians Have Bicycles?' The Yanks are not going to let the snub die down.

Mrs Carpenter-Phinney came out of retirement in 1981 especially for this race. Six hours later, her husband would finish fifth in the men's 120 miles event. She said afterwards: 'This is my last race. I had thought it would be a great way to go out. After 12 years in international sport, I still can't believe I've won. I was a pioneer in women's cycling, and I worked very hard for this day.'

But not as hard or as long as Eileen Grey. This first-ever women's cycling event in the Olympics was a private triumph for her after almost 40 years of campaigning for women's equality by the benevolent Englishwoman. As the ginger-haired American stood on the victory podium waving to the cheering and whooping crowd, she owed a piece of that gold medal to the president of the British Cycling Federation, who had spent much of the last 12 years relentlessly pursuing an awed Lord Killanin. Repeatedly, Killanin had taken cover and run, insisting that the Games must not be bigger – even though, as long ago as 1971, Avery Brundage had admitted that the women could not indefinitely be kept out, following Mrs Grey's major breakthrough in bringing about a women's world championship in 1958. Her first demanding letter to the IOC dates back to 1957 and it has been her cheerful combination of charm and persistence that has prevented her lone efforts from losing rather than winning friends, of whom she has many.

One of them is the general secretary of the international amateur federation, a beaming Polish-Swiss, whose enthusiasm in the euphoria of the closing stages was as much for the innovator by his side clutching her camera, insisting she could never have done it without the support of her now retired husband, Walter, as for the scenes of jubilation around the course. This was fanned very soon by the news that President Reagan had already been on the telephone with congratulations for the first American gold medallist of the Games.

It is sometimes hard to understand how anyone finds the altruism to work as Mrs Grey has done all these years, often paying her own expenses when travelling around Europe. When she first started competing, there was not even a national championship for women, who were accepted as members of the then National Cycling Union but rather regarded as good company for men on cycle touring. By the time the first national championship arrived in 1947, Mrs Grey was pregnant and her competition days were over. Ten years later, she brought about the first world championship by telling the International Cycling Union that the women would organise their own if they did not get official permission.

The turning point for the Olympics came when Juan Samaranch, an expansionist, succeeded Killanin. Samaranch would double, not halve, the Olympics if he could. And on Sunday you could see why. Over half an hour after the medal winners had crossed the line, three Korean girls, matted with sweat and hollow-eyed with fatigue, swayed up the finishing straight to receive warm applause from the crowd, most of whom could not point to Korea or, say, Austria, on a map, but were giving the Olympics everything they could. Third World development in sport will soon be a revelation.

Many had doubted Coe's ability to challenge for a medal again in the Olympic Games, following intermittent illness for two years. Retaining his title was a triumph greater than first winning it. Four years later, the British Board would deny him the chance to run a third time, in Seoul.

CUTTING SHORT THE SCEPTICS

The Times, August 1984

Los Angeles: Before John Walker and Sebastian Coe left the UCLA village for their respective finals on the last day of track and field events at the Coliseum, Walker, the 1,500 metres champion of 1976, privately apologised to Coe for his statement some time ago that no great athlete ever lasted at the top for more than two years, and now added that he thought Coe would win.

Steve Cram, the world, European and Commonwealth champion at 1,500 metres during the two years of Coe's continual health problems, had said earlier in the Olympic fortnight that nobody would be able to last seven races over two distances in the abrasive acid and heat of Los Angeles' polluted air. Joachim Cruz, the 800 metres champion, has not: but after Coe had electrifyingly kicked clear from Cram in the last 120 metres of a record race, Cram was the first to pay tribute to a unique performer. 'I'm satisfied. I enjoyed the race. I couldn't do anything else,' he said. 'Seb was brilliant. I didn't think he'd have it in his legs. I'm pleased for him.' It is the recognition of the calibre of his performance by other athletes which will most gratify Coe, because a successful defence of the title, which he gained in Moscow, has not been achieved in this Blue Riband of Olympic events since before the First World War. It was the perfectly gauged race, run in a time which lowered Keino's 1968 Olympic record, the more remarkable because at this time last year Coe was in hospital with a serious blood disease and did not start training again until Christmas.

The unseen heroes of his victory, which had the American crowds out of their seats, are a bunch of anonymous Haringey club runners – John, Gary, Perry, and Dennis – whose selfless relay running ahead of Coe in training in the wretched winter months of January to March enabled him to recapture the endurance which would withstand the seven races.

The 800 metres series arrived, he says, without any disrespect for Cruz's record-breaking run, two races too soon. It was those four two-lap races that gave him the sharpness for the 1,500 metres, and it was only following the first round of the longer race that he had, briefly, any discomfort.

There is no belittlement of Cram, the silver medal winner, in emphasising Coe's exceptional comeback to repeat his silver and gold in Moscow. No British runner at any distance has won more than two Olympic medals. Although a couple of months ago he was not sure of selection, he confided after Saturday's race that, so confident was he feeling during the development of tactics in the race, he fastened onto Khalifa, Scott and Abascal when they successively led the field, and had to discipline himself not to make a break with 270 metres to go, but to bide his time. 'The Olympics is a competition to win, not to put at risk.'

For a variety of reasons Coe is more satisfied with his Los Angeles gold medal than with Moscow's, not least because his father, Peter Coe, putting an affectionate arm around him afterwards, would say with mock seriousness: 'I couldn't find a single thing wrong with that performance, except you didn't dip at the tape.' Several minutes after the semi-final, in which Seb had foolishly eased over the last 30 yards and two fast finishers had nearly passed him, Peter, close to retirement age, was still visibly trembling with anxiety, and said to a friend: 'If you see him first, thump him.'

What neither son nor father had revealed prior to the Olympics was that by mutual agreement they had for the last month separated: not as coach and athlete, not tactically, not temperamentally, not permanently, but simply to take away the stress caused by their differing personalities and concern for each other, so as not to jeopardise the effort. Seb knew that in the emotional turmoil of the Olympics, which can make or break competitors, he had to be his own man mentally. Peter acknowledged that change in his son when, discussing the significance of Seb's sharp semi-final performance, he said: 'The person who knew better than I or any judge that he could win was himself.'

In the coming weeks Coe will run several 1,500 metre races

and at least one 5,000 to explore his intended switch. His main target now is the European 5,000 metres at Stuttgart, in 1986. But before his season is out he would like to try to regain the 1,500 world record, lost by Steve Ovett to Sydney Maree last season then regained.

For Ovett, it was a sad conclusion to his Olympic career. His courageous, almost belligerent insistence on coming back from illness in the 800, against the advice of his wife and some medical advisers, was doomed to failure, and he dropped out of the race shortly after the bell with a recurrence of his breathing difficulties. Both Coe and Cram commiserated with the world record holder afterwards. 'It was very brave of him to step out after the 800 and I hope he finds out what his problem is when he gets home,' Coe said.

Khalifa, of Sudan, set a fastish first lap of 58 seconds and down the back straight for the second time Scott suddenly jumped into the lead, Coe moving in behind Khalifa as they went around the third bend. Scott said later that he was determined to make it a fast race and not just a kickers' finish; but his boldness served only to assist Coe and condemn his own chances. Scott led for just over a lap, passing the 800 metres mark in 1:56.8, eight seconds faster than the split time in Moscow, but with a lap and a quarter to go Abascal, then Coe and Cram swept past Scott, with Ovett pulling through into fourth place at the bell.

Around the penultimate bend Ovett was obliged to drop out. Down the last back straight Abascal clung to his lead, but into the bend was passed by Coe and then Cram as the former held off the latter's challenge. Coming into the straight Coe kicked for a second time then a third, and raced away from Cram, covering the last lap in 53.25, the last 300 in 39.32, the same time as in Moscow. His mood as he crossed the line had not the same ecstatic relief as four years ago, but the satisfaction was deeper. 'It was a coldly calculated race for me from start to finish,' Coe said. 'It was the best I'd felt for two years, and took me back to the form of 1981, which I've not touched since then.'

LYLE SLAYS THE DRAGON OF ST GEORGE'S
The Times, July 1985

They had said Sandy Lyle is too gentle and nice a man to be a champion, that he too readily accommodates himself to coming second because life is too short for regrets. No killer streak, they had said. On a gloriously benevolent summer's day at Sandwich, the kind when you long for the clock to stand still, Lyle conquered the ferocious Royal St George's, and the doubters.

He so nearly, agonisingly, justified the reputation of being the most agreeable loser in the game when, on the fringe of the 18th green, he fluffed a simple chip up to the flag, the ball rolling back towards him almost reproachfully. Lyle uncharacteristically sank to his knees in dismay, striking the turf with his betraying club. It seemed that fame might slip away at the very moment he had encompassed it. Yet for 17 holes his equanimity had been his ally, not his weakness. In pursuit of golf's most historic prize, I think I heard him swear once, ever so mildly, when he dropped a shot at the 13th.

Never had those in the game doubted his ability. He has always been a sweet striker of the ball. It was almost as an afterthought that last year, having spent quite a bit of money on a new house, he slipped off and recouped it in a few weeks in America.

You could not yesterday have found a more pleasant pair of men than the one about to become champion and Christy O'Connor, the first day's hero, to follow round the course on such an afternoon of swaying fortunes. O'Connor would lean his head sideways following the line of every drive as if, to be sure, it might look a little better from that angle. It looked pretty good, from any angle. Lyle smiled a little sheepishly, like a small boy slightly embarrassed by all the attention at his own birthday party, at the crowd's encouragement and applause as the players approached each succeeding green.

'Good luck, Sandy,' the voices echoed from outside the ropes as Lyle set off down the first fairway. He promptly sliced into the rough, shanked a second into rough and took five to go one over. He looked as undisturbed as if it was any old Sunday four-ball. Yet both players from there on exhibited uncommon steadiness, woods and irons flying like arrows against an azure sky, only the greens proving a frustration. At the second, eighth and 12th Lyle could have had birdies, his first putt missing by less than the width of the ball and stopping dead. In an excess of emotion, he actually screwed up his eyes at the eighth and slapped his thigh at the 12th.

The charm of the round was the companionship of two men enjoying an occupation which has few rivals when things are going well. They would discuss their respective lie, the wind, the proximity of photographers, the perversity of chance. When they both birdied the seventh they smiled at each other like boys who had just found a fiver.

The turning point in their respective fortunes came at the 14th. Both hooked into the crowd, Lyle having the worse lie and being forced to wedge out short to safety. But from the back of the green where his third ended, Lyle holed from 50 feet for a birdie, while O'Connor was par, his first putt stopping four feet short. The wind was now a zephyr. On the elevated 15th green came the nicest touch of the day as O'Connor stepped forward to remove a piece of loose grass in the line of Lyle's 12-foot putt. To a great roar, Lyle holed; O'Connor took two putts, having been nearly bunkered, for a two-stroke difference on the hole. Now O'Connor became sombre, understandably.

O'Connor dropped another stroke at the 16th and now was the passenger of the partnership as they moved towards the rumble of the crowd gathering at the last two holes. Lyle ensured his par at the 17th with a long uphill putt to within two feet. The sun was now burning down at the climax of the week and the crowds were alight with excitement. As Lyle stepped on to the 18th tee, the sun in his eyes, he pursed his lips and exhaled as he gazed down at the finishing arena. He knew he might be the winner but he barely paused as he drove down the middle straight and true. He would have liked to have avoided that final flaw, no doubt, for he had played almost without fault till then.

THE MAN BEHIND THE CLASSLESS MASK
The Times, August 1985

The public school, middle-class conventions of his upbringing have been carefully cloaked by David Gower with the classless contemporary mannerisms of a social cosmopolitan. Yet no one, including perhaps the man himself, is quite sure what is the real Gower. The current England captain of cricket, who this morning in the sixth Test at the Oval hopes to guide his team to the winning of the Ashes, is a complex sportsman: known to all, yet truly known by few. Even the chairman of the selectors, Peter May, is said to find it difficult to communicate with him.

As a distantly viewed public figure, there is something of the politician David Owen about Gower. Able, intelligent, popular, there is flexibility in his nature, in seemingly wanting to be all things to all men, which leaves people unsure: gregarious yet private, personable yet emotionless, an ardent modern professional with the almost lazy aura of an old-fashioned amateur, a winner without the killer instinct.

His fascination with cats and leopards is perhaps indicative of his character. 'They have a serenity,' he says. So, occasionally unduly, does his leadership. There are times, watching him fielding at mid-off, when he appears to be observing the conflict rather than directing it. Yet after three Test series as a comparatively youthful and somewhat reluctant captain, there is little doubt that he is maturing. Ray Illingworth, the former England, Yorkshire and Leicestershire captain, under whose wing the schoolboy Gower entered first class cricket, says: 'He is undoubtedly improving, as shown by his handling of the last few overs of the one-day match against Australia at Lord's, and his judgement in the Trent Bridge Test. He would no doubt say he got the job a year or two earlier than he wanted it.'

Chosen at 27 to succeed Bob Willis last summer when almost simultaneously he had replaced Roger Tolchard as Leicestershire captain, Gower was prepared for the West

Indies series at home to be gruelling. It was. England were overrun, but he felt they should have done better in the match at Lord's. His own performance with the bat fell short; at least in part because of an early season infection, sustained in a finger injury against Derbyshire, which characteristically he at first declined to take seriously. A specialist has said that 15 years ago he could have died from it. Ill for a month, he started playing again too soon, attempting to find form for the Tests, was never really fit, and after a brief holiday led the team in India, hardly a rest cure. His batting remained, for him, sub-standard; and he was a less than diligent captain when England moved on to Australia for the superfluous one-day series. At times, too, he was touchy in handling the Press, resorting to the flippancy which is his self-defensive mechanism. An interviewer once wrote of him that 'he is so laid back he is almost comatose.'

Gentle iconoclasm has always been evident. At King's School, Canterbury, he was never a school monitor, yet when asked at 15, reprovingly, by his housemaster what he thought he would be doing in 10 years' time, is said to have replied that he would be captain of England. Berated as a teenager by Illingworth for the casualness of his dress, he once mockingly appeared at breakfast in a dinner jacket. He made an indifferent start as vice-captain to Willis in 1983–84, informal in dress and punctuality, but latterly as captain he has never put a foot wrong at such formalities as embassy receptions – before disappearing off to a disco.

Gower adapts, chameleon-like, to his circumstances, which adds to the enigma of who he is. He was born in Kent of a family with long colonial service, including a judge and an admiral, with traditions of duty from which he is clearly not immune. Following a childhood partly spent in what was then Tanganyika, he returned to English preparatory school and thence to King's, achieved three A-levels, failed Oxbridge, and went to read law at University College London. He has discreetly played down his background and speech: his mother has been quoted as saying that she long ago recognised that he had one accent with the family and another with friends. The everyman's voice of a Smiley.

The decision, when Leicestershire successfully approached Kent for his signature, to forego a law degree for full-time cricket, may well have accentuated the social ambivalence for someone who found it easy, and more acceptable, to conform to surroundings than conventions. He quite enjoyed being regarded in the early 1980s as one of the rebels, identifying with Botham; unconcerned that traditionalists at Lord's gritted their teeth if he appeared at nets in a T-shirt. He was of another world, another age, compared with the established figures of the MCC. 'He mixed very easily,' Illingworth says. 'When he was young, without being cheeky he had the self-confidence to speak freely with the older professionals.'

If Gower was with them in spirit and ambition, he was still somehow not *of* them. The players, then and now, liked him and enjoyed playing with him, but he was largely reluctant to talk about cricket. His articles for *Wisden Cricket Monthly* are as likely to refer to restaurants as to the game. He enjoys the good life, and will search for champagne at inflated prices in up-country India. His cultural tastes are as catholic as his behaviour: in the house near the Leicestershire ground where he lives with his girlfriend he is as likely to listen to Brahms as to rock, reads avidly and most days does the *Telegraph* crossword. Someone who knows him well says that, though he would not care to admit it, Gower does not consider his life ends with cricket.

Be that as it may, he is one of the most illustrious lights in the game. The secret of all games is timing. In tennis, the great players such as Perry, Hoad and McEnroe take the ball early. Great batsmen often take it late. Maybe Gower does not take it as late as the famed Ranjitsinhji, but he is likened to the debonair Compton, and to the legendary Woolley, likewise a left-hander from Kent with a similarly upright stance, who was the quintessence of style. Hutton has said that Gower does not have Woolley's ability to demolish an attack, leaving the bowlers not knowing where or how to bowl. Yet Gower, admittedly on covered wickets, has scored 5,228 runs in 75 Tests so far compared with Woolley's 3,283 in 64.

The next five years will determine whether he is a good batsman or a great one. He is no ruthless accumulator, such as Boycott or Bradman, and is apt to try difficult shots regarded by some as irresponsible merely to prove he *can* play them. 'He was the greatest youngster anyone could have seen,' Illingworth says. 'A marvellous timer of the ball. He was tactically poor at first, weak at playing spin, but such was his timing he soon improved.' In his first Test at Edgbaston against Pakistan in 1978 he memorably hooked his first ball for four, scored 58, and subsequently became the youngest Englishman since May, in 1951, to score a Test century. His 187 during eight hours for England against the West Indies in 1981 disproved that he cannot concentrate; as did his double century a fortnight ago.

Captaincy undoubtedly did not come as easily to him as does the game. There are those at Leicester who say the team looked more purposeful under Tolchard, yet this season Gower has several times shown himself ready to take a risk which Tolchard would have eschewed. Mike Turner, the Leicestershire secretary, recalls that Illingworth, when captain of country and county at the age of 38, needed time to adjust after a Test match to the lower key of the county championship, and that Gower, 10 years younger, is experiencing the same problem. Yet it must be doubted if England would have called upon him had he not already been made county captain, even if preferably he needed to have waited a year or two longer for both. Brearley, England's last outstanding captain, was, like Illingworth, in his 30s.

It seems unlikely that Australia, if unaided by the weather, can deny England at least the draw they need to take the series. A more searching examination of Gower's leadership will come in the West Indies this winter in an environment of sharper hostility than has been provided by the Australians. Will Gower be able to control, on and off the pitch, one of his predecessors as captain, the rogue elephant Botham, who was absent during the successful tour of India? Gower has written of Botham that 'you seem to get the best out of him by letting him have his way when setting the field or bowling a spell.' That policy has not always proved strategic this summer, during which Botham has often been erratic. With his growing influence, Gower is establishing within the England team a coterie of supporters and some of them, such as his admirable vice-captain Gatting, would be happy to see a team ethic more vigorously imposed on the egocentric Botham. Can Gower, or indeed anyone, achieve that?

France morally deserved to win an unforgettable match: yet it was Brazil who would probably have defeated West Germany in the semi-final.

A CLASSIC GAME OPENS WAY FOR FRENCH REVENGE

The Times, June 1986
BRAZIL 1   FRANCE 1
(France win on penalties)

Guadalajara: It is doubtful if the first half-century of the World Cup saw a more eventful match than Saturday's quarter-final between France and Brazil. And the second half-century will be fortunate to see its equal. The two teams defied the ferocious temperature of 120 degrees in the Jalisco Stadium, and each other, to reinvigorate international football with a classic tussle which will be talked about for years. Whether France can recover their mental and physical fibre in three days after such an epic, to avenge the semi-final of 1982 when they meet West Germany again, keeps this competition in a state of fascinated anticipation.

Over two hours and a half, including the wretched necessity for the nevertheless spellbinding execution by penalty shoot-out, there were the dramatic qualities of many sports. No 15-round world title bout, nor match-play golf taken to the 19th, nor five-set tennis final fluctuating on every point, nor Olympic race decided in the last few strides, nor Test won in the last over could have had more suspense. It was one of those rare occasions which makes my occupation uniquely pleasurable, yet how to recapture the emotions, skills and courage which flowed back and forth across the sunlit pitch? I have not seen a better match in eight finals, nor one played in such a marvellous spirit: only one single mean foul, sheer desperation by Carlos, the Brazil goalkeeper late in extra time, amid mutual generosity which put many teams here to shame. As in all great sporting moments, the quality of the losers contributed as much or more than that of the winners. How we grieve for Brazil: such a flourish, yet no reward other than admiration.

The match swung from end to end throughout, almost with the rapidity of ice hockey, and one knew not how the players sustained the momentum in their fifth match at altitude in three weeks. There were 16 scoring opportunities created by Brazil to 15 by France. In some matches there are none.

On Friday, Joao Saldanha, Brazil's former manager whose marvellous team of 1970 was taken over at the last moment by Mario Zagalo, insisted this team was better than four years ago. It was stronger defensively and more balanced, with Elzo, of Athletico Minas Gerais the foundation of the midfield – 'the man who carries the piano', Saldanha said evocatively. What heroics were performed by Elzo and Branco for Brazil; by Bossis, Amoros and Fernandez for France, in the shadow of more famous reputations.

Brazil developed with every successive match, and if France, who provided thrilling performances against the Soviet Union and Italy, were their first opponents of quality, they unleashed within minutes all the traditional, instinctive touches which make Brazilian football so appealing: the enticement and the acceleration clear of a tackle by Junior, Careca and Muller which puts the opponents momentarily out of the game, the half-volleyed trap-cum-pass by Julio Cesar at the back or Socrates as the fulcrum of attack, which transforms apparent innocence into danger. Bossis, unexpectedly swapping sweeper/marker roles with Battiston, was for half an hour or so being pounded by Careca as Junior and Socrates ceaselessly primed the guns like powder-monkeys. There is no team which can play as Brazil do when in the mood.

Suddenly France, the masters for four or five years of silken midfield embroidery, were worried stiff by the shielded first-touch which was wrong-footing them. After 17 minutes, Brazil scored the most breathtaking goal of the finals yet, a ripple of passes between Socrates, Branco and Josimar, a first-time exchange between Junior and Muller and a final thrust by Junior sending Careca through a stricken French rearguard. It was the first time France had been behind since they played the Soviet Union, and it stung them into response.

At last, in the 46th minute, France's rhythm clicked: Giresse, the oldest of 10 players in the match in their 30s, slipped the ball to another of them, Rocheteau, who was finding a new lease of speed, clear on the right; and his early low centre was deflected off Edinho, Stopyra's goalmouth dive confused Carlos, and the ball ran free. Platini stole through unnoticed, and with all the calm of a training stint in a deserted stadium tapped into the net.

The second half contained sufficient incidents for half a dozen matches. Zico replaced Muller with 17 minutes to go, and with almost his first touch sent Branco through on an overlap. Out rushed Bats, spread himself across Branco's path, missed the ball and hauled him down. Unwisely, Zico, not yet in tune, moved up to take the penalty. Behind Zico's back, Platini signalled to Bats' left and Bats took the hint to parry the shot. Brazil's chance to win in normal time had passed.

Extra time. We wilted in the shade in 90 degrees. Both sides continued to hurl themselves at each other, but their legs were beginning to crumble. A last glorious pass by Platini, the most memorable of the match, sent Bellone clear, only for him to be manhandled off the ball a yard outside the area by Carlos. A blunder by the sweat-soaked referee, Igna of Romania. Carlos should have been sent off.

The whistle went. The unenvied penalty kickers assembled in the centre circle drained and blank-faced like actors being asked to audition after running a marathon. Socrates had the first kick saved by Bats, and France were 3-2 up when Bellone, with moral justice, scored with a rebound off the post and back off Carlos' head. Platini skied his shot, to level the situation, but Josimar slammed against a post, and stoic, dependable Fernandez atoned for Platini's miss. So now France must meet the West Germans to claim the place in the final which they deserve. It will be a better final if they do; and France have a score to settle with Schumacher.

BRAZIL: Carlos; Josimar, Edinho, J. Cesar, Branco; Elzo, Socrates, Junior Alemao; Muller, Careca. Subs: Silas, Zico.
FRANCE: J. Bats; M. Amoros, M. Bossis, P. Battiston, T. Tusseau; L. Fernandez, M. Platini, A. Giresse, J. Tigana, Y. Stopyra, D. Rocheteau. Subs: J-M. Ferreri, B. Bellone.

In the World Cup finals of 1982, Maradona had been, like Pelé before, mercilessly kicked and provoked by Belgium and Italy. In 1986, though defiling his reputation with a handled goal against England, he was truly in a class of his own.

POSITIVE WAY TO TAKE THE WORLD CUP
The Times, June 1986
ARGENTINA 3   WEST GERMANY 2

Mexico City: Not a great final, until the last quarter of an hour when a combination of Argentina's fragility in defence and West Germany's habitual capacity to turn their back on the odds and come from behind gave the match its final flurry of anxieties and frenzied action. It was good for football that the team which throughout had placed their concentration upon playing football, upon being positive, should be the winners, and that they lived dangerously at times was all the better for the spectators.

It was a final distinguished, if by nothing else, by the performance of the Brazilian referee Filho, who kept the play closer to a correct interpretation of the laws than anyone, if I may be forgiven for saying so, since an Englishman in 1974, when Jack Taylor gave a penalty against the home team in the first minute and they still won. If we had had such diligence with the whistle, such an understanding of players' intent and what is and is not fair, we would have avoided that awful first hour in Madrid – with another Brazilian – while in 1978 Holland would probably have beaten Argentina, whose gamesmanship was unchecked by an Italian.

Not so now. Of the six bookings, five were for dissent or time wasting. Matthaus was booked after only 22 minutes when he hacked at Maradona's heels well after the ball had been despatched, and that served to restrain the Germans' latent capacity for intimidation. It was appropriate that Argentina should go in front in the next minute from a free kick, for the Germans were being a shade too confidently contemptuous to get 11 men behind the ball and hope that Argentina would eventually run out of inspiration.

It was a match also notable for the errors of Schumacher, Germany's goalkeeper from Cologne who likes to think himself the most professionally prepared, physically and mentally, in the game. He seriously misjudged the swing on Burruchaga's free kick which moved away as it dipped into the six-yard line, and was met unerringly by Joe Brown. On Argentina's second and third goals, Schumacher was strangely inert when drawn towards the ball first by Valdano cutting in from the left and then, in instant reply to Germany's equaliser, when Burruchaga swept in from the right. It was a rare trio of misjudgements.

Many critics have been saying that without Maradona, Argentina were relatively insignificant opposition. I had felt, since seeing them pace themselves through the first round, that they were likely to be able to adjust their game to produce what was necessary, certainly within the context of this competition. Germany, with their relentless marking, proved to be the most obdurate; but some marvellous, flowing first-time moves at close quarters between Burruchaga, Valdano, Maradona and Enrique thrilled the Azteca crowd and enticed Germany into committing repeated infringements, so that a succession of free kicks swung the

193

tide against them. Burruchaga was a delight, springing forward from midfield onto Maradona's promptings like a cat off a wall, to such effect that Maradona himself could most of the time be happy to play the subsidiary role. Just now and then he would remind Germany that he was by a distance the outstanding performer of 1986.

Germany suffered to some extent from exactly the same problem as had England: getting so many men behind the ball demanded that extra pace and accuracy was needed on the counter-attack, and being currently without threatening forwards, they mostly could not find it. They were too dependent on Briegel's initiative in surges out of defence, but after the first half hour he became less significant. Argentina's one-touch play was exacting a fearful strain on Germany's defensive running and covering.

Less than they did against England, Argentina only began to play for time after Rummenigge had stabbed the ball home at a corner with a quarter of an hour to go. For a reason which would not become apparent until the post-match crescendo of victory had calmed, Brown, Argentina's sweeper, strangely stayed on the field in spite of a shoulder injury in the 52nd minute. He continued bravely to hold the fort with timely interceptions, yet was increasingly in pain and under pressure, and it seemed extraordinary that he should still be allowed to remain when Voller equalised. In that moment you would not have given Argentina an earthly to win in extra time: but Maradona and Burruchaga provided the instant answer with the final goal.

ARGENTINA: Pumpido; Brown; Cuciuffo, Rugger, Olarticocchea; Batista, Giusti, Burruchaga (Trobbiani 90); Enrique, Maradona, Valdano.
WEST GERMANY: Schumacher: Jakobs; Forster, Eder; Brehme, Matthaus, Berthold, Magath (Honess 62), Briegel; Rummenigge, Allofs (Voller 46).

SILVER LINING TO SOME YEOMANLY SERVICE
The Times, August 1986

Thursday was a mixed sort of day. The car wouldn't start

because the battery was flat, which complicated an early breakfast interview with a chap from Royal Lymington before the day's fleet set off from Cowes. Round about lunchtime, a turbulent Solent, whipped by a Force Six, was lapping disconcertingly round my armpits somewhere near the Bramble Bank, halfway between Southampton and the island. At the time I was supposed to be in a boat. Such an occasion is termed 'broaching'. In the evening, my mind too genuinely a shade blown, I managed to put five gallons of derv in the car. It is not a diesel.

Not every cloud at Cowes this week, however, has been without a silver lining. The boat's skipper, who as a commodore of the Royal Ocean Racing Club has an answer to such situations other than firing a flare, got us ship-shape in no time. A couple of his crew, who had been swimming about like castaways amid a chaos of ropes, spars, a horizontal mast and language fit to make Mrs Whitehouse emigrate, returned on board in immaculate order; little time was lost, a vertical profile was resumed, and on a spinnaker run at the end of 30 miles, Yeoman XXVI beat Tim Herring's Backlash for the Squadron's gun by a distance no farther than I could have thrown my full wellies.

I've seldom had as much fun without laughing. Admittedly, my sailing is more a matter of who gets up early to go and buy the bread in St Peter Port or Camaret, or unblocking the ship's loo with a wire coathanger. Not the least remarkable part of this Class I race was that the 86-year-old Sir Owen Aisher, a veritable old man of the sea, sat in the stern throughout, as upright as the Needles lighthouse, alongside his son Robin at the helm with no concession to age other than woolly gloves. When it was all over he had a beer and sailed back to Portsmouth.

Robin Aisher is one of the last of the top flight 'amateurs' of yachting, with enough knowledge and experience to have helmed his own boat in an Admiral's Cup. One of his contributions with the RORC has been the introduction of the Channel Handicap, a rating measurement which can be obtained by standard production family boats of, say, 30 feet for only £25 instead of the £500 or more necessary to have an international ocean rating. He believes that this will help offset the gap that is developing between the amateurs and the new breed of professional yachtsmen, which will increase even more with the advent of individual boat sponsorship.

Yeoman XXVI has almost as much technology below deck as a television broadcasting unit. All around above deck, electronic digital screens blink at you through the spray like an airport departure board. A matter of some alarm is that the light displacement, a configuration of contemporary design, has so little buoyance for'ard that the broach was precipitated by the mere weight of two deck-hands on the bow preparing for a gybe. The nose went under as far back as the mast-step, the 45-foot boat halted from 10 knots and slewed: the mast could have snapped. One of the crew observed later that he wasn't sure if he'd fancy the middle of the Atlantic in such a sensitive craft.

Few people can afford such complex gadgetry, and indeed the whole problem of yachting in Britain is how to overcome the public concept of its seeming financial and social exclusiveness. As was remarked this week by a club official with a conscience: 'The major clubs on the south coast are like social fortresses, with their guns pointing inland.' For a democratic expansion of yachting, the British have to move towards the pattern in France in the relationship with the local council. Mostly in Britain, in the edgy balance between 'town' and 'yachties', the council understandably tend to identify with 'town', and are grudgingly helpful. 'Sailing boats disfigure the jetty' one council contradictorily ruled on a mooring request.

Royal Lymington has a waiting list: but whereas potential social members wanting to dine have to wait, those wanting to sail are quickly admitted. Ten per cent of the 3,400 members are under 21, paying only £9 per annum. On Wednesday, the club is open to any child from seven to 16 in the town: and has been swamped by those anxious to avail themselves of the 15 Scow dinghies. 'Every club should be asking whether it is doing a good job for its community,' a chap from Lymington says, gratified that the club is now qualified as a Royal Yachting Association teaching establishment. 'So many youngsters would like to sail, but don't know how to start or haven't the means. They're like tennis players without rackets.'

Yachting, like golf, is strong on traditions of etiquette. It is imperative that this is not sacrificed in the breaching of social barriers. The natural tendency when a youngster who has just won a dinghy race appears in the bar in soaking clothes is to say 'get out' rather than 'well done'. It would be retrogressive if the yacht clubs were overrun: they need to become more cosmopolitan in outlook, but not unduly common in standards.

COE PUTS CRAM IN SHADE
The Times, August 1986

Stuttgart: Sebastian Coe is an 800 metres champion at last. With a perfectly judged race from the back of the pack, shadowing Steve Cram until the moment came to strike off the last bend, Coe triumphantly won the European title at the third attempt, after two previous silver medals. A month before his 30th birthday, his victory was the sweeter for being achieved at the expense of the man regarded, currently, as unbeatable. Indeed, Cram was pushed into third place by young Tom McKean who achieved a personal best, and there must now be doubts about Cram's recovery from recent muscle problems. He seemed to be in pain in the tunnel after the race which questions his ability to defend his 1,500 metres title.

A euphoric Coe said afterwards that the misfortunes and the misjudgements of the past eight years are melting away. 'It's all I've ever wanted!' Those five words said so much, for his failures at this distance – at which he holds the world record – have weighed heavily in spite of all the other compensations. Though he had won the Europa Cup of 1979 and 1981 at 800 metres and also the World Cup in 1981, he has long felt wretched that he might have to retire without ever having proved himself in a championship. To do so at 30 is exceptional.

It was another miserable day. The sky was a uniform grey above the green hills surrounding the stadium, and the three British runners returned from the warm-up track unrecognised beneath the hoods of their tracksuits as late arrivals at the stadium passed them outside. Peter Coe, who had been giving a few last words of encouragement, said as his son disappeared towards the dressing-room: 'He's in the best shape he can be against a man who has all the aces – those five extra races in Edinburgh, four years in age and no illnesses. We'll see.' (Coe had had flu during the Commonwealth Games.)

All the seats in the stadium were full, the crowd huddled beneath umbrellas, though the rain eased as the runners stripped off for the start. Strangely there was not a single East German in the field. Coe was drawn on the inside, which no runner likes in this race. 'It gives you all the disadvantages,' he said, 'because if you go off too fast you can find yourself in the lead at the lane-break when you don't want to be, in the middle of the field you can get boxed and if you hang back you can get out of touch.' He is not likely ever to forget his error in Moscow.

At the end of the first bend Braun, the home favourite, led from Druppers, the Dutchman, Collard, of France, and Kalinkin, of the Soviet Union. Going into the second bend Coe was seventh, ahead of the Pole, Ostrowski, and keeping his eye on Cram. Coming down the home straight for the first time McKean had taken up third place ahead of Collard, with Coe sticking close on the heels of Cram. At the bell it was still Braun at the front from Druppers. Into the third bend Cram made as if to accelerate, but momentarily found himself boxed, and Coe had to run wide almost into lane three so as not to get barged. This gave Cram room to make his move. Down the back straight they were fourth and fifth behind McKean, and on the crown of the last bend all three British runners swept to the front past the West German and Dutchman.

Coming into the final straight Cram had moved wide to go

past McKean, but then, 90 metres from the tape, Coe produced that renowned kick. His training has been going as well as he thought. Changing down a gear he accelerated past Cram, took McKean with about 50 metres to go and held his rhythm to win by a stride. Behind him Cram had been labouring, his shoulders rolling and with none of the poise he had shown as recently as last week in Birmingham. Coe said afterwards: 'At the bell I felt optimistic. When the break hadn't come with 300 metres to go I felt able to relax for the next 100 metres. I knew I could only lose now if my own form went in the finishing straight. At 200 metres to go, I was into my favourite territory.'

In that memorable last lap, the splits were 52 seconds for 400, 37.8 for 300, 24.7 for 200 and 12.4 for 100. The times of Britain's medallists were respectively: 1 min 44.50 sec, 1 min 44.61 sec, 1 min 44.88 sec.

A clearly dispirited Cram said afterwards that he would not be able to say anything about the condition of his calf problem until the morning. 'When I didn't have the strength to get past Tom coming off the final bend I knew I was unlikely to be able to beat Seb. I've not been feeling at full strength since I came here, the way I was three or four weeks ago. I tried to go earlier in the race, but on the day I wasn't good enough.'

Against the impossible odds of being born in a 'low' country, Martin Bell, and his younger brother Graham, have a distinguished record, culminating at the Olympic Games in Calgary, when Martin's eighth place would be Britain's highest ever achievement in an Olympic downhill.

THE DOWNHILL SLOPE EASES FOR BELL

The Times, December 1986

Val d'Isère: As they climbed into the cable car to go up to the start of Saturday's Super-G race at Val d'Isère, Wirnsberger, of Austria, congratulated Martin Bell on his sixth place in the World Cup downhill the day before. Bell is still turning over in his mind whether it was a gesture of admiration or condescension: was Wirnsberger saying in effect, 'not bad for a Brit!'

To be British in Alpine skiing is to be irreconcilably on the wrong side of the tracks: never mind that the English first converted a mountain dweller's means of transport into a sport and Swiss shepherds used, in Saas Fee, to throw stones at them. Bell, 23 last Saturday, launched himself into competitive skiing a few years ago with as much credibility as a Czechoslovak midshipman entering Dartmouth. He's hoping to break the mould.

Bell's emergence in the front rank, with the potential to win a medal in February's world championship or the Olympic Games in Calgary in 14 months' time, is akin to the Netherlands beating England at Lord's. He is not quite sure how the Alpine traditional élite are reacting to it. In recent months, having earned some modest sponsorship through his fifth and sixth places at Åre and Morzine in last year's downhill series, Bell has been accompanying Resch, of Austria, and Alpiger, of Switzerland, at functions of ICI, whose name appears on their equipment. Resch and Alpiger, he has sensed, had a slight, if unspoken, superiority in their manner. Last Saturday, Resch was eighth and Alpiger 12th.

For those who watch *Ski Sunday*, with its anaesthetising Christmas card glamour, the realities of a downhill are unimaginable. This year, for the first time in his career, Bell came to the start of the European season with a mastery of the fear from which no competitor is ever free. 'The fear is always there, but this year it was a lot less', he says. 'It's a matter of feeling *secure* at speed. Wirnsberger has been at it 12 years, yet he says that every time he sees the *Mausefalle* drop at Kitzbühel, he shakes.'

Last year, Bell admits to finishing 10th in his first race. The year before, he crashed in his first training run. 'This year, I didn't have to adjust, emotionally, as much. I felt more at home. It wasn't so much the confidence gained from last year's results, but the slow build-up of experience.' Although he came 36th and 37th in two races in Argentina at the end of the summer, he feels they acted as a therapeutic staging post between March and December. At 100 kilometres per hour, experience is everything. By the time the Olympics come here, in 1992, Bell will be only just 28.

His immediate ambition – although he did not talk about it over the weekend at the informally British-run, club-style Hotel Moris here – is to win next Saturday's race at Val Gardena, his favourite course, in the Italian Tyrol. Having finished less than a second behind Zurbriggen, the winner here, he knows that he is within range of an achievement that would be unique in British skiing.

'The difference in him this year is that he seems a happier person,' Alistair Scobie, the British team manager, says. 'With the sponsorship Martin's now getting, he is less hard-pressed financially, and that has made him more relaxed to be with.' Throughout the years on the circuit, Bell, his brother Graham – now recovering from a serious knee operation – Nigel Smith and Ron Duncan have been partially paying their own way. Now that Martin Bell has some income, the British Ski Federation have opened a separate account in his name prior to setting up a trust fund.

It is ironic that just at the time when Britain produces a potential medallist, the Federation should be in dire financial difficulty. Gordons Gin, their sponsors, pulled out in the Distillers/Guinness shuffle, most of the officers have resigned, and even with added Sports Council assistance, the men's and women's Alpine teams are operating on less than a quarter of the budget of, say, the Americans. This means that Bell still has no personal assistance to service his skis, as the stars do, and is dependent on help from Hans Gapp, an Austrian working with the Canadians. Combining training with the Americans means that the British get some assistance on valuable split-timings, but they continue to live hand-to-mouth. Two helpers, John Vaitkus and Alan Thompson, work for expenses only and a succession of enthusiastic doctors take holiday time to join the circuit. Are you listening, Richard Tracey and your lady leader?

'Communication is still a problem within the Federation,' Bell says. 'One of the helpers is now going to have to switch to the women's team, even though they would prefer to remain with us. Timing the different sections on the slope, a thankless task of sitting in the snow and freezing shade for several hours taking split-second times, is so important in judging whether your technique on a particular turn, or your skis on a straight, are making you slower,' Bell says. He needs to know his 'straight line' ski speed, and all this comes down to having the back-up people, even though he is now ranked fifth in the supply of individual skis by Fischer of Austria, one of his sponsors.

It is a measure of Bell's improvement, and expectation, that he can be considering how to achieve the best preparation for the Olympics. For the world championship, in Crans Montana, he knows he must continue improving. 'Val d'Isère won't matter if I have a bad time at Kitzbühel the week before,' he says.

It was at Kitzbühel that Graham crashed last year, and his long lay-off has set back his confidence. He is here with the squad, training. Two years ago, it was Graham making the news when he was second in the world junior championships. When Martin complains of demands on his time, Graham gently reminds him that one bad season will give him all the free time he needs! 'Graham's had amazing patience,' Martin says. 'He's been hoping by now to have caught up with Smith and Duncan, but he's still several seconds adrift, lacking the confidence to be settled at faster speeds.' The sponsorship running Martin's way does not make Graham's tribulations any easier to bear.

> The demands of Oxbridge admissions tutors, misguidedly orientated towards academic exclusivity, have resulted in deteriorating sporting standards that were once almost uniformly international.

DECLINE IN SPORT AT OXBRIDGE
The Times, December 1986

At Cambridge in the 1950s you could sit down to a three-shillings-and-sixpence lunch at the Hawks Club any day of the week among a group of international performers in half a dozen sports: a brains trust of table talk for which, gathered in a television studio today, Mark McCormack would demand a five-figure fee. They included household names in major and lesser sports – May, Barber and Dexter from cricket, Marques, Mulligan and Arthur Smith from rugby, Marsh and Huddy (golf), Masser (rowing), Barrett and Warwick (tennis), Maitland and Cockett (hockey), Lyon and Broomfield (squash), Hildreth and Dunkley (athletics). It was the same at Vincents Club in Oxford in the era of Cowdrey, Davidge, Brace and Derek Johnson. Pegasus, the joint football club, produced 21 amateur internationals including several, such as Tanner, Pawson and Pinner, who played for League clubs.

Now, Oxbridge performance has declined relative to national standards, partly because overall national levels of ability have risen and partly because the structure of the student population has changed, with more women and less emphasis on sport. Nowhere is the situation more critical than in cricket. The Test and County Cricket Board has recently warned Oxford and Cambridge that their first class status may be at risk. In rugby, which during a century at Cambridge has produced 300 international players with some 1,900 caps between them, Oxbridge now clings to its status by the increasing enlistment of postgraduates – which is also true of rowing at Boat Race level.

In today's varsity match at Twickenham, Oxford are relying on the scholarship schemes which attract international players with the academic qualifications to take further degree courses; soon Cambridge will be in the same position. Although Cambridge could, from recent seasons, field an England line of backs, the total of 84 caps by 10 players between 1974 and 1984 compares badly with the 291 caps of 32 players in the previous 10 years. The future worries Dr Alan Tayler, rugby senior treasurer at Oxford, who says: 'We could not hold our heads above water [in senior fixtures] if we relied on undergraduates.'

Five factors produced the decline, sufficient for a group of ex-Cambridge industrialists to have refused to help raise money for a projected £8 million sports centre at Cambridge unless there is a change in admissions policy. The factors are: the end of National Service meant younger and physically less mature undergraduates; a changed admissions policy put less emphasis on sport; increased training at outside clubs lured undergraduates away from Oxbridge and into the clubs; a proportional rise in women students cut the available pool of sportsmen; and the decline of school sport meant fewer university entrants with a sporting background.

The trend produces a dilemma not merely for Oxbridge sport but, as a minority of dons now recognise, for the fundamental attitude of the two universities towards their very function. Intellectual excellence must be the aim, but fewer than 20 per cent of undergraduates gain first-class degrees. The nationally available appointments for researchers and lectureships are diminishing: jobs must be found for the majority gaining second-class degrees. Employers increasingly look for those with self-discipline, personality, gregariousness, and a sense of collective responsibility, as well as brains. Such characteristics are strongly evident in those with sporting achievement.

John Butterfield, distinguished physician, Master of Downing College and president of both rugby and cricket at Cambridge, says: 'I believe sportsmen make good citizens.

What we are looking for [at Oxbridge] is leaders. It is valuable to know, from sport, the experience of losing.' John Hopkins, Downing admissions tutor in Arts, says: 'There are half a dozen colleges [out of 30] who want people with energy, whatever they are doing.' And Dr Alan Tayler, St Catherine's, Oxford: 'Below the level of distinguished scholars, what are our criteria? We want people who will benefit from the system, and go on to do something.' Colin Kolbert, barrister and tutor of Magdalene, Cambridge: 'A poll would show that academic performance by Blues is above the university average. Those sent down have usually done nothing in *any* field. There are no unemployed Blues, but dozens of unemployed English firsts.' Charles Wenden, fellow of All Souls, Oxford, with 30 years' experience in international university sport, and Christopher Taylor, bursar of Newnham, Cambridge, are emphatic: the maintenance of a high sporting profile is essential to Oxbridge public identification.

Many senior academics are indifferent, even hostile, to sport, resenting the lack of recognition they had as non-sporting students. Subconsciously, are they getting revenge? Wenden says: 'Maybe the attitude of the past 20 years [among tutors] has turned the corner.' Maybe not. Michael Risman, younger brother of Oxford's full-back at Twickenham today, son of Bev, grandson of Gus (both famous internationals), gained three As at A-level, and Oxford rejected him. Cambridge, shrewdly, did not.

For Steffi Graf the Grand Slam has been not so much a dream as an inevitability.

WHEN WINNING IS A FAMILY AFFAIR

The Times, December 1986

She has been called, in recent months of universal acclaim, *The Woman Borg*. The girl who will topple Martina Navratilova. In her first tournament for under-eights in Munich, an umpire called a point in favour of her opponent on a shot that was blatantly out. She cried in disbelief, and the tournament organiser told her father she would never be a player. That was the last time Steffi Graf cried on court, though she has shed tears a few times after a match. 'Crying is normal and spontaneous, it is healing,' Peter Graf, her father, says. He is also her coach. It is a parent-child relationship in competitive sport as unique, and at the present stage as successful, as has been the father-son Coe partnership.

As with the Coes, the parent has been criticised for driving the child too severely, yet Steffi, like Sebastian, is emphatic that the intensity of the partnership is at her behest, under her direction and control. 'I need him, he's most important to me, but he wouldn't be so close if I didn't want it,' she says. When she lost the Virginia Slims final to Navratilova recently, her eye tended to seek him out in the crowd, where he tries to sit anonymously. 'I don't need advice or coaching,' she says, 'just to know that he is there. It makes me feel comfortable, especially at the big meetings.' Some would say that the inherent strains in such a relationship when she is 17 – reflecting, possibly, an insecurity in the world outside tennis – will magnify as she matures, mentally and emotionally, over the next few years.

Yet to listen to the two of them talking, off duty so to speak, in the family home alongside the tennis and bowling club where all the winter practice takes place, is to believe the relationship is balanced and relaxed. The father seems protective rather than proprietorial. 'There are people who are jealous, who disapprove because I am father-coach-manager,' Peter Graf says. 'Yet I know what is right for her, I know her mentality and character.'

Earlier this year, Peter employed Pavel Slozil, the former Czechoslovak Davis Cup player, as full-time practice partner for his daughter. The intention is to modify her fundamental baseline game to include a more flexible, all-court serve-and-volley style which is imperative if she is to displace the seemingly impregnable Navratilova. Though she beat Navratilova in the German Open and lost a thrilling semi-final in the US Open after having three match points, she lost the Slims final in three straight sets.

Peter, an outstanding former club player, had intended to retreat but Steffi will not let him go. The day I called on her at Bruhl, outside Heidelberg, she was serving, again and again, at Slozil from a bucket of 50 balls, and from midcourt volleying his returns to the baseline corners. Formidable stuff. Yet she is, allegedly, a difficult person in training. 'I have to coach the coach,' Peter says with a smile. 'Pavel is still learning that Steffi is reluctant to talk during practice, that she just wants to concentrate and slam away the winners as she does in a match. He has to discover how to handle her.'

There is, indeed, a remarkable difference in her manner on and off court. Her focus, when playing, is absolute. I had arrived at Bruhl early and when she came off court she said, almost abruptly: 'Yes, we are meeting. At five.' An hour later, showered and relaxed, she was a slightly coy, smiling, relaxed schoolgirl, not the phenomenon who is the fourth prize money winner of the year ($455,000), third in the rankings and second in the Slims points table. Her ambition this year had been to win one tournament. She won eight.

When she was 10, she told the chief national coach, who had said she was too unemotional: 'Either I play or I laugh.' It is the self-generating discipline of which champions are made. 'I cannot smile when I play,' she says. 'The fun for me is in ending the point.' When she wants a laugh, she practises left-handed.

Her wish is not to be rich (which, relatively, she already is), or famous, but to master the game, to play it beautifully. Perfectly. 'I want to be a baseliner who can come to the net when it's necessary. To be able to do what *I* want on the court, what *I* feel like.' Her personality is expressed through her racket, though she is not the impersonal, inscrutable machine that Borg was. She knows she has not a waiting mentality, that the match has to be played *her* way. That is why the silent winter weeks will be spent volleying against Slozil. 'I have to work at serve-and-volley. I don't really know as yet where to go. Against other volleyers, in the past, they have known I won't come in. If I did, I put more pressure on myself.' Now, she is strengthening the serve: slower swing, more snap. Taking risks. Navratilova does not hit passing shots that well, she knows.

Will she, like Borg, Austin, Jaeger, become prematurely burned out? No, her father says emphatically, because she wants to win points in six or seven strokes, not 30 or 40. And she does not have the spinal strain of a two-handed backhand. The intention is to keep the quality high and the tournaments low.

So far as it is possible to be normal in contemporary professional sport, Steffi seems pretty normal. Her parents, her younger brother Michael's humour, her two dogs: such conventional family surroundings should help.

FIGHTING CASH BECOMES THE HERO OF AUSTRALIA
The Times, December 1986

Melbourne: As Neale Fraser, Australia's captain, said in friendly jest at the post-Davis Cup banquet: 'Where on earth did *he* come from?' Mikael Pernfors, yet another remarkably-gifted player to emerge from the rich forests of Swedish tennis, contrived to plot a momentous climax to the 1986 final with Australia, yet ultimately lost to a truly redoubtable competitor. It was an historic last final at Kooyong.

Bob Hawke, Australia's Prime Minister, may not be the race-form expert of international tennis, yet it was no inappropriate comparison when he suggested that Pernfors reminded us of Rosewall: the innocuous serve, the short-back-and-sides and modest physique, combined with a service return and with passing shots which would win prizes at Bisley.

The quality of any outstanding sporting winner is dependent, almost always, on the quality of the loser. For two sets Pernfors, aged 23, the United States national collegiate champion who has jumped in one season from 164 in the rankings to 11, played tennis as special as anyone present could remember. Yet Pat Cash came back to beat him, memorably, 2-6 4-6 6-3 6-4 6-3 and thereby give Australia a winning 3-1 lead. On Saturday, Cash and John Fitzgerald, had unexpectedly won the doubles in four sets against the recent Albert Hall winners, Anders Jarryd and Stefan Edberg, with Edberg once more a shadow of his normal self.

You may not like Cash. Indeed, there are plenty of Australians in this continent of rugged extroverts who would not choose him as a desert island companion. However, in this Davis Cup final – sponsored by NEC – Cash, at 21, has shown himself to be one of the sternest and most courageous competitors of this or any era. No Australian in the history of the Cup has won a singles from two sets down. For almost an hour and a half, Cash must have thought that Butch Cassidy and Sundance were together down the other end of the court. The shots went peppering past him – cross-court, down the lines, overhead – to leave him stunned. Six times he surrendered his service. Cash's difficulties made Paul McNamee's embarrassment at his destruction on Friday less painful. 'Pernfors played the best tennis for two sets I have ever encountered,' Cash said afterwards. Mimicking Cash with his white Apache headband, Pernfors had set about his rival from the outset, breaking his opening service with two wicked lobs, and almost sprinting to change ends.

Within six games, at 2-4 down, Cash recognised the need for new tactics, staying back and frantically slow-balling to give Pernfors less pace off which to drive his stinging passes. To no avail. Pernfors again led 4-0 in the second set and should have taken it 6-2, but squandered two set points as he snatched at successive, comparatively simple, forehand and backhand, dropping his own service on a double fault.

Cash was stalling all he could, keeping Pernfors waiting at

the start of each point within legal limits. Inch by inch he edged back into the match. In the first and third games of the third set, Pernfors had break-points on Cash's service but failed to take them, then lost his own service in the fourth game. Cash was beginning to serve better, occasionally aceing; Pernfors to return less accurately. By sheer willpower, Cash kept forcing forward to the net whenever he could, grunting with the effort as he went for the low volleys under the pressure of Pernfors' top spin. He did not crack.

The tension among the 12,000 crowd was as sensitive as a primed mousetrap. A fault on first serve by either player would bring a spatter of applause just from nervousness. There was the expectation of a boxing hall, the chanting of a football stadium: yet conventionally as well-mannered as were the players. The emotion became almost unendurable in the critical seventh and eighth games of the fourth set. With Cash leading 4-2, Pernfors survived two break-points and five deuces to hold on for 4-3, and then had Cash love-40 in the next game: three points for four-all. With unflinching concentration, Cash hammered down three first serves to reach deuce, and held the game. 'I didn't think about it,' he said. 'I just concentrated on my first serve. If you think about situations like that, you'd go nuts.' There were those among the spectators who were.

The final nail, as Pernfors ran out of strength, came at 2-2 and 30-all in the final set. How marvellously over three days Cash had played the key points! Now Pernfors volleyed deep to the forehand corner of the baseline, only for Cash to respond with a running forehand pass down the tramline which clipped the baseline. Next, still under pressure at the net from Pernfors' probing, he played a cruel stop-volley to break service for 3-2. It was effectively over. As Pernfors served at 5-3 to save the match, to save the tie ... to save the Cup which Sweden had held for two years, the tree leaves rustled in a gentle breeze under the cloudless sky of a perfect day. The crowd was gripped in silence at the climax of a great match. Cash came in like an ogre: a smash, a backhand volley at the net, another smash and he was the hero a nation needed to soothe the pain of simultaneous cricket ignominy.

'The Davis Cup means more sacrifice and more pain for less pay,' Cash said. 'But it's worth it. I would never have to be paid to be there.' If that was a mood he had shared magnificently with Pernfors, it was something which, maybe through no fault of his own, had not touched Edberg, the world's No 4. In the dead fifth match, he beat McNamee in straight sets; but his mental frailty, against Cash on Friday, and again in the doubles, had cost Sweden their title.

THE GAME OF LIFE
The Times, January 1987

Fremantle: It is eight in the morning. The previous evening, Dennis Conner, the man whose defeat opened the gates of the America's Cup, had gained the fourth straight victory on Stars and Stripes in a best-of-seven series against Tom Blackaller's USA to put him in the Louis Vuitton challengers' final. Now, as the gulls screech for an easy breakfast from a handful of early picnickers on the promenade, Conner is already back at the San Diego dock: an amateur who is meticulously professional. The first race against Kiwi Magic is more than a week away.

He leans his big, ponderous frame backwards in the chair behind his desk, and inserts several eye drops. In a face ravaged by tens of thousands of hours' exposure to sun, wind and salt, the eyes are permanently bloodshot. 'They hurt continuously,' he says. He wears a welding visor for protection, his skin is cracked and crumbling in spite of daily ointments when out on the water and he worries about the possibility of skin cancer.

Here is a man who gives his body and soul to his hobby. Some would call it his obsession. He will be giving even more these next few weeks in the attempt to take the Cup back home: to California, not Manhattan. He is relentless, preoccupied, and brilliant; sensitive yet mostly undemonstrative. Somehow, his interior decorating business and his family have coped. 'You can rationalise everything,' he says

211

laconically, 'but the America's Cup is not really the right thing to do if you want to be father of the year.' With a pleasure addict's bravado, he says he has not doubted the wisdom of his sailing investment for one day of the past 27 years.

He is a private man, sometimes given to hostility: against, among others, the ebullient Blackaller, whom he regards as shallow, a mere sprinter among marathon runners. 'Fortunately, the America's Cup is not about bullshit,' he says dismissively of Friday's losing semi-finalist. He has, too, a poor opinion of the media, as Daley Thompson does, for not understanding his sport in detail; though, in contrast to Thompson, he concedes he has a responsibility to try and educate them. 'It's a shame they don't work as hard as I do,' he says meaningfully, casting his beady, bloodshot gaze upon the correspondent of this newspaper, which somehow managed, by inadvertent midnight editorial malfunction, to report his demise as skipper of America II at the end of the third round. I make our due apologies with real sincerity.

One of my enduring memories will be that final, heartbroken Press conference he gave after defeat in Newport: deserted by the officials of the haughty New York Yacht Club, left to carry the global flack on his own. He had just about managed to keep back the tears then. 'It wasn't fun,' he says. 'But that's their style. I was carrying the flag. There's no purpose in flinging mud their way. The fact now is that I'm still here racing, and they're back in New York.' Losing in 1983 was an emotional event, he admits, but it did not get in the way of his competing again. He could either feel sorry for himself, or win it back. 'I like sporting events and I had no remorse. I had just had a slower boat.' The voice carries an undercurrent of menace for those still in his way this time; those who may think he again has a slower boat.

Though he carries, with all those years of experience from Olympic medals and two America's Cup victories, an ease of *savoir-faire*, the motivation generated by defeat runs turbulently beneath the surface. 'This mission is very emotional. The whole reason of our being,' Robert Hopkins, his tactical consultant who follows each race in the Dory, says. In Newport, Hopkins worked with Victory '83. 'A third of the squad, like Tom Whidden, the tactician, Jon Wright on mainsheet, Kyle Smith on grinders, Scott Vogel in the bow and John Marshall, were all with him in Newport. Dennis lives every moment of every day, we see it all the time,' Hopkins says.

Aged 44, Conner has been up against many younger helmsmen here, the whiz-kids of the daily match-racing slog. In the 24-hour cycle, the older man's mental maturity has not the same value as on a round-the-world race. 'At the end of every race he is completely exhausted, you can see it in his face, his speech, his posture,' Hopkins says.

No syndicate, and no individual, has put as much thought or planning into this campaign as Conner and Sail America, under its president, Malin Burnham. Conner had four new boats constructed and is emphatic that such a programme, based initially in Hawaii, is being proved correct: that the development graph will reach a peak at the right time.

'I've been saying since 1979 that a two-boat programme (minimum) is essential,' Conner says. 'The last four syndicates in the competition have all had good trial horses. Our testing and trialing in Hawaii made obvious sense, both logistically and for the weather pattern there.' Based in Hawaii, he and his crew could travel overnight, could easily freight new gear, sails and keels, and could bring their families; they could be sure of constant wind and sea conditions similar to Fremantle's, yet all-year-round instead of two or three months only. 'Without being in Hawaii, we couldn't have accomplished our design programme,' he says.

Conner also believes there was a tactical advantage in being absent from the fleet racing world championship last January – won by Australia III (later abandoned by Bond) with New Zealand second and America II, third. A strong performance then by Stars and Stripes would have forewarned the others. 'The championship was a non-event,' he says off-handedly. 'If we had blown off the others, revealed them to be off the pace, they would have had time to learn and to rebuild. Instead, they've been living in bliss, like America II.' The jibes at NYYC are gentle but sharp.

It is clear that Conner believes he is coming to the boil at the right moment; that he has something yet to reveal to Chris Dickson with US 55, the fourth of his new boats; that he considers Dickson to be a shade cocky, and should not talk quite like he does. 'I've been around,' Conner says cagily. 'There are so many games being played out there.' He reckons he would have qualified for the elimination finals even if he had not bothered with the first series in October.

The intrigue of the racing fascinates him, like a poker-playing gambler. 'It's getting better, because the game is becoming more interesting all the time,' he says. 'New York losing the Cup was the best thing that's ever happened. The Cup is happy!'

Vast Australian horizons and vertical lift frighten the life out of me.

FLIGHTS OF FANTASY ARE MADE OF THIS
The Times, January 1987

Benalla, Victoria: 'Just pull that little yellow lever on the left,' the instructor behind me said matter-of-factly, 'and we're away.' 'Fine,' I replied casually, while swallowing with a dry tongue and wondering how I would find the nerve to move anything more than an eyeball. We were at Benalla, in Northern Victoria for the 20th world gliding championships. Or rather, I should say, we were *above* Benalla. Some 2,000 feet above it, or twice the height of the Empire State building. Benalla, with its rural 9,000 population, was looking about as big as Trafalgar Square.

The alternatives confronting me certainly concentrated the mind, not to say temporarily froze the limbs of this first-timer. At that moment we were being towed in our two-seater glider by an old Piper Pawnee, a former crop-spraying plane, and leaping about as though on a sledge behind Red Rum at Aintree. If I pulled that yellow lever, we would peel off into nothingness, two men wedged into a transparent thermos flask, drifting about an azure, cloudless sky. I felt close to my maker.

Tremulously pulling the lever to release the tow line and allow this aerial AA van up ahead of us to return to the airfield and tug some more competitors up into this opalesque, silent freedom, the thought briefly arose whether my building society would consider this a reasonable leisure pursuit. Reassuringly, I convinced myself that, of course, only racing was risky.

Only racing? We dived away to starboard in a steep bank, and suddenly I was looking at the parched terrain through the top of the little cockpit dome. Often when sailing I have longed to be a gull, but now I was not so sure. Yet within a minute or two, coming to terms with this profound experience, I was beginning to enjoy it.

The voice behind me was a great help. John Spura, a mechanic who emigrated to Australia from Europe, has been an instructor for five years or so. What would I like to see? he enquired, as if we were on top of a sightseeing double decker bus. As much as he could show me, I answered with totally hollow bravado. Although I had achieved some sort of temperamental equilibrium on behalf of our readers, I stopped short of accepting his offer to try the controls; still clutching my pen and notebook, I said I wanted to take notes. It must be said they were mostly taken by memory.

The privilege was to be experiencing the kind of conditions for gliding largely unknown other than in the great land masses of Southern Africa, Australia and America. Ingo Renner, a German-Australian and the current world open champion who will be defending his title when the racing starts on Sunday, thinks nothing of setting off on a day's 1,000 km course. In Britain, it is not uncommon for none of the competitors in a 250 km event circuit to make it back to the finishing line, running out of lift and being forced to land out in a field: *aux vaches*, as the French say. In Australia, it is rare for the majority of competitors not to complete a 500 or

700 km course. I was about to discover why.

The glider pilot's ability to stay airborne depends on finding upward currents of warmer air to provide lift. Thermals. In Western European climates, these may occasionally reach two or three knots, some 200-300 feet lift per minute, rising off a stubble cornfield or large flat-roofed buildings. With the dry earth's crust of much of Australia, conditions are ideal. Although the town of Benalla, where a new state gliding centre has recently been opened, has pleasant green parkland, a golf club and many thriving residential gardens, the surrounding bushland is as dry as a cheese biscuit. Visiting foreign gliders were being obliged to replace their steel tailplane skid-plates for brass ones, so as not to ignite the grass landing strip. Australia has more thermals than England has umbrellas.

Behind me, John Spura said he had spotted another glider spiralling upwards, and we ought to go and investigate. As in powered flight, once a glider is above a couple of thousand feet, there is little impression of speed. Even when the speedometer is registering 80 knots or so, you appear to be almost hovering.

Suddenly, as we approached the other glider, there was the sensation of being on the upward section of a big dipper: a huge thrust under one's seat. The variometer, which measures the rate of climb or fall, was reading between plus eight to 10 knots. In little more than 30 seconds, we climbed from 2,500 feet to 3,300 feet, two or three times the rate of climb of a small powered aircraft. At the controls, John made the exclamations of someone who has just unwrapped a Christmas gift of rare vintage claret, and kept us in a rising left-handed corkscrew. I pressed my knees against the side of the cockpit, glanced uneasily at the violently rotating countryside beneath and hoped that our Romanian model IS28-B2, with 7,000 hours on the clock, was well maintained.

As thermals reach upper, cooler air, they expand and slow until they reach a ceiling. Approaching 4,000 feet my instructor levelled off, and then demonstrated 'dolphin' flying, by which you gain forward speed in a straight line and repeatedly lift the nose, dropping back towards the stalling speed of 38 knots, so as to maintain altitude as much as possible. Such a manoeuvre is fine, maybe, if you are at the controls, but for a passenger can induce the consternation of a cross-Channel trip to Boulogne in a Force Eight gale.

The skies and the horizons in Australia are prodigious. The air is so unpolluted you can see 50 or 60 miles even at lower altitudes. Around us, in the distance, were Mt Buller, the skiing resort, and the 4,000-foot Buffalo Plateau. Gently, we cruised down to 1,000 feet, entered the obligatory approach circuit of the airfield, coasted in over the rooftops, and after some 40 minutes bumped back onto earth. John said I'd done well for a first trip, and I said I was more concerned that he had done well. The next day during practice an Australian and an Irishman collided in a thermal, though they landed unharmed. They do say it's a safe sport.

> The fingers of the Olympic Movement stretch to the farthest corners of the globe: even to the enchanting South Pacific.

FOAMING TORPEDOES
The Times, March 1987

Pago Pago, American Samoa: The United States territory of American Samoa, first ceded to America in 1902, yesterday received their Olympic flag in formal recognition of their National Olympic Committee (NOC), and their Government burst into song. It was one of the most beautiful moments in a lifetime of reporting sport. The Samoans have voices as ringingly melodious as the Welsh ... they sing with their souls, in close harmony and without instruments, and would, I suspect, win the gold medal at any Olympic Eisteddfod.

Their recognition by the International Olympic Committee

(IOC), with the approval of the United States Olympic Committee, provided them, as it does all such tiny nations, with a day of rare pride. Juan Antonio Samaranch, the IOC president, was accompanied by Ati Lutali, the Governor Chief, and John Samia, the NOC president, to the legislative centre where the Senate and elected representatives awaited them in collar and tie and lava-lava, the national costume skirt. The vocal welcome was not a total surprise, for the delegation had just arrived from Western Samoa, where for two days they had been festooned with flower garlands of intoxicating scent, and with Polynesian melodies. The farewell in Apia saw Cardinal Pio, a man of serene Christianity, take part in a formal Polynesian breakfast dance after conducting Mass.

It is no revelation to say that the South Pacific captures your heart. A member of Sweden's Admiral's Cup team at Cowes in 1985 kept heading south, via the Canaries and Galapagos, and is still enjoying a tranquil life here on board his boat. 'It is better than North Atlantic weather and Swedish taxes,' he says.

Pago Pago is one of the world's most scenic natural harbours. Mariners who glide through the narrow deep-water entrance and turn to port are confronted by a haven two miles long and half a mile wide lying beneath tree-covered cliffs a thousand feet high. The United States first approached the independent kingdom to use this port as a naval base. Sadly, the harbour is now disfigured by massive tuna-canning factories which provide 98 per cent of American Samoa's exports.

Mr Samaranch was treated to one of the most spectacular competitions in sport, regrettably not an Olympic event. The Samoans are currently training for the long-boat championships on flag day, 17 April. The boats, once warring craft and massively but finely built in wood, nowadays cost £7,000. They are 92-feet long and are driven by 48 oarsmen, who are kept in rhythm by a drummer in the bow.

The championship course is over three miles beyond the reef at sea, a challenge requiring exceptional strength and fitness. Boats represent a village or district. Yesterday, Pago

Pago Eagle was challenged by Nuuli Satan, which arrived dramatically through the rolling swell for the start at 7.30 a.m. The delegation was perched in vacant spaces at bow and stern in the two craft, though Philip Coles, an Australian IOC member and three times an Olympic canoeist, took one of Satan's oars: and paid with blisters.

It was an exhilarating experience as two lines of huge knotted muscle drove the boats through the water like foaming torpedoes at more than 12 knots. What an Olympic sight this would be. Over a one-and-a-half-mile course inside the harbour, rival blades clashing frenziedly several times, Eagle won by half a length. So impressed was the IOC president that he asked Mr Coles to arrange for two fours' shells to be sent to the new NOC to give them a taste of conventional rowing. Tolani Teleso, Eagle's coach and the professional at the local golf course, is delighted at the prospect. A former international rifle marksman in the United States Army who coached members of the 1968 Olympic team, Teleso is one of three professionals coaching Samoan long-boats. Few sportsmen are fitter than the Samoan oarsmen, who have normal jobs and train at daybreak and again in the evening.

The island's new Olympic status is especially gratifying oneupmanship on Hawaii, their long-standing rivals. Now the Samoans can send their own team to Seoul next year, however modest, from their 30,000 population, while Hawaii, with a million inhabitants, remain just another US State. Samoan boxers will not disgrace themselves: they won two gold medals and three silver at the Oceania championships last year.

The cloud on the horizon, however, lies in the disorganisation among some officials of the new committee. John Samia, who has worked for 30 years to keep sport afloat in American Samoa, is now elderly, and too many of his successors have no idea of the difference between Government departments and sport. They must learn fast.

Mike Tyson finds it difficult to get an opponent who can give him a decent fight.

A HUGE YAWN
The Times, March 1987

Las Vegas: The one undisputed fact after Mike Tyson's one-sided world heavyweight championship victory over James Smith is that it was a huge yawn. I have seen more punches landed in 40 minutes of a disorderly rugby match. The fight has diminished the winner, in part through no fault of his, and it will take not one but several victories for him to recover his reputation. Talk here yesterday of Frank Bruno being a possible contender against Tyson on 30 May can do Tyson little good and Bruno even less and is confirmation of the poverty of opposition for a formidable young man who has, however, much still to learn.

The contest which was supposed to bring the re-enrichment of boxing, and particularly of the heavyweight division, was an anti-climax of monumental boredom, not to say public deception. The so-called 'Bonecrusher' would hardly have cracked an acorn as he backed away for much of the 12 rounds, of which he won only, possibly, the fifth: and none according to the judges.

Tyson's points victory may have added Smith's World Boxing Association (WBA) title to his own World Boxing Council (WBC) crown – which he won so dramatically against Trevor Berbick – yet, instead of further prestige, the only additional ingredient to his reputation is one of doubt. Against an opponent five inches taller and who shamefully did not want to fight, the alleged 'Iron Man' could not produce the blows to terminate either the bout, the boredom or the justifiable booing of a 14,000 crowd.

Smith, who comes from Magnolia, North Carolina, and has

a degree in business administration, assuredly pulled off the biggest deal of his life, following his flattering acquisition of the WBA title from Tim Witherspoon. Several times during Saturday night's walkabout, Smith could be seen talking to Tyson. We must assume that one of the things he was saying was

> *Nothing could be finer*
> *Than to be in Carolina*
> *With a mill ... ion.*

Such purses for a loser should carry a forfeit clause for defective contribution, although, frankly, I never supposed Smith carried the armoury to trouble Tyson. What had not been evident, as it now certainly is, was that Tyson the fighter might not be a boxer with the wit to deal with large, stalling opponents with a longer reach. He is only 20: time will tell.

However, we can no more for the moment place him in the same category as Louis or Ali than equate Norman with Nicklaus. Tyson's currency, and heavyweight boxing, has taken a fall. And he knows it. 'I feel very bad about the booing. I want people to see me at my best,' Tyson said afterwards, looking as if he had just risen after a night's peaceful sleep. 'The heavyweight title should have prestige, but how can you bring boxing alive if you just hang on? I think you should expose yourself. Smith wasn't there to win, but to survive.'

There were some who, not unreasonably, considered the champion was making excuses for an inadequate performance when he said: 'I've now got to suffer the criticism, I've got to deal with it [the public's frustration].' Personally, I thought he was speaking with sincerity, for he had vainly pursued Smith throughout the ungainly fight.

Smith's Press conference afterwards was as lame as his performance. 'I did the best I could,' he said. If that is so, then Don King – a promoter of himself as much as of boxers, and one who manages interminably to talk exaggerations without drawing breath – should be prosecuted under the American equivalent of the Trades Descriptions Act (the 'the truth in advertising' laws). Smith, stated by the official programme to be 'one of the most explosive and devastating fighters of modern times', landed one punch in the first round and one in the last, and in between missed with a couple of uppercuts ... Peashooter Smith. When he caught Tyson with a right in the 12th, by then it was too late for him to be exposed by testing Tyson in an open fight. Smith was, at least, gracious enough to admit that Tyson had 'nailed me early on, he's very quick.'

Tyson's plan was to get inside Smith's superior reach of 11 inches and to weaken him with short left hooks and body blows. This immediately worked, and in the second round he opened a cut on Smith's left eyebrow. Yet after one punch from Tyson, Smith would immediately clinch, and was twice warned for holding; though Tyson was equally guilty of holding with one arm while attempting to hook with the other.

The booing had begun by the third round. Partially, this was directed at Tyson for blatantly hitting after the bell in the first two rounds (and he did again in the ninth). In a close decision, the compulsory point lost each time could have cost him the fight. By the fourth, Smith was feebly backing off, and by the sixth, he was circling so far from Tyson that the crowd was demanding: 'Fight!' The inaction continued, and in the 10th somebody near me yelled: 'Let 'em go another 12.' When it was all over, a disgruntled fan observed that they had danced together so long it was time they kissed each other.

Tyson had fallen in the seventh when he swayed out of the way of a swing from Smith, tried to counter-punch, and lost his balance.

The notion that Bruno could be in line to take on Tyson, now that his forthcoming fight with Page has been cancelled because of Page's cut eye in training, is unimaginable; although Seth Abraham of HBO network television suggested this was possible. Nobody should do that to Bruno, remembering that he was defeated by Smith, who, in the words of that American sage of the ring, Barney Nagle, 'gave the worst heavyweight defence I can remember in a fight that went the distance', and Nagle's memory goes back to Louis.

People have to learn to handle natural forces, Ted
Tinling says. Boris Becker, like others before and since,
found emotional life a strain.

FINDING FAULTS IN A LOVE GAME
The Times, June 1987

Sharing with someone of the opposite sex the same front
door, and all that goes on behind it, is not that simple, as
parents are forever telling their children. The arguments will
now be raised, throughout West Germany, throughout
tennis, and not to mention within the entourage of Boris
Becker, whether it was right to banish Benedicte Courtin, his
girlfriend, back to Monaco for the duration of the
Wimbledon championships.

Defeat will not make Becker that much poorer at the bank,
but he will undoubtedly be poorer in spirit. For a long time.
Maybe for all time. His identification with Wimbledon has
been the essence of his personality, the ultimate expression of
his magnificent athletic gifts. To have won twice as the
youngest ever, and now to lose in the second round will be an
unimaginable wound to his self-esteem. Becker lost, to an
opponent of no consequence, for a variety of reasons, and all
of them were apparent beforehand. They were apparent to
those closest to him, who had talked of the problems, and
they were apparent to knowledgeable observers. It has been
evident for more than six months that Becker had receded
from his peak.

The reasons are both mental and physical. Thirty years ago
young players such as Hoad won Wimbledon, but Hoad was
never burdened with the colossal strain of tournaments, and
of money-making, in the full glare of publicity around the
globe for almost 12 months a year. The mental burden,
however, and the strain of being the most famous player in

the game when still a teenager, is even greater. Just as a teenage girl is well able physically to bear children but may be unprepared emotionally to cope with motherhood, so it has been an almost intolerable imposition for Becker, from the age of 17, to carry the Wimbledon crown. He has worn that crown with dignity and even maturity, but that is not to say that fame was comfortable. He retained that dignity yesterday, being generous to his opponent in defeat. Yet fame, in taking away privacy, removes also from one so young some of the ability to handle life's other facets. Becker has suffered.

Romance was bound to enter his life. He's handsome and personable. But he could never have the quiet, unobserved romance of others of his age. It is no criticism of Miss Courtin to say that she has, for Becker, been a problem. She was older, and had had previous romances. For Becker, it was something new, with all the glorious excitement and uncertainties that surround these moments. Inevitably, Miss Courtin came between Becker and his coach. She came between Becker and his manager. And there must be the possibility that she came between Becker and his game. It would be unnatural if she did not. Ask any boxing or football manager.

Was he, in the event, better off with or without her? 'A player needs those closest to them emotionally during the tournament, to be supportive,' Billie Jean King said this week. 'But it is essential that they are totally supportive. Otherwise, forget it.' Miss Courtin liked the glamour of the circuit, but tended not to sit as an unobtrusive observer. You can see Becker's eye follow her during his matches. Obviously, the advice of Ion Tiriac, Becker's manager, prevailed. Benedicte went home. And Boris lost.

Ted Tinling, that doyen of tennis and the most perceptive of observers who has known personally almost every famous player, man and woman, for 50 years and has advised many on their emotional traumas, said last night: 'If it had been down to me, I would have let Benedicte stay. It does not do to interfere with natural forces. People have to learn to handle them.' It is something which Becker and his manager will ponder for a long time. He should have our sympathy.

Once more, the ultimate prize eludes Ivan Lendl and so does the crowd's sympathy in the 1987 Wimbledon men's final.

SIREN OF DOOM WAILS AT LENDL
The Times, July 1987

At about 4.15 p.m. there was the sound of an ambulance siren outside the Centre Court main entrance. It might well have arrived to bear away the luckless Ivan Lendl, who on the fiery, biscuit-brown court had been torn limb from limb by the concentrated tenacity of Pat Cash.

When it was all over, and Lendl was already hurrying to catch the next Concorde home to hide his pain for a few days in New England, the figure of Ian Barclay emerged into the Wimbledon footlights. The silver-haired Barclay is Cash's coach. He has been around a while, and some promising youngsters have prospered in his care. 'If I have a thousand pupils,' he said with a pleasant lack of ostentation, 'I find one winner. Pat is a winner. He's the best competitor I've ever seen. He just doesn't know how to step back from a crisis.'

From the age of 11, Cash has been guided by this quietly-spoken man, but together they have been through the innumerable frustrations of Cash's injuries. Repeatedly during the teenage years, Barclay was told that Cash would never make a player. He has proved the critics wrong. 'His temperament was never an obstacle to me,' Barclay says. He believes that the kind of competitive streak in his player was what was needed to produce Australia's first Wimbledon men's champion since 1971. Barclay recalls that at the age of only 15, shielding a doubles partner in the final of a junior tournament, Cash had 'played like a demon'. Only the prolonged absences, he thinks, have delayed until the age of 22 Cash's rise to yesterday's pinnacle.

The fascination was the pressure which Cash imposed on his opponent. Barclay argues that in the modern game, if a player has one weakness, the better opponents will cut him to pieces. Is Lendl's weakness, after two consecutive Wimbledon final defeats, in his head?

There was no doubting the tension in the Czech-American: all those tedious preparatory twitches before every first service, rotating balls in his hand repeatedly before putting one of them in his pocket, straightening the strings of his racket, applying sawdust to the handle, mopping his forehead with his wrist sweatband and then again on his shoulder, tapping imaginary dust from his shoe soles, rotating his head as though he had a crick in his neck and finally bouncing the ball half a dozen times. The sympathetic may feel for Lendl in his tribulations, but there was no doubting with whom the public's heart lay. The majority were rooting for the ebullient Cash.

The world's No 1 simply could not cope with the determination of the man staring him down from the other end of the court, hammering services at him, forcing him to lunge and grope at volleys. 'He played very well,' Lendl said. 'He mixed it; I hardly knew where the ball would go. He played better in every department. He has less power than Becker, but he's more strategic.' It was just after the ambulance had been heard that Lendl for the first time found a sequence of four games, during which he broke Cash's service and led 4-1 in the third set. It did not last. At 3-5, Cash hit two stunning backhand returns and Lendl's briefly flickering light was extinguished.

It is true that the difference at the top in most sports is mental, and Cash has been having the benefit of consultations with Jeff Bond, the sports psychiatrist from the Australian Sports Academy at Canberra. Cash paid tribute to the benefits he had gained: notably over the 48 hours before the final, during which he admitted his feelings in anticipation of the match could hardly have been lower. Yesterday morning his legs had felt like jelly. That never was apparent once the match started.

Azinger's bunker on the last hole of the British Open hands the title to Faldo.

AGONY OF SILENCE FOR THE VICTORS AND LOSERS

The Times, July 1987

Sport is characterised by a throaty roar of acclaim: at Twickenham, Aintree or Wembley, at an Olympic final or at Madison Square Garden. There is nothing to compare, however, with the massive, breath-held silence of 20,000 people at Muirfield awaiting yesterday's agonising outcome at the final hole between Nick Faldo and Paul Azinger.

Sad, courageous Azinger. An almost funereal pall hung over the crowd as the luckless American arrived at the final green, bunkered to the left, to attempt to rescue a dream that had so wretchedly disintegrated over the two last disastrous holes. In a few moments his young, lean face perceptibly aged. Seldom have triumph and disaster been so unbearably held in the same palm.

Yet none should doubt that Faldo played a champion's round one stride ahead of his rival. With home expectation enormous, with his own ambition pumping, his nerve and his head still held steady. His sustained round of unbroken par contained moments of heroic calm without which the afternoon might have run away from him. It must be hoped that the champion's crown he deservedly now wears will enable him to be more relaxed off the course.

It is a reflection of the strained relationship between Faldo and the media that, with some 170 armbands available to walk the course with the players, fewer than a dozen yesterday followed the leading Briton, and this had extraordinarily diminished to four or five by the last six holes. It would be difficult to say whether that was an indication of disaffection or of the proclivity of the Press for working, at stroke-play events, from the tent.

Faldo must be praised for overcoming a few difficult years, on and off the course, for working diligently without immediate encouragement at modifying his swing with Dave Leadbetter, his coach, and for showing a champion's resolution when his chance came for the sweetest of prizes. To be popular is not essential to success; let us hope this triumph gives breadth to his personality.

What was shown transparently yesterday was character under the stress of competition. Faldo came to the first tee with a previous best performance of fourth in 1982, fifth last year and seventh twice. Consistency would now be the key. He was partnered by Craig Stadler, that portly American who must give his tailor a trying time. For him it was not to be a happy day. Starting at four under par, his challenge soon evaporated. He has an endearing way of looking at departing, miscued shots as at some lady with whom he has had an argument: half bitter, half nostalgic.

It was another day more suitable for fishing than golf. A grey sea mist rolled over the course, penetrating one's clothing, but thankfully the wind was nowhere near as fierce as it was on Saturday. Faldo's attack was quickly apparent. Commendably straight off the tee, he was within inches of having birdies at the first five holes. As the surge of the sea drummed in his ears at the fifth, he heard that Azinger was now seven under, then eight under at the seventh.

If, unknowingly, the chance to have taken the title with more comfort had slipped away over those early holes, the core of eventual success came from the seventh to 11th. With a cross-wind at the seventh, Faldo put a five-iron into one of those fearsome bunkers to the left of the green, but escaped to within five feet of the pin. Bunkered again at the eighth to the right, he saved par again by dropping the ball dead for a single putt. At the ninth he again missed a possible birdie,

breaking off in hesitation when preparing a three and a half
foot first putt: and missing. Bunkered at the 10th, he came
out to within two feet.

Now, at the 11th, came perhaps the shot that won the
trophy. His second left him close to the green but obstructed
by a huge bunker with the hole hidden behind it on a slope
running back towards him. He rolled his chip round the
hillock to the left but the ball did not swing back far enough,
and left him with four feet downhill requiring a surgeon's
care. The ball dropped. Now he knew that Azinger had shed
two strokes of his lead and from the 13th to 17th Faldo gave
nothing away as the mist turned to the finest rain. At the 17th
you could barely see the grandstand from the tee. From 30
feet he putted to within 15 inches. With every shot the
pressure was growing on Azinger behind him. And so to the
18th, where Faldo fluffed his birdie: and Azinger met his
nemesis.

The African Games in Kenya herald the emergence of
black sporting ceremony.

DIGNIFIED STYLE
The Times, August 1987

Nairobi: You hear it said, around the world, that Africa, with
all its problems, is a lost cause. Certainly that accusation is
made against African sport, beyond the wealthier Arabic
northern states. On Saturday, Kenya and their blood brothers
booted the cynicism out of bounds. The opening ceremony of
the fourth All Africa Games was a heartening, rewarding
festival of optimism, pride and emotion. It demonstrated
that, given time and encouragement, black Africa is able to
stage major public events with some style.

The Kenyan organising committee may have lived uncomfortably close to chaos up to the last moment, the programme may have run almost an hour over time. Yet the continent, and the race, which so often considers it is scorned by the global community, exhibited the most dignified of faces. The teams of 39 out of 45 states – almost double the attendance at the previous first three Games – colourfully marched into the stadium with a mood of formal friendliness that characterises the Commonwealth Games: which so many of these teams' governments had seen fit to boycott last year.

Daniel Moi, the President of Kenya, made inevitably political references in his speech to open the Games. His truest comment was that of all Africa's resources the most important is its people. It was people who made the opening ceremony an occasion of serenity and simplicity. Africa, like every continent, has its deceits, greed, exploitation and inhumanity, but the ordinary people of Kenya gave this ceremony an unaffected charm.

It is perversely tempting to suggest that, while in some places they slaughter each other, African tribes, free of material corruption, are among the last civilised peoples on earth. Here was none of the martial precision of Moscow in 1980, or the showbiz extravaganza of Los Angeles. We had 3,000 school children from Nairobi and Mombasa, some no more than 10 years old, circling the stadium hand-in-hand in rhythmic exercise. No one was to know their uniforms were completed only that morning by factories working round the clock. They formed maps of Africa, and of Kenya, in the red, black, green and white of the national flag. We can be sure that among them was another Keino, Boit, Jipcho, Temu or Rono.

Starehe High School brass band, with that typical biscuit-tin harmony of the Boys Brigade, beat out a strict tempo for a squad of gymnasts. 'A very well disciplined school,' said my beaming companion. It was the discipline bit that made him proud. Then came the regional tribal dancers, imposing in their various costumes. And, having travelled many miles, they would not go away, despite all the pleas and arm-waving of the on-field stage managers. A tribal dance is not something to be meddled with for television schedules. President Moi's speech would have to wait. Finally came a choir of 600, whose melodies belonged to the tranquil beauty of an African dusk.

Kenya endured three postponements of the Games, awaiting the completion of China's gift: a $20 million stadium and their first synthetic track. This somehow was not mentioned on Saturday, but who admits borrowing the money to get married if it's a marvellous reception.

Regrettably, the audience this week will be almost exclusively African. I hope I live to see the day when black Africa is able to stage an Olympic Games. To achieve that, however, they will need progress, discipline and diplomacy: none of which come easily to them.

On the bi-centenary of MCC, does the game have more gentlemen than cheats?

WAXING LYRICAL ON A GAME OF HUMAN POETRY
The Times, August 1987

Eloquence is heard, poetry is overheard, John Stuart Mill, the philosopher, said. Eloquence supposes an audience, but poetry is unconscious of the listener. MCC's bi-centenary match celebrates a game which, more than any, abounds with poetry.

Cricket, of course, is not indifferent to an audience. How often has not Botham played to the gallery, though here is a man whose performance, in spite of himself, has poetry within its eloquence. The spontaneous players down the years have been born with an innate spirit of adventure, who conceded nothing to public expectation or demand, giving away their wicket with no thought of tomorrow. Macartney, who would score a Test century before lunch; Woolley, who in consecutive innings at Lord's in 1921, against Gregory and McDonald, hit 95 and 93; Constantine, who at Sydney in 1930 took six for 45, including Bradman, Fairfax, McCabe and Kippax; Botham, who beat the Australians so memorably in 1981; they, together with such as Sobers and Miller and Viv Richards, made cricket a game of beauty.

In no other sport is it so true that style is the man. Compton, reproved as an apprentice for his technique by a diligent Middlesex coach, rejoined with impatience after another flurry of runs: 'Never mind the left leg, where was the ball.' Constantine, one of the greatest of all-rounders, having rejected at 23 a career in law, said upon retirement: 'Had I plodded back to the lawyers' parchment den, I should perhaps have been wise and successful in interference, and never have known the ecstasy of fulfilment.'

Neville Cardus, who numbered Lord Birkenhead and Sir Thomas Beecham among personal friends, and as a critic acquired a profound knowledge of music, said: 'I have met far more interesting characters amongst the cricketers than amongst the musicians of England ... No living English musician, critic or performer is half the work of art to look at and to experience as C.B. Fry. I would rather go into a pub with half a dozen north country cricket professionals than into all the studios or Athenaeum and Savile clubs in London. I have tried both, so I know.'

Cricket played spontaneously, not for national prestige or personal gain, is one of the purest activities invented by a man's mind, a synthesis of body and soul as moving as Louis Armstrong. Where lies the next 200 years of MCC, post-Packer, post-television, post-Pakistani condemnation of umpires?

If cricket has become by definition a game for cheats, it were better that it be buried now with dignity than descend into a formalised approval of the Artful Dodger. MCC, caught in the cross-fire of racial tensions, perhaps alone is capable of designing and preserving the future. But where are their leaders, and where the goodwill upon which they will depend?

Someone inquired of a colleague of W.G. Grace if it were true that the great man was a cheat. No, was the reply, he's far too clever for that. The story goes that at Worcester against an opening pair, who had become entrenched on a hot and cloudless day, W.G. exclaimed to one of them: 'Just look at that flight of duck!' The batsman stared unavailingly into the sky. 'Must have gone behind those trees,' W.G. murmured, and then, to his flagging bowler: 'A quick couple of half-volleys while his eye still has the glare of the sun.'

Thankfully, the distinction between gentlemen and players was removed, yet as an 11-year-old, with the privilege of having once been bowled at in a net at the Saffrons by Miller and Hassett, I never conceived of a difference. All cricketers were gentlemen. The day may come when none of them are. That must not be allowed to happen.

I was there. The taking of Ryder Cup 27, the first time in America.

A MOMENTOUS OCCASION
The Times, September 1987

Columbus, Ohio: America has just staged one of the most enthralling sporting events of all time: and has hardly noticed. Worse even than New York's *Post* and *Times*, which carried only nominal reports, one of yesterday's breakfast television sports newscasts did not even mention the cliff-hanging, unique, 15-13 Ryder Cup defeat. It was thought more important to show pictures of empty National Football League stadiums, where the players earning an average $230,000 a year (about £140,000) are on strike. The irony of such an attitude could not have been more pointed. Not only was the 27th Ryder Cup a stupendous competition fought at a summit of technique by 24 of the world's top players, but it was between millionaire money-earners playing for nothing but each other and their national pride.

It is my privilege as well as my job to be at many international events, yet I have witnessed no Wimbledon, no Olympic Games, no World Cup of football where for three days I lived, minute by minute from breakfast till teatime, in such suspense along with a crowd of 20,000. And all the time in a setting of enchanting natural beauty.

More than that, there is another aspect which many Americans do not fully appreciate, not only because of their baseball-football-basketball obsession: though in this they are in company with many others. It is that professional golf is almost the only major sport in which the players unwaveringly stick to the rules.

A unique part of the tournament has been not only America's first home defeat but, as always, the sight of famous players sitting, sometimes anonymously among the crowd, to watch and then encourage their colleagues, following the conclusion of their own matches. In every way the Ryder Cup is the essence of sport, in the way we sometimes see it in Olympic relay races: which matter most to those running them. The insular glory of an individual achievement, however great the satisfaction, does not have the enduring warmth of a team triumph. That is why, emotionally, Tony Jacklin values the last few days even more than his own victories, famous and rich though they made him.

It has been a revelation, in the European team, to see Lyle and Langer, Brand and Rivero playing together like brothers. To see Olazábal, the boy of 21 from San Sebastian, demonstrating the maturity of a 30-year-old, the way Ballesteros always promised he would. To watch Darcy, splendid, shy, self-effacing, from Delgany village outside Dublin, holing that downhill putt for the moment that made, for golf and Darcy, history.

'T'lad should retoire temorrah,' a tipsy compatriot, one of hundreds who made the trip, happily suggested as a noisy evening swayed towards dawn at the Muirfield Village club.

Darcy continued blinking and nodding and smiling. And Olazábal, himself drunk with fatigue more than champagne, would again mimic his Irish colleague's rolling head; and do another little Spanish rumba of personal celebration.

They have been, the Europeans, a fine bunch of characters. Doughty little Woosnam, promising he would bite the Americans' ankles, proceeding with Faldo to do it, and then promising to get drunk for a week. Disciplined, restrained and correct Langer, half smiling at the closing ceremony, having come back for his half with Nelson. Ebullient Torrance, rising once more when it mattered on the final day. And Ballesteros: the matinée idol he is, and playing like Apollo.

It always requires, it seems, a Pearl Harbor to wake up the Americans. The America's Cup defeat – almost equally memorable at Newport – galvanised them into action, and Muirfield Village 1987 will probably do the same. They went home muttering threats. 'The Ryder, it seems, is suddenly a major,' Dick Fenlon, columnist in the *Columbus Dispatch*, condescendingly wrote yesterday. Those 12 Americans who lost knew that beforehand, and that is why they were smiling through clenched teeth as the trophy was handed over on that unforgettable, sunny September afternoon. As Lord Derby, president of the PGA, said, it will be a wonderful recollection to be able to say: 'I was there.'

During a visit to Canton, I discover the Chinese, and others, are astonished by news of intended FA commercialism. Thankfully, the proposal was dropped ... for the moment.

FINAL INDIGNITY OF THE DRINKING MAN'S TEAM

The Times, November 1987

Canton: I have just had dinner here with international sports administrators from nine different countries in three continents. One of the main topics of conversation has been the extraordinary news that the English Football Association, fathers of football, once the trustees of sportsmanship, have allegedly sold their soul to a beer company. The unanimous view in Chinese, French, Israeli, Flemish, Spanish and German, not to mention English, is that the FA has departed from all sanity: that no money can buy what it has just given away. The FA has pawned its historic competition, plus its national team, and will never henceforth be able to afford to redeem the ticket.

We are given to understand, from 10,000 miles away, that the new leaseholders are a brewery. Well, I suppose that is no less than appropriate for what could be said to have become the drinking man's team. The FA has capitulated, quite recently I believe, to the very forces which, over the past 20 years, have already destroyed their international image on the terraces. England now drinks rather better than it plays football. The FA could be said to be in league with the devil.

The FA Cup has been respected, and envied, for its name and its style throughout its history of illustrious clubs such as Aston Villa, Preston North End, Wolverhampton Wanderers, Arsenal, Manchester United, Everton, Tottenham Hotspur and Liverpool: around the globe. It is one of the last bastions of true sport, 116 years old, and has been disposed of like an old bedstead to a scrap merchant ringing his bell.

Li Menghua, the Chinese Minister of Sport, who first became deputy minister in 1958, asked me what was the secret of England's traditional success. He is presiding here over the sixth Chinese National Games, at which 6,000 competitors are striving at 44 different sports. He asked: 'What's the secret of English football's historic appeal? I would love to know, because football is the biggest sporting motive the people of China know.' It would have been a proud claim to have said that England's tradition was built, above all, on the spirit of the players. Yet what will become of that spirit when the game has become, say, Foster's Footy? To what further indignities may the FA yet sink now that it has tossed away its crown jewel?

The Australians among us tonight bemoaned the coarseness inflicted upon the Melbourne Cup, the equivalent down under of the Derby, by an insensitive and greedy brewery that has disfigured with advertising a fine horse race. Before we know where we are, the grass of the centre circle at Wembley will be impregnated with the motif of some lager which has rendered the spectators incapable any longer of appreciating a great sport: reduced by liquor to booing the opposition's national anthem, cheering an opponent's injury and abusing an impartial referee. That is the FA's wretched coincidental bonus. Will the England team bonus for winning now be free pints for life? Will the little giant-killers down the years such as Altrincham, Blyth and York still be inspired by an alcohol trophy?

The only remaining unblemished major British competitions are now the Open golf and the Wimbledon championships. The FA's argument, no doubt, is that, unlike the R and A or the All England Club, it has to maintain a permanent international senior team and the expensive junior side which produces the next generation of World Cup players. Yet money alone does not generate such teams: as we know from tennis, where Wimbledon's huge profits handed to the Lawn Tennis Association have not unearthed a champion in the 50 years since Fred Perry. With the price that the FA now charge at Wembley, and with its income from the World Cup, it surely cannot claim to be in the same plight as humble Wales. I do not believe that a reported figure of £12 million over three years is either unavoidably necessary or can cure the various ills that confront English football. If the FA is so hard up, it has been spending too much and planning too little.

Its priorities are not money in the bank, but having the guts to stand up to disciplinarian issues which Bert Millichip, the chairman, is seemingly willing to duck. Millichip has previously said the FA Cup would never be sold. So much for his promise.

Ted Croker, whose time as general secretary has seen the unscrupulous marketing of England shirts and socks to the parents of schoolboy footballers, claims that the FA is prepared to market a job lot to sponsors of the Cup, the team and the school at Lilleshall. It is a job lot of officials that should be disposed of. The Olympic Games may have surrendered to the irresistible march of professionalism, but it has yet to admit advertising to its arena. The World Cup in football is not yet, in name at least, the Coke Cup.

I sit here beside the Pearl River, in one of Asia's most luxurious hotels, built in a joint venture between the Red Chinese and opportunist but shrewd developers from Hong Kong, and witness a remarkable transformation in the ideological face of Communism. Yet the Chinese, with the wisdom of millenia, still understand the inner values of human endeavour and objectives. And the English, at this moment, frankly puzzle them.

'If I didn't do this I'd get fat and lazy,' says the man with a difference who missed a bronze medal by split seconds.

WILL TO SUCCEED STRIKES A RESONANT CHORD

The Times, February 1988

Calgary: Peter Young is a likely lad from Dagenham. A piano-tuner by trade. Does a bit of most sports. Running, rowing, spot of canoeing now and then, that kind of thing.

Enjoys his pint. The other day he was out here skiing. He says it is the best sport he's ever done. Cross-country. You know, where you seem to go more uphill than downhill, slog yourself silly till you're nearly sick. Fun for those who are fit, though. The best bit was, he met the guv'nor, as he calls him. Juan Antonio, that fellow who runs the Olympics. Smashing bloke. Stayed to watch the whole race.

Mind you, a pity about that fourth place. Just another seven-tenths of a second faster over five kilometres and he'd have had the bronze. Medals? Well, he doesn't want to sound flash, but he's got a load back home, from bits and pieces. An Olympic exhibition medal would have been nice. Still, mustn't grumble. It is a good life. Specially when you are blind.

Peter lost his sight when he was two years old. At blind school, he wasn't particularly musical, but decided on piano-tuning because it gave him freedom. He could be his own boss. He laughs. 'It is just a question of hearing,' he says. 'You don't really have to know G from C.' He travels by public transport. Finding his way to clients' addresses isn't difficult from the Tube or bus station, if he has proper directions. House numbers can be tricky. If they're raised figures, he is okay. 'But if they are painted, I am in trouble.' He is 32 now, got married a couple of years ago. Kathy works at the Midland Bank. He met her at the ice skating rink.

A while back, one day when he was running, the Blind Sports Federation said there was some skiing at Beitostolen in Norway. That's a bit keen, he thought; downhill and all that. Anyroad, why not give it a go. It turned out to be cross-country and that was where he met Jan Knutsen. Jan's in ICI Chemicals, a sales rep. And was a volunteer guide: skiing a few yards in front, shouting back instructions and warnings, leading touch-shoulder round obstacles. They have been together as a pair since 1983. Jan drops in at Dagenham when he is in London two or three times a year.

Peter's been to four Physically Handicapped Olympics. He was eighth in 1980, got the bronze with Jan in 1984, and was fifth last month in Austria. They finance themselves, though they occasionally manage some fund-raising: a bit of sponsored marathon running, say. Peter did three hours 40 minutes in 1983, the same year he took part in the Devizes to Westminster canoe race. 'If I didn't do this kind of thing,' he says, 'I'd get fat and lazy. But apart from a sense of fulfilment, it increases your spatial awareness, your mobility and reaction. You're sharper. It makes you feel that much damn better. Two hours of this, a shower, and you've earned a pint.'

The winner this week was Hans Aalien, of Norway, a computer scientist in the final stages of a master's degree at Oslo University. He's 29, and has been blind since birth. He has been skiing for 14 years. Arne Homb is his guide. They ski once or twice a week, and have run together a lot. But Hans is going to have to get a new guide for running. He is now too fast for Arne. Receiving the gold medal from Samaranch, hearing the Norwegian anthem: that was good.

'I beat Hans skiing once,' Peter reflects, as he gets changed for the evening party.

A Canadian helps an American beat a Canadian with a sublime combination of grace and technique.

BOITANO IS IN A WORLD AND CLASS OF HIS OWN
The Times, February 1988

Calgary: The judges seemed not to have noticed. Confronted by Brian Boitano's majestic free programme in the men's figure skating, they gave him the gold medal almost by accident: by the tiniest of margins. A 20,000 Saddledome audience, at a fever pitch of expectation for Canada's first gold medal from Brian Orser, was left in limp disbelief. The Canadian majority among them had also failed fully to appreciate the sophistication of America's first winner at these Olympics.

240

Orser, who last year had taken Boitano's world title and was silver medal winner behind Scott Hamilton in 1984, was crestfallen. Yet while he had come out to skate, a shade histrionically, for the gallery and for a gold medal, Boitano, with unprecedented poise, had skated for himself and for posterity. 'It didn't matter to me whether it was gold, silver or bronze,' he said uniquely. 'I came to give a performance, the best of my life if possible. I did, and for me, that was it.'

He had been first of the final group of six medal contenders. After rapturous applause, he had left the ice, returned to the dressing-room without watching the remaining five, and had packed. What happened now, he said, had not mattered. Orser, his wan face tight with dismay, looked along the Press conference table with aching, uncomprehensible eyes at his triumphant rival. For Orser, the medal had mattered so much more than the performance. Boitano, by contrast, had skated as though in a world of his own, indifferent to the crowd: athletically agile yet in an artistic trance.

To my unspecialised but instinctive eye, the difference between them was apparent, and equally subtle as between silk and satin. 'He was too sophisticated for the judges,' Sandra Bezic said of Boitano. Bezic, a willowy blonde Canadian of Yugoslav descent, was ninth in the 1972 Games at Sapporo, aged 15, skating with her brother in pairs, and subsequently fifth in the world championship. She is now a prominent choreographer. Nine months ago she started to work with Boitano: with magical effect. He had been, always, an exemplary technician, the world champion in 1986. She revealed his heart and soul. 'What I did was give him the confidence to be himself,' she said, her deep Adriatic eyes aglow with satisfaction. 'He needed that confidence to bare himself, he was afraid, the warmth wasn't there. But he was ready to absorb what I had to give.'

To the music of Carmine Coppola and dressed in the dark grey uniform of a 19th-century Legionnaire, Boitano expressed the moods of a soldier: introspective, romantic, resolute, morbid, victorious. Here was Hamilton and John Curry blended into one. 'It was emotionally everything I hoped it would be,' Bezic said. When Boitano revolved in three long backward leaning circles – the spreadeagle, in which Curry did a single turn – it was a sublime combination of grace and technique.

Both men had been under intense pressure of nationalistic expectation. Orser, long afflicted by nerves, had been in consultation with a psychologist. I can think of few more severe tests for the solo sports performer than to go out on the ice in front of that huge audience in an ice hockey stadium. Going out to bat against Lillee or Hall might be worse.

It was ironic that a Canadian, Bezic, should have conspired in an American victory, though this is the nature of so much coaching in international sport. It makes nonsense of the reprehensible headlines condemning Christopher Dean as a traitor for coaching the French. You would have supposed that Dean and his partner had done more than enough to repay Nottingham for any assistance provided on the way up.

THE BREATHTAKING CATHEDRAL OF
AMERICAN GOLF
The Times, April 1988

Augusta, Georgia: As you drive the 120-odd miles of gently-wooded landscape from Atlanta to Augusta, Pearl Bailey's *Georgia on My Mind* fills the senses. The aroma of pine needles, the air full of bird song, that friendly Southern languor, which pervades even a trucking pull-in, makes it the most agreeable of American states.

Take a wrong turn as you eventually slide off the Bobby Jones Expressway and you could be back in the Depression. Peeling weatherboard bungalows, dry as cheese rind, have a forlorn air on their broken brick piles. Old black men, hair grey with years, and small children slumber on the verandas in the afternoon heat on old car seats. Voluminous automobiles rot like stranded whales in the back gardens, their wheels overgrown by weeds.

It seems a one-horse town, for all the evidence here and

there of new business; not the resort it once was at the turn of the century for Southern gentry from Atlanta, seeking a warm, sea-level winter residence. The best hotel in town has the forsaken mood of King's Cross station on a Sunday in December, and the night is punctuated by the melancholy of goods-train sirens. The main street meanders out of town, over the Savannah river, past little bait-and-tackle shops offering hunting licences, past wooden white painted Methodist chapels, and one of several huge signs proclaiming 'Real Men Don't Hit Women'.

And then, suddenly, down a drive on the left, you discover the golfing Mecca created by the man who they say was greater than Nicklaus; a sporting oasis more naturally perfect even than Nicklaus' own Muirfield Village in Ohio. It is a partial coincidence, as Charles Price describes in his history of Bobby Jones' triumphs and of the Augusta National, that the club is a horticultural as well as a golfing masterpiece.

When Jones, son of a well-to-do lawyer, uniquely won the Amateur and Open championships of both Britain and the United States in 1930, he decided not to turn professional but to create a private club, primarily for winter use, away from his home of Atlanta and where, in the words of Belloc:

The men that were boys when I was a boy
Shall sit and drink with me.

In the midst of the Depression and with Wall Street in panic he found, such was his name, the backers. By chance, he found, in Augusta, an abandoned horticultural nursery, founded the previous century by Baron Berckmans, of Belgium. Of his first visit, passing down the magnificent avenue of magnolias, still serene today, and into the manor which is the clubhouse, Jones later wrote: 'When I walked out onto the terrace and looked down over the landscape, the experience was unforgettable.' It still is.

With his co-designer, Alistair Mackenzie, he fashioned a course that, like the greatest of American screen goddesses, is voluptuous, enslaving, enigmatic and occasionally destructive. Its fairways, greens and shrubberies are so perfect you dare not discard a spent cigarette, never mind a candy paper. Two oaks, maybe 300 years old, dominate the clubhouse terrace, while around the course gigantic firs, as ageless as Grecian columns and many entwined with wisteria, give dappled shade on the velvet grass. Berckmans' grandson was re-engaged by Jones to give each fairway its blazing borders of colour: camellia, cherry, jasmine, peach, juniper, crab apple.

Modest to a fault, Jones did not wish the title of 'championship' for the initial invitation tournament of 1934 – 'championship of what?' he asked – but inexorably it became known as the Masters; past and current major champions invited automatically, only the foreign entry selected, sometimes controversially, by discretion. Victories of the greatest golfers compounded its pre-eminence – Hogan and Snead twice each, Palmer three times, Nicklaus six, Player, Watson and Ballesteros twice each.

There are fewer (45) than half the usual number of championship bunkers, the subtlety achieved instead by fairway hillocks. The huge vistas, on a course with twice the conventional acreage, are often breathtaking. The par-four fifth hole climbs onto a wide sward, like Arundel cricket ground. As you gaze down the par-five second, into the huge bowl of the centre of the course, the crowds swirl around the third, eighth and 18th tees and the second, seventh and 17th greens like battle scenes at Waterloo.

It is possible simultaneously to watch the first and ninth from beneath four giant magnolias, each with a spread of 60 feet, while on benches on the fairway, just beneath the dropping, short sixth tee, you can simultaneously observe the sixth and 16th greens surrounded by a sea of azaleas: mauve, crimson, pink, white and flame.

Beauty and deception envelop the 11th, 12th and 13th. The 11th green lies below hillocks, surrounded by water to the left, bunkers behind. The short 12th is over water into what might be a private garden at Frinton-on-Sea; a herbal, sand-circled dartboard. The dog-leg 13th, skirting a brook, is the venomous par four-and-a-half champion maker. Not for nothing is this threesome known as Amen Corner.

> The greatest bunker shot in the history of golf, hit by
> Sandy Lyle on the last hole of the last day, makes him
> the first Briton to win the prestigious Masters.

LYLE APPLIES GENTLE TOUCH IN VICTORY
The Times, April 1988

Augusta, Georgia: The jargon of golf these days, when you
have just watched your chances plummet through the
floorboards, is that you have to 'regroup'. It is a word that
sounds straight out of West Point or Sandhurst. Patton or
Westmoreland would approve it.

When Sandy Lyle arrived, with an eight-under-par
two-stroke lead over Mark Calcavecchia, at what is regarded
as the definitive phase of the Augusta National course, and
proceeded to drop one shot at the 11th and then, plopping
into the water off the shoulder of the green, two at the short
12th, his expression was not so much 'amen' as a mortal,
blood-curdling 'aaarrghh'. There were not a few uncon-
trolled whoopees from the home crowd. Calcavecchia,
playing a hole in front, watched his putt roll round the rim
and drop for a birdie at the par-five 13th to go six-under.
Coming up behind, Lyle then bunkered his approach, came
out to 20 feet and missed the first putt to take a five.

It was a particular pleasure to walk this final round on what
was to be an historic afternoon with Herbert Warren Wind,
veteran correspondent of the *New Yorker*, to whom Amen
Corner owes its names. At this stage we were waiting,
fascinated, as were the millions watching on television as well
as the thousands thronging the course, for Lyle to 'regroup'.
And seemingly it was not happening.

It is difficult to read the mood of this tall, unblinking but
slightly shy-looking Englishman from Shropshire, whose
parents' Glaswegian blood affiliates him to Scotland. He

could be playing an artisans' evening four-ball. It is a characteristic which makes him both so likeable and, maybe, so good. He is said to be unflappable.

We had seen the steadiness in the outward half. Starting the day six-under, Lyle birdied the second and also, with a 20-yard chip from among the crowd at the back of the green, the fourth. There were brilliant recoveries at the seventh and ninth. Driving into trees at the seventh, a brave short-iron high through the foliage found a bunker; a wedge reached the green, and a curling 12-footer saved the par. Off the fairway again at the ninth, a glorious seven-iron rolled to within two feet for a birdie three, to turn two up. He was, someone observed, just about to reach the 'wall' to which marathon runners fearingly refer. And thence, via disasters, to the 14th, where Lyle has a par four.

As Lyle gazes down at the 15th green, from where his drive rests comfortably on the ridge, observing Calcavecchia remain six-under, Herb Wind voices the thought that the next couple of strokes will probably determine whether or not Lyle will be champion. Lyle is in range for a possible eagle; and is still in range of a birdie when his approach runs just off the back of the green. Yet when he arrives, to appreciative applause from the now immense crowd, his shoulders seemingly slump, a suggestion of resignation. It is to prove misleading. When his little chip grazes the hole, he slams his visor on the ground: though he will later say, in an admission of rare histrionics, that it had been 'putting a show on'.

Nevertheless, from seven feet past he misses the one back, takes par, and goes to the 16th still a stroke down on Calcavecchia. His fine seven-iron to the short 16th, that idyllic azalea-decked arbour, rests some feet above the pin on a notoriously sloped green where in the past four days there have been few birdie twos. Lyle makes it: all square.

It is the most tranquil of late afternoons, the sun sinking from view, as Lyle reaches the 17th. A distant roar tells us Calcavecchia is on the 18th in two. As Lyle lines up his 20-foot putt from the beard of the green, dwarfed by the pines standing sentinel around the back, the stillness among the thousands watching is that of a museum. He two-putts. The rest, as they say, is history: the bunker; the seven-iron so cleanly hit it takes not a grain of sand; the backwards, downhill roll towards the pin that is like a hand stretching out with a Nobel Prize; the final birdie putt.

A single historic stroke divides two men, but back in the interview room there is a marked cultural difference. When analysing his final round, Calcavecchia, though in no way boastful, uses the expressions 'great', 'real good', 'perfect', 'nice', 'so easy', 'my favourite', some 50 times in relation to his shots: American positive thinking.

Then comes the fellow in the spanking new, august Augusta green, smiling an almost apologetic, satisfied smile. He had, he says with courtesy to accepted cliché, managed to regroup after the 12th: yet he remains immovably honest. He declines to agree he is the best in the world, because 'there are a lot of other good players'. He would have to think about the possibilities of the grand slam.

The American Press are pleading with him, in effect, to shout yippee and he simply will not. Calcavecchia has generously said his rival is 'real patient'. They had talked a bit beforehand. Sandy had given him all that English stuff: you win some, you lose some, old chap, you know. 'I've never seen him doubt himself,' Calcavecchia said. 'I'm glad he's going home.' Lyle has given himself, and certainly has given me, an afternoon of magical memories.

Dan Maskell, the reassuring voice of tennis, has proved that he is more gent than some of the gentlemen.

A GENTLE VOICE IN THE GAME
The Times, June 1988

Dan Maskell, in the words of someone who has known him since he embarked on his professional career as a full-time ball boy at Queen's Club in 1923, is popular because he epitomised what so many of the English believe they would like to be. Courteous, modest, understated. His carefully modulated voice, known to millions since his first televised Wimbledon broadcast in 1951, has that quality which, without ever stating as much, always charmingly reminds us that tennis, however turbulent or epic the match, is still only a game.

Some might say that Maskell, still illuminating at 80 the most widely discussed event in England's sporting calendar, was nice to a fault. Extremes of misbehaviour have never brought from him anything more censorious than 'Oh dear'. This English reluctance to advocate punitive measures is perhaps a characteristic of those establishment figures whom, by social metamorphosis, he has come to be seen to represent.

We are now witnessing the new McEnroe with added whiteness; yet in Maskell's autobiography (*From Where I Sit*, Collins Willow, £14.95) he can only say of the devil's disciple at his worst four or five years ago: 'More likely to be remembered not for his tennis but for some truly appalling behaviour ... if only the authorities had made him pay the penalty ...' and so on. You cannot but wonder how Maskell, whose kindly manner never allowed him to say 'no' to anyone, would have fared as chairman of a disciplinary commission!

Maskell is fascinating on two counts: primarily because he has seen, played against, advised or commentated on every great player from Tilden and Lenglen to the present day, but also because, as a working-class boy from Fulham denied a full academic education by family impecuniosity, he penetrated the bastions of social privilege in that period between the wars when upstairs and downstairs were mostly unbreachable.

His judgement, whether coaching some of the foremost men and women – most notably, perhaps, the pre-war Davis Cup team with Perry and Austen – or commentating, has always had that calm, sensible assurance which makes fine teachers. It helped make him, too, a rescuer of broken limbs and minds as senior rehabilitation officer for the RAF, for which he was awarded the OBE. Not, it should be said, for guarding Hastings Pier from imminent invasion with a rifle without bayonet or bullets.

Threading a racket handle through the net and projecting six inches above the tape just inside the sideline, Maskell helped Perry perfect his blocked backhand passing shot 'until he could hit the handle almost at will'. What Maskell may have lacked in authority he makes up for in his celebration of anyone's skill, conveying this to the viewer without the near hysteria common to television.

He manages to make even McEnroe seem civilised: 'The finest tennis I have ever seen' when beating Connors in the 1984 Wimbledon final with 'reflexes as fast as any player's have ever been' and an instinct that 'was the stuff of genius'. Maskell places McEnroe sixth in his all-time list, headed by Laver, Budge, Tilden, Perry and Borg, and including Cochet, Borotra, Rosewall and Connors ... but not, controversially, Hoad. The other morning, at about the time some are still abed, I caught him just before he headed off from Dorking for his 453rd unbroken day's commentary at the championships. Why no Hoad? The reply was predictably professorial: 'I always felt Lew was spectacular to a degree that few were more so, but there wasn't a consistency in his career – the quality of Jack Hobbs, for instance.'

Maskell's life has been a social document of our times. The fourth of eight children, whose mother died in childbirth at 47; a mechanic-turned-publican father who used to give cycling lessons to the gentry at Queen's Club for a shilling to extend a modest wage, and whose children called him 'sir'; discipline at elementary school in which all were punished unless the guilty owned up, in an era of horse-drawn fire engines and London fogs where you could get lost in your own street; seaside holidays and repertory moral melodramas; and joining Queen's Club, being unable to afford grammar school fees, where he enjoyed 'the sense of good breeding and orderly management that pervaded the place'.

Maskell says he will continue until the adrenalin ceases to be stirred; his, by the tennis or, unlikely, the BBC's by him. This Wimbledon is exciting him more than for a long time. 'It's so open.' What distinguishes Maskell from some of the

249

establishment members he joined is his unfailing generosity of spirit.

If there was a time for Bobby Robson, England's manager, to go, voluntarily or by request, it was following the débâcle of England's performances in the European championship. He was without credibility: even if it was later learned that Lineker had had hepatitis.

ROBSON'S DELUSIONS OF GRANDEUR TURNED TO DUST
The Times, June 1988

Frankfurt: On the evidence of the past week, on and off the field during the European championship, I do not expect to live to see England again in the semi-final of an international tournament, never mind winning it, whether I reach three score years or 80. Indeed, they will be fortunate during that time even to qualify for the World Cup – if they are allowed to try – because it will take 25 years to put right what is wrong with English football, let alone what is wrong with England.

If the performance of our spectators has again, predictably, been a disgrace, the performance of our players has been, less expectedly, an embarrassment. The spectators are guilty of wilful malice, the players only of incompetence. The first factor will not spontaneously improve; the second will probably decline still further.

It is therefore to a degree irrelevant who is the national team manager. The players available, thanks to the style of schoolboy and then club football, and thanks to a continuing absence from European competition, are not good enough. Yet it has to be asked why Jack Charlton, with less talent in his squad than Bobby Robson, achieved relatively so much more; why Houghton, Aldridge and Whelan played to their Liverpool form for Ireland, and Beardsley and Barnes below it for England?

Charlton played 35 times for England and Robson 20. But the difference last week, I suspect, lay not in what they knew or in their experience, but in knowing what they wanted; and in the players knowing clearly what their managers wanted. Charlton recognised from the start three years ago the limitations of his squad, and he played to its strengths. Robson, believing England to be better than they are, played to imagined strengths and discovered they were not there. The success of the qualifying matches was a discernible illusion. The failure of Beardsley and Lineker was partially predictable (in the office sweepstake, I had put England down to score only three goals – they got two – because I thought the midfield and defence would be vulnerable).

The sober prediction is that in the immediate years ahead, the only effective way for England to play will be like Wimbledon, because they do not have the skill to play like the Netherlands, Italy or West Germany. To try would be a presumption; especially when most of our League managers, including Robson, believe that Graham Roberts is a good player. To be fair to Robson, he has always *wanted* to play good football. He brought Muhren and Thyssen to Ipswich. But with England he has never been wholly sure how he wanted to play good football.

There is no one in England at present who can pass a ball like Peters, or Brooking, except for Hoddle. Yet Hoddle is such an amalgam of brilliance and deficiency that he can never be more than a substitute to exploit tiring opponents. Hateley is not a substitute for anyone: his style demands a different function from half the team – long, high balls, Wimbledon-style – which was the way Robson thought he wanted to play for four years until circumstances forced his hand after two matches in Mexico.

English football will produce the occasional Lineker, Francis or Keegan – who played successfully alongside Latchford – but the way League football is played, it will produce more players like Latchford, Withe, and Hateley. Therefore, the way to play internationally is bound to be with an old-fashioned tactical centre-forward, who you hope can play with the accuracy of Hurst rather than Hateley. Charlton used the veteran Stapleton.

English football continues to drive relentlessly down its own lonely path, being followed slavishly at a distance by Australian and United States football. Not one in 20 Football League directors could so much as tell you who Leo Beenhakker is, never mind go and watch his football with Real Madrid and consider employing him. I endeavoured 12 years ago to persuade Arsenal and Everton to appoint respectively Miljanic, of Yugoslavia, and Cramer, who had just finished with the European Cup champions, Bayern Munich. Philip Carter flew to interview Cramer but could not match Continental salaries. In confidentiality, I never wrote the Cramer story.

What has happened over the past 15 years is that English clubs, though playing largely their own way other than at Anfield, have partially adapted to foreign habits and the possession game; and with strength and self-discipline have won European matches. That experience was reflected in the England team, an experience no longer available. Watson of Everton, for example, who is an average but intelligent defender, would have improved substantially with a dozen foreign cup ties. Hooligan violence has handicapped his career prospects. The FA returns home moaning about the Press coverage. Robson can hardly complain. He enjoyed predominantly sycophantic reviews before the competition, and then the team played badly. Tabloid coverage is admittedly mixed. Some correspondents might expect to find Azeglio Vicini at the Chelsea Flower Show rather than on the Italian trainers' bench; but Ken Bates and the rest really cannot blame the hooligans on Fleet Street's coverage of the game.

We were collectively reproached during the 125th anniversary banquet for inaccurate reporting, but ever since the *centenary* the FA has been failing to deal firmly with hooliganism on and off the pitch. It cannot say violence is society's problem and not its own. For more than 20 years it has helped to form society as it now is.

> The House of Commons proves that hooliganism has spread to every corner of society.

ROUGH RIDE FOR THE NIMBLE DRIBBLER
The Times, July 1988

The House gathered on Tuesday night for the Social Credibility Cup, a competition that will determine whether Colin Moynihan, the Minister for Sport, is an old-fashioned inside-forward, beloved on the terraces for crowd entertainment, or a ruthless tackler bent on promotion at all costs, playing in a cost-efficiency formation.

Attendance was poor; sport has never been a crowd-puller at Westminster, never mind that it is a billion-pound industry generating more jobs and revenue than, say, the gas or DIY trades. Notable figures from each side of the House only appeared, after wine and preferred conversation elsewhere, in time for the vote, with as much unconcern as if they had missed a darts social.

Behaviour, it must be said, had not been good. The Opposition fans, with Bernie Grant a visible ringleader backed by the under-privileged Celtic fringe, leapt up and down demanding to know what the Minister was doing about racist chanting or about South Africa, who didn't appear on the team sheet; and when they got no response proceeded to howl and heckle as vigorously as any quorum of Alf Garnetts at Upton Park. No one person could hear what any other person was saying and the Deputy Speaker repeatedly had to call for order. It was unnerving to consider that such standards of debate govern our lives, though I suppose this was just further evidence that hooliganism has spread to every corner of society.

Behind the Government goal, those who bothered to turn up seemed mostly asleep, content to let the Minister infuriate the Opposition with his nimble dribbling. The Minister does show a tendency to hang on to the ball too long, and he gives the occasional hospital-pass. The Opposition intercepted the ball in a flash when he talked of swimming pool management needing to show a profit, when everyone knows that a swimming pool is the Glenn Hoddle of any local authority team: decorative and expensive but will never show a gain.

Yet the Minister, lacking inches, had to dodge some blatant professional fouls – 'Been to a football match but never saw it' and so on – typical of the four-letter chanting to which we have become accustomed. No doubt the Minister would like to earn a reputation as the Prince of Dribblers, but he was not helped by the absence from the bench of his heavyweight centre-back, the Home Secretary, and his team captain, the Environment Secretary, who only appeared for a chat in the dressing-room when it was all over. The Minister showed all the signs of being coached by his chairwoman, with a preoccupation on transfer values.

John Carlisle showed some neat footwork on the Government wing, but as everyone knows he has been tapped by the Pretoria scouts; nobody takes him seriously, which is a pity because his tactics on behalf of the ratepayers are sound. When Carlisle, with justification, referred to the yobbish shouting behind the Opposition goal, Michael Foot, the oldest season ticket-holder in the stand, stumped off in disgust. He had asked a serious question on the cost to League clubs of the Government's card membership scheme.

Denis Howell, a popular long-serving one-club man, had led the attack for the Opposition. He isn't as penetrating as he once was, and may soon move into the non-League game. Nowadays he stands around the centre circle, shirt unbuttoned at the navel, shorts sagging slightly, acknowledging friends with a wave or a smile, and attempting to whack the ball in, like the veteran Ronnie Rooke of Arsenal once did, from

40 yards. The power is still there but the aim is less sure, and he was unconvincing on the inefficiency of the membership scheme which the chairwoman and her Minister are determined to introduce. Howell's comparison between membership cards and pornography clubs was tenuous to say the least.

David Evans, a utility player representing both the Government and Luton Town, as its chairman, stepped on to the field only to find he initially had two left feet. We heard all about Denis Compton and inadequate modern wickets. Evans' voice sounded from a long way off, though Luton is not far north of Watford. Eventually he reached, as the commentators say, a critical scoring chance: the membership scheme works admirably at Luton, families are coming back, and the town is once again a safe environment on a Saturday afternoon. But his negative square-passing approach-play on cricket and tennis had left everyone drowsily wishing for the final whistle and a return to the supporters' club bar, so his point was lost.

David Blunkett, an extra-time substitute for the Opposition, leapt off the bench aiming shots at unprotected morality areas of the Minister's net. Yet he made Roy Hattersley's common mistake of attributing football thuggery to this Government's term of office when we all know that it really began during Harold Wilson's premiership, and, anyway, it is irrelevant to any current political hue.

By the end of the match, the teams had been unable to agree whether the increase in national sports participation from 17 million in 1978 to 23 million today was attributable to the Sports Council, local authorities, the Government, or simply the fact that people, employed or unemployed, have increasing amounts of time to devote to leisure. Howell made the sensible plea that there should be an All Party committee to seriously investigate the needs of sport.

The match ended with Brian Wilson abusing the Minister, and being labelled despicable in return. The Opposition were defeated by 277 corners to 205, nobody scored a memorable goal, and we left the House feeling that the Opposition needs some coaching in manners and the Government in sincerity.

> The stakes for which Manchester bids against Athens for the Olympic Games of 1996 stretch far beyond running tracks.

TAKING GOLD IN A GREATER GAME
The Times, September 1988

Seoul: The governments of Britain and the United States remain alone in the world among developed nations not to realise the political, social and commercial value of international sport, which is about to be demonstrated by South Korea. The US still has sporting success because it has four times Britain's population and immense private corporate wealth from which to sustain sport. Britain is now among the poor relations of international sport in almost every respect, as demonstrated by the derisory reaction of the Commonwealth Games Federation here yesterday to Cardiff's bid for the Games of 1994, awarded to Victoria, British Columbia, by an overwhelming majority. Cardiff never had a chance.

Seven years ago Dr Kim Un Yung, adviser to the Korean embassies of America and Britain and deputy director-general to the President's office, and also himself president of the World Taekwondo Federation, realised that his country could make an impact without parallel upon world awareness by staging the Olympic Games. Korea was already advancing through the ranks of the world's industrial producers, yet no single event could expose the nation to global publicity as could the Olympics.

With the support of General Roh Tae Woo, an emerging figure of domestic political power, Kim went to the Olympic Congress in Baden-Baden, West Germany, in 1981 to bid for the Games this year. The field was open. Munich had been terrorised by the Israeli massacre and Olympic security had become a nightmare. Montreal had the African boycott, Moscow the West boycott. Additionally, Montreal had run up a bill in 1976 under Mayor Drapeau, thanks to over-ambitious construction and workforce strikes, that the ratepayers would be paying into the next century. Los Angeles had been the only bid, by a private business consortium, for 1984.

The unknown Koreans got the vote when environmental protesters from Nagoya, Japan, the other candidate, lined the streets of Baden-Baden. Within three years Korea, with government money, had built a main stadium second to none in the world. By 1986, as host to the Asian Games, it had completed a unique complex of modern sports facilities. The swimming pool was unsatisfactory? They would build another by the time of the Olympic Games. Their new equestrian centre, to be used this fortnight for the first time, is without comparison.

The fee negotiated for American television rights, $300 million, might have been half of what Korea was led to believe it could get; but other incomes from ticket sales, sponsorship, sale of Olympic Village flats and so on would ensure Korea did not lose on its investment.

The risks might have been high, but so were the stakes. Korea was challenging Japan (its former colonial master), Hong Kong and China on the battlefield of commerce and politics, as well as striving to out-distance its North Korean neighbour and to prove its ultimate independence from America. The Olympic Games would achieve a level of publicity for its efforts which a million television commercials could never buy.

The danger was that North Korea, inflamed by envy of the South's favourable exposure, would attempt to fuse the magic lantern by persuading China, the Soviet Union and other Socialist states, to stay away. But China was changing, and so was the Soviet Union. China went to the Los Angeles Games and then, a critical move, to the Asian Games in 1986 here in Seoul: the Pyongyang reliance on Socialist solidarity was holed below the water-line. Not only that, the Soviet Union, East Germany and others had discovered a serious setback in incentive, through absence from the Games, within their social system of privilege and advance for an army of sports performers, coaches and doctors. *Glasnost* accelerated a change in attitude to the South Korean regime.

Astute negotiations by Juan Antonio Samaranch, president of the International Olympic Committee, seemingly keeping the door open for North Korea to compete, had already enabled Socialist countries to contemplate their own participation, never mind the absence of diplomatic relations. The thaw in the cold war began and, to the acute embarrassment of North Korea, harmonious relations between South Korea and the Communist bloc are advancing rapidly.

To South Korea, the staging of the Olympic Games has been like the success of Jaguar at Le Mans in the 1950s. They had, and have, to produce the goods for the public, but their name, for much of the past four years and for almost every hour of the next fortnight, is on a billion lips. Kim's imaginative and almost anonymous bid seven years ago may in time prove to have been as profound an influence on the balance of Asian commercial affairs as Japan's staging of the Games in Tokyo, the first in Asia, in 1964. That, too, was a calculated commercial campaign. The fact that South Korea's sporting achievement, reaching out to challenge the former dominance of Japan and the new power of China, is faster growing than in most countries, is almost incidental. South Korea is expected to be among the top eight medal winners.

What is inexplicable, and what some may regret, is the contemporary link between sport and money and social (structural) development. It is a link of which the Manchester committee, led by Robert Scott, the theatrical entrepreneur who is here to evaluate Seoul's organisation, is well aware. An Olympic Games in Manchester in 1996, the Olympic centenary year, could help reshape and revitalise the north-west of England beyond all expectation: just as it would reshape Athens, Greece's suffocating, under-developed capital. Athens needs to celebrate its own centenary more out of social necessity, for the redevelopment that would be generated, than out of any historic sense of pride.

Toronto and Atlanta are equally enthusiastic. Ever since Los Angeles made a profit of $220 million, there is no shortage of volunteer cities. The Olympic Games, for better or worse, are a colossal commercial force; and from the unexpected victory yesterday by tiny Lillehammer of Norway, population 25,000, in the bid to host the Olympic Winter Games of 1994, it is abundantly evident that Manchester has a realistic chance, if it is not blighted by the confused British record on the anti-apartheid issue that wrecked Edinburgh's Commonwealth Games and, to an extent, Cardiff's attempt this week.

Mrs Thatcher should take note that the campaign (unsuccessful) by Paris two years ago for the 1992 summer Games was personally led by Jacques Chirac, and that here in Seoul the Norwegian final presentation to the IOC was fronted by the Prime Minister, Gro Harlem Brundtland; and that of Öster-sund of Sweden, the runner-up yesterday, by King Gustav. Cardiff's courageous, vain effort, backed by the city council, was hopelessly overwhelmed by the $86 million guarantee from federal and provincial governments for Victoria.

The Olympic Games present not merely an Aladdin's lamp to host cities: they are a bull ring of intense action for commercial operators. Visa, the credit card organisation, has put $14 million into the Calgary/Seoul sponsorship programme organised for the IOC by ISL Marketing of Lucerne, and has spent $25 million worldwide to advertise its involvement. The Minneapolis/St Paul company, 3M, one of America's largest, in an attempt to raise its image outside the States, invested $15 million in the IOC package, with a further $50 million in worldwide advertising back-up. 3M's marketing analysts will decide in November whether the results justify repeating the process for Albertville/Barcelona in 1992. They are looking this time for a 10 per cent increase in market awareness.

It is perhaps time that the mandarins of Whitehall came to recognise that there is rather more to sport than running fast in a circle or putting on a pair of swimming trunks.

> A wonderful contest between Silivas and Shushunova in
> the women's all-round gymnastics was marred by the
> absurdity of arbitrary marks of fractional difference.

JUDGING PERFORMANCES ON THE MAT
The Times, September 1988

Seoul: The women's individual all-round gymnastics final
produced an amalgam of beauty, excellence, prejudice and,
ultimately, an absurdity. How else can be described the
wonderful performances of Elena Shushunova, of the Soviet
Union, and Daniela Silivas, of Romania, and their separation
in determining the gold medal for the former by 0.025 of a
point, or less than one 3,000th part of their totals, on the
arbitrary opinion of six judges. No logical person can happily
accept such a refinement of human discretion.

Certainly Adrian Goreac, Silivas' coach, could not willingly
accept it, and said so when asked at the official Press
conference after Shushunova had received the gold medal:
one of the most prized in Eastern European sport. Goreac
had been asked to give an opinion on the low mark awarded
Silivas on her final exercise by Nellie Kim, the Soviet judge
and herself a former champion. Goreac said, with evident
feeling: 'My own unofficial opinion is when sportsmen or
-women receive a 9.8 we are not taking it very well. A 9.8 does
not express a high level of endeavour. Such low marks do not
express this level of sport.' In other words, he implied,
Romania was paying the price of what we cannot be sure –
perhaps Romania's lack of solidarity in turning up in Los
Angeles four years ago.

Shushunova's coach, Viktor Gavrichenko, had tried to
interrupt the question, telling the experienced Norwegian
journalist he should instead ask the judges. Shushunova's

pert little face, hitherto all smiles and assurance alongside the despairing, pale, childlike Silivas, now fell into an expression of self-doubt and annoyance. It must be likely that every gymnastic expert in the Olympic park stadium, competitor, official or observer, will have known the verdict was questionable. Silivas, in fact, beat Shushunova on the day's four exercises by the same tiny margin she lost the medal, on account of the 0.050 points which the Russian carried forward from the preliminaries.

Silivas, aged 17 and Romania's replacement for Nadia Comaneci, led by 0.025 points going into the last exercise, the vaulting horse. To this untutored eye, her leap, spinning and twisting like a salmon, was faultless: the judges gave her 9.900.

Of six judges' marks, the top and bottom are discarded and an average taken on the middle four. Kim's persistent low marking would push into the average the other lowest mark. In popular sports it is clearly impossible to have judging panels that exclude anyone of the same nationality as any of those competing, yet the vulnerability to prejudice in arbitrarily measured sports – boxing, figure skating, diving, dressage, gymnastics – is too evidently prevalent to pass notice.

It was, nonetheless, a spectacular competition between the two, however much at the end one might feel sorry for the little Romanian with the doll face and milkmaid's heavy hands. Although Shushunova performed with style her switched-hands grip in the asymmetric bars, Silivas had the edge with the first 10.

On they moved to the beam. Shushunova, with those incredible backward somersaults landing blind on one foot, scored a fraction higher, Silivas losing balance for a split second and being forced into an involuntary turn. Yet at times she kept contact with the beam with entwining legs like an ivy creeper. Look, no hands!

Silivas led on points as they performed their floor exercises. Shushunova, in her leotard of almost elderly sophistication, mauve, grey and black, utilised a Russian dance to give rhythm to a bewitching sequence; a delectable 10. Silivas was her equal, perhaps even superior, corkscrewing in mid-air, somersaulting incredibly from a kneeling position, all to a jazz rhythm. Another 10.

Finally they were at the vault. Silivas, still leading, was drawn first, spinning like a coin, with barely a touch of the horse as she cartwheeled three times, yet received only 9.950. Shushunova was drawn last of the group of six. She warmed up meticulously, and was clearly relaxed as she chatted to her colleague Natalia Lachtchenova, who had a fall on her first jump. Shushunova's first run was as good but no more so, it seemed, than that of Silivas. It was a decisive 10. The photographers crowded her. Silivas, a few yards away, sat on the floor, expressionless, and hardly glanced when Shushunova walked by: one of them forever a national heroine, the other forever a runner-up, and all by the discretionary flick of a judge's finger on an electric button.

What most depressed me, looking back, was not the dubious marking, but the blank, programmed look of the medal winners when they appeared behind the microphones: conditioned to cliché replies, seemingly unable to comprehend or respond to questions other than the obvious; looking forward to no more, as Svetlana Boguinskaia, the bronze medal winner, admitted, than coaching the next generation of automated geniuses.

EXCEPTIONAL EFFORTS SINK REDGRAVE AND HOLMES IN DESPAIR
The Times, September 1988

Seoul: Seldom has a bronze medal earned by such exceptional ability brought so little satisfaction. Steve Redgrave and Andy Holmes were silently drinking champagne in a deserted boat-house, following their coxed pairs, and from their expressions you would have supposed they had just won a one-way ticket to Devil's Island. Michael Spracklen, the British chief coach, who has trained Redgrave throughout his career, embraced Holmes, but the empty stare remained: a

262

man who has seen the summit of Everest from 500 feet and not made it.

Brian Armstrong, the team manager, stood looking on, not knowing how to intrude on private contemplation. 'Never in modern times has there been anyone to win two medals,' he said. 'Several tried this time, but no one else reached two finals. Six times in a week they have rowed 2,000 metres, with two semi-finals within an hour.'

Redgrave and Holmes, perhaps the greatest names in British rowing history, had just succeeded in the most Herculean task any two competitors ever set themselves. By their own terms, they had failed. They believed their gold and bronze in the coxless and coxed pairs should have been a double gold. They had worked for four years with a strange combination of friction and harmony; utterly dependent on each other, yet regularly questioning each other. 'It is a functional relationship they have,' an observer in the athletes' village said yesterday. 'They have been under enormous tension, arriving here earlier than anyone. They're both fairly irascible. They are not easy partners.'

Holmes was the more rational in the trough of their disappointment. 'Considering that two months ago I thought I was a write-off with my back injury and that Steve would have to row in another boat, two medals is something to be pleased with,' he said.

It is sad that yesterday they were disconsolately going about the mechanics of preparing to return home. They had attempted the impossible and come within three seconds of doing it.

On Saturday in the coxless pairs final, they had crushed the formidable Romanians, Dragos Neagu and Danut Dobre, leading from start to finish, attempting to preserve themselves and remain fresh for yesterday when they would meet the exceptional Abbagnale brothers of Italy, four times world champions.

When the start came, Redgrave and Holmes were last for the first 500 metres. 'The horsepower just wasn't there,' Redgrave said. 'We have the horsepower, but not after six races.' Slowly they ground their way back into the race,

Redgrave's massive shoulders setting a long stroke which recovered the lost ground. By 1,000 metres the Italians were a length clear but Redgrave and Holmes were overlapping the Bulgarians, lying second.

At 1,500 metres, the British boat was almost level with the fading Bulgarians, but the East German pair, Steit and Kirchhoff, were sweeping through from fifth place. In the final, desperate burst, Redgrave and Holmes, coxed by Pat Sweeney, gained second place, only to concede it to the East Germans. The Abbagnales had the gold by two seconds. The margin between silver and bronze was one second. Holmes' head sank on his chest as they crossed the line. Redgrave's eyes, as he stood waiting to receive their medals, were grey with fatigue.

What of the future? They will take a holiday for a few weeks, then reconsider their position. 'It all depends, I suppose, on whether we can get the financial backing to make it worthwhile,' Holmes said. Maybe, who knows, Redgrave will revert to his previously failed ambition to be a single sculler. Their stresses together might not endure for another four years.

These were the Games of the African runners: of Ereng, Rono, Ngugi and Kariuki, winners respectively of the 800, 1,500, 5,000 and 3,000 steeplechase, and of Wakihuri, second in the memorable marathon.

HAZE OF DISBELIEF
The Times, September 1988

Seoul: With almost biblical simplicity, Paul Ereng, who as a boy was a cow-herd, came down from the high plains of Kenya to win an Olympic gold medal yesterday. If we are astonished by the improbability of his victory, Ereng himself is still reeling in a haze of disbelief. He not only beat Cruz, the defending champion, but the legendary Aouita, and for hours afterwards he could hardly comprehend the reality of what he had done. Never having competed in a 800 metres until this year, Ereng is yet another phenomenal Kenyan runner. Mike Koskei, the national middle-distance coach, estimates that Ereng can run 1 min 39 sec, some two seconds below Sebastian Coe's seven-year-old world record. 'That's what we are aiming for,' Koskei said with a laugh.

Ereng's victory, running through from the back of the field after the final bend, past a host of famous names, is partially a story of sacrifice by Nixon Kiprotich, his colleague. Under Koskei's direction it was planned that Kiprotich, a front-•runner, would create a fierce pace that would destroy Barbosa and Cruz, the two Brazilians. Because Barbosa and Cruz had planned with their coach, Oliveira, to wring the speed out of Aouita by the 600-metre mark, the way was paved for the emergence of the least-heralded hero since Bikila's first marathon triumph.

Yet the real story lies in how Ereng ever came to be here. Born in Turkana, a remote, tiny village in the Rift Valley without electricity or roads, he grew up on mostly-arid pastureland, tending the herds in between lessons at the most basic of primary schools. An alert boy, he was given a scholarship to Starehe boys' school for the underprivileged, founded by Bill Griffin, an Englishman, in Nairobi.

At about the age of 15 Ereng started to run competitively and four years later was spotted, as a moderate quarter-miler, by an American scout. He was offered an athletic scholarship to the University of Virginia, at Charlottesville, the alma mater of Thomas Jefferson. Fred Hardy, the university coach was convinced he was a potential 800-metre runner. Ereng had so far run a 45-second 400 metres. 'I did not have a great record at 400,' he said yesterday as he gazed a trifle bewildered at an array of more journalists in one spot than he had previously seen. 'When I first tried 800 at the start of this year, I was running around two minutes and felt discouraged.' Well he might, with women nowadays beating

1 min 54 sec. Then he ran under 1 min 50 sec. 'After that I felt good. I realised I was dependent on speed, not endurance.'

Nothing more might have been heard of him this year, had not the *Standard* newspaper in Nairobi spotted one or two Reuter reports with some encouraging times in national collegiate track meetings. The Kenyan federation decided it had better send him an air ticket to come home to attend the Olympic trials. He finished third and was selected. 'I didn't really know whether I needed more races to give me more experience. On the other hand, by running only two big races this year, the NCAA final and the trials, I'm not really drained.' There lies a lesson for such as Aouita and Cram, who are without doubt seriously over-raced and suffering for it.

Ereng prepared for the Games under the guidance of Koskei. 'We were doing 600s and he was running 1:16, so I knew he was in good shape,' Koskei said yesterday as his runners warmed up for the 10,000 metres final. Kipkemboi Kimele, who was to win the bronze, cheerfully went to find Koskei out on the warm-up track, only 10 minutes or so before his own race.

'When Paul was doing 47-second repetitions over 400, with only seven minutes' rest, I was confident for him,' Koskei said. When Ereng was 16, Koskei had given him his first pair of spikes. The rest is history. Ereng's run off the peak of the last bend, coming through the gap that had been created ahead of him by Elliott running wide to challenge Cruz, was the most perfect piece of timing since Wottle's in Munich 16 years ago.

Ereng can now expect to be honoured by his national president with the Order of the Burning Spear – the highest civilian decoration – on Independence Day, 12 December. Whatever else may come his way, he has won 50,000 Kenyan shillings (about £3,000) in prizes donated for gold medallists by Kenya Telecommunications, a brewery and a government minister. He may receive much more in due course. The most precious reward he has, however, is a slice of history.

WHY LEWIS MUST BE REGARDED IN THE CORRECT LIGHT

The Times, September 1988

Seoul: The disgrace of one great athlete is tending temporarily to obscure the excellence of another. We ought not to overlook that Carl Lewis, the rival whom Ben Johnson beat in the controversial 100 metres final before disqualification, is possibly the supreme natural athlete of all time, even judged alongside the legendary Jesse Owens.

That is certainly the opinion of Tom Tellez, Lewis' coach. Yet the silver medal Lewis won in yesterday's 200 metres, defeated in a close finish by his compatriot and friend, Joe DeLoach, is seen by some as failure, ending Lewis' attempt to win four gold medals in successive Olympic Games. That would be a harsh judgement on five days of exceptional performances in the 100 metres, long jump and 200 metres.

Lewis, since I first saw him as a teenager competing in Zurich, has had a beautiful, lissom shape, with none of the muscular definition of a particular kind that makes one suspicious of certain other athletes. He ran like a deer from the time he first emerged because he had a deer's natural grace and balance.

In 1980, aged 19, he was denied the Games in Moscow, for which he had qualified in the long jump, coming only fourth in the 100 metres trials. He was then primarily a long jumper. 'Running the 100 metres was simply ancillary, a beneficial sideline to long jumping,' Tellez said. 'It was only after 1980 that he decided he wanted to be a serious sprinter as well.'

Tellez is convinced that Lewis' determination to compete in all four events again, as in Los Angeles, and as Owens did in 1936, contributed to yesterday's defeat: especially the decision to jump all six times in the long jump final and not only once as in Los Angeles, which unfairly earned him widespread public criticism. Lewis, aged 27, won on Monday with his fourth jump, and injured an ankle on his fifth. There was a tight interval, additionally, between the long jump and

267

200 metres heats. 'I didn't advise him to take six jumps,' Tellez said. 'But the first three were not so good, and anyway he wanted to do six. Myricks [who came third] is always a danger. Yet bowing to public opinion may have cost Carl the gold medal today.'

That is not a coach's sour grapes. Tellez is also coach of DeLoach. 'I didn't have any idea that Joe would win until he did, not with someone like Carl running,' Tellez said. 'I knew that Joe would have to run a perfect race, which he did, and that Carl would have to be tired, which he was.' Besides these two, Tellez has trained such outstanding Americans as Baptiste, Banks, Tully and Floyd.

Over five exceptional days Lewis had run four 100 metres races, four 200 metres races and nine 60-metre approach runs in his preliminary and final long jump rounds. The end product had been an American record in the 100 metres of 9.92 sec, bettered only by Johnson's world record, set last year in Rome, of 9.83 sec and the disqualified 9.79 sec; the sixth best long jump of all time, 8.72 metres; and the fourth fastest ever 200 metres of 19.79 sec. Lewis was entitled to say at his Press conference, 'I'm happy with my performances.'

He was reluctant to discuss the fatigue factor. He did not know how much it cost him, and it didn't matter, he insisted. DeLoach, aged 21, had run an Olympic record to win by four-hundredths of a second. In the final 10 metres, Lewis had visibly flagged, his stride shorter and stiff. Yet that is the equivalent to saying Vivien Leigh was ugly one day merely because she had a cold.

Tellez was sadder than Lewis, to whom he is something of an uncle. Their homes are within walking distance of each other, and the relationship is close, though not closed. 'I'm not his guru, but I know this race was big for him,' Tellez said, although Lewis betrays no signs of regret. Tellez merely reflected that he now knew Lewis could not take all those jumps *and* the 200. It is not possible, he said, to do all the necessary training for both. The 200 requires stamina work, running 500s and 600s. Some weeks Lewis will have only one long jump session. Tellez believes, however, that Lewis can still challenge for medals in Barcelona in four years' time; but not in four events. 'It depends what he wants,' he said. 'I hope he can diversify away from athletics, find himself new challenges.'

We are standing on chairs at the back of the main stadium's open air, makeshift and inadequate interview room, together with Lewis' mother. Tellez is observing his man with a mixture of affection and fascination. 'Whatever he does, in my opinion he's the greatest ever,' he says. 'A phenomenal runner.'

COURAGE ALONE IS NOT ENOUGH FOR TOILING THOMPSON
The Times, September 1988

Seoul: Daley Thompson is a wise old owl. Aged 30, he has been 12 years at the top in international decathlon competition, and although hampered here by a previously undisclosed thigh strain received a few days ago, he knew that the opposition was also off form. So for two days he kept going, gambling that he might steal a medal. His fortitude helped produce a thrilling climax to the event yesterday, despite the lowest scoring in an Olympic Games since 1972.

Thompson finished fourth, denied a bronze medal on the last event by a strong 1,500 metres from Dave Steen, of Canada. The winner was Christian Schenk, of East Germany, aged 23 and a medical student, with a total of 8,488 points. Schenk had been fifth in last year's world championships. Torsten Voss, also of East Germany, who had won in Rome, was second. 'If everyone else had been doing well, I would have dropped out,' Thompson said afterwards, his left thigh strapped like a burst waterpipe. 'I'm really upset. More so than in Rome last year.' In Rome he had finished ninth, also when injured.

The depth of his competitiveness, which has won him eight major championships, was doubly evident yesterday. After the high hurdles and discus he was still lying third overall, his overnight position. Then, on his first attempt at the pole vault, his pole snapped in two places on lift-off – a rare and unpredictable occurrence with a glassfibre pole. It damaged his left hand and inflicted the kind of emotional jolt upon the nerves which might finish a lesser man. He shook himself like a half-drowned dog, cleared the bar at 4.70 metres at his second attempt, and went on to record 4.90 metres, which was below his best but enough to retain fourth place. Voss had now moved ahead of him, with Plaziat, of France, maintaining second position.

With a personal best in the javelin of 64.04 metres, Thompson heaved himself back to third, though around him other positions were fluctuating. Schenk and Voss were in front, but Plaziat, with a poor throw in his worst event, had fallen to seventh. The danger for Thompson now lay immediately behind. Tim Bright, an American who cannot make up his mind whether to be a pole vaulter or a decathlete, had climbed higher and higher in the vault until he reached 5.70 metres. He had finished fourth in the Olympic pole vault trials, and his height yesterday would have placed him seventh in the open pole vault the day before. Also threatening were Pavel Tarnovetski, of the Soviet Union, who was third in Rome, and Steen, now in eighth place and 120 points behind Thompson, but with a strong 1,500 metres potential.

Bright's prolonged vaulting on his own had thrown the schedule awry. The first round of the javelin throwers had concluded while Bright was attempting 5.80 metres. When Thompson and the rest finally got to the line for the last race at 9.20 p.m. the competition's second day had been running 13 hours. A full-scale dress rehearsal of the closing ceremony was being delayed.

The Press and television ranks were still packed in hundreds, a testimony primarily to Thompson's reputation; never mind that, in his one blind spot of immaturity, he still treats the Press with ill-mannered discourtesy. He has latterly refused to speak to *The Times*, for instance, because my colleague, Pat Butcher, excluded Thompson – correctly, as it proved – from his medal forecasts.

But now, for all his injuries, he was running with characteristic guts. He slotted in at the back of the field alongside Bright, who needed to beat him by some 10 seconds to take the bronze, and 10 yards astern of Tarnovetski, who had to beat him by more. Way out ahead, Steen was the unknown factor. On the final lap Thompson somehow managed to accelerate, left Bright and Tarnovetski behind, and had the 13th fastest time of 4 min 45.11 sec. But Steen, two years his junior, had recorded 4:23.20, the fourth best time, and had taken the bronze behind Schenk and Voss.

Thompson limped away, a dispirited figure. 'I don't want to make excuses, but I have this little injury,' he said, trying to put on a brave face. Two defeats have dented his image of invincibility. There is no knowing how much a wife and child have reduced his competitive thirst, his incentive to train for countless hours each week. 'I'm going to continue – for another two or three years I reckon.' The voice was optimistic, yet seemed not to measure what will be required to come back. Schenk will get better while Thompson's snap in the explosive sprinting and jumping events has declined.

He has reached that point at which, even when fit, courage alone cannot carry him through. He can, however, look back upon a unique career. The recognition of that yesterday came with the handshakes from his rivals before they went their own ways off into the night.

A GOLD MEDAL FOR THE GAMES MASTERS
The Times, October 1988

Seoul: As I walked away from the closing ceremony of the 1988 Olympic Games, just before the end, a haunting oriental chorale still drifted upwards to the night sky. I was more than ever in love with Korea. Confronted with the largest Games in history, they had been the perfect hosts. The debt which the Olympic movement owes them is immense. The Koreans have the organisation of the Germans, the courtesy and culture of the Orient and the sense of money of the Americans. They can hardly fail. It is undoubtedly true that the Games always tend to bring out the best in a host nation, but few, if any, have given so much, and on such a scale, as have these remarkable people for the past two weeks: or, should I say, for the past seven years.

The worst had been expected. The International Olympic Committee and its president had been condemned for allowing the Games to go ahead here. Yet what has been achieved by a nation that 30 years ago was a bomb-site, and when it was awarded the Games in 1981 was a pariah to most Socialist countries, is phenomenal.

The North Koreans did not terrorise us, the Socialists did not boycott, the students threw only a handful of token petrol bombs. The only injuries we have are our telephone bills in a city where it costs almost as much to have a suit cleaned as to have it made. Even the Korean autumn has smiled upon us delightfully, someone pointing out that for the past two weeks it has been raining in Nagoya, the Japanese city to which Seoul was preferred.

The largest Games in history – in size, technology and publicity – have been an exceptional success. There has been a degree of friendship, from the level of foreign diplomacy down to local taxi drivers and shopkeepers, which may come to be seen as a milestone in social and political history. These Games may have had more influence than can yet be estimated.

There was a scandal which vibrated to the farthest corners of sport and throughout the population of Canada but which, in the long term, will, optimistically, prove to be a significant deterrent to others. It was nothing to do with Korea.

Considering some of the logistical problems, mostly accentuated through lack of language communications, the Koreans were more helpful, more accommodating than the hosts of any other Games I have attended. In spite of the intensity of security, I was admitted to the gymnastics hall when I had forgotten my accreditation card and was allowed into the regatta course competition area in a taxi without a private badge, on each occasion with careful scrutiny. I cannot imagine such understanding flexibility having taken place in Montreal, Moscow or Los Angeles.

The Games of Seoul provided competition facilities without

parallel, setting a standard that Barcelona, or any other city, will find an immense challenge to equal. The Koreans advanced the public perception of the Games more than anybody since the West Germans in 1972.

The achievement of the South Korean team, finishing in fourth place in the medal table, could have one profound influence upon the future of the Games during the next 12 years. It is unlikely that China, which finished 11th, would wish to stage the Games of 2000 if it could not expect to be the highest Asian medals winner. Japan, incidentally, finished 14th, and was hugely embarrassed by Korea in the judo competition, hitherto an exclusive Japanese domain. When you look around, and 80 per cent of the population seems to be under 35, the nation's potential is unlimited.

The friendship of these Games has overflowed. At the closing ceremony Arabs and Israelis walked round the track with total informality, side by side. Such anti-Americanism as there has been among the Koreans has been largely inspired by the NBC inquisitorial television coverage of boxing, a sore point since the blatant American bias of judging in 1984.

The closing ceremony was as colourful as the opening ceremony, tasteful and elegant. The Koreans have a cultural tradition in music and singing, in theatre and dance, which makes their ceremonial accomplishment no surprise. They welcomed us and bid us goodbye with such warmth that it is sad to be going. At one stage in the closing ceremony it looked as if the uninhibited disorganisation among thousands of athletes in the arena – the worst offenders being the British – was going to get out of control, yet the Koreans handled the situation with a discretion that few would have managed under the eye of television. With competitors swarming around them, the ceremonial dancers smiled as benignly as ever.

The philosophical conception behind many of the Koreans' actions is such as to make Europeans feel humble. In what some might regard as a frivolous or shallow life spent following sport, this has for me been a fortnight of exceptional courtesy and co-operation: as Juan Antonio Samaranch said in his closing speech, the best and most unified of Games.

> The worry for Bruno was that he might not survive against Tyson. The worry for Tyson is that he may not survive against himself.

ANXIETY FOR THE CHAMPION
The Times, February 1989

Las Vegas: I am sorry, in a sense, for Frank Bruno. There is much more reason this morning, however, to be sorry for Mike Tyson, which may sound an odd thing to say about the man who has just emphatically re-established himself as undisputed world heavyweight champion. More than ever, though, I am sorry for boxing.

The best bout at the Las Vegas Hilton on Saturday evening was the WBC superflyweight title contest between Azumah Nelson, of Ghana, and Mario Martinez, of Mexico, a minor classic in which Martinez, narrowly beaten by the champion a year ago, gave another courageous and skilful challenge before the fluctuating bout was stopped in favour of Nelson in the twelfth. The audience, gorged on the commercial hype and gambling on the imminent main event, hardly noticed these splendid contestants.

Do not be seduced into any feeling that Bruno was noble or unlucky. As a boxer, he is not worthy to be mentioned in the same breath as Tommy Farr or Henry Cooper. What he managed to achieve, as a no-hoper, was a dignified and brave exit that lasted, improbably, for five rounds in the course of a financial sting, following which he should retire richer and wiser.

Because Bruno was a European contender around whom tickets and television could be sold in a muddled heavyweight field, the commercial circus granted him a shot at the title. If Tyson had been an inch or so more accurate with the second right-hander which put Bruno down in the first 18 seconds of the contest, it would probably have been all over within the first minute. As it was, the combination of Tyson's slight rustiness after eight months out of the ring and Bruno's ability illegally to lock his left arm round Tyson's head and hang on for much of four rounds extended an encounter which had only one possible outcome from the first bell.

Terry Lawless' main contribution was to have one hand permanently at the ready to fling in the towel the moment the rain of Tyson's fists became no longer acceptable. For tunately, the referee, in the pulverising fifth round, acted even more swiftly than Lawless, and if the record will show that Bruno finished on his feet, that was only because the referee was holding him up against the ropes after Tyson had all but knocked his head off.

To Bruno's credit, he absorbed more punches than had been supposed possible, thanks in part to the referee's long-winded warning for an illegal punch on the back of Tyson's neck in the first round, which gave Bruno another invaluable 12-second breather.

The background of the year-long on-off saga of this match is that Bruno and his handlers have made a killing from the mismatch – Jarvis Astaire and Mickey Duff looked uncommonly anxious during the moments beforehand – and Tyson has landed himself in the hands of one of the most objectionable men in the clouded history of this sport. Watching Don King cavorting around Tyson this past week, manipulating Press conferences, gratuitously insulting people and patronising his new charge, has been to witness a formidable heavyweight champion becoming ensnared in surroundings which may ultimately prove more threatening to his stability as a man than those from which he has recently freed himself.

The failing marriage to Robin Givens may have been doomed from the start; but Tyson's additional abandonment of almost all the contacts with the Cus D'Amato stable, which had rescued him from being a hoodlum and made him into a champion, seems almost equally ill-advised. King, his son Carl, and the multitude of handlers assembled around the champion under the presumptuous title 'Team Tyson' will consume a colossal slice of the champion's earnings; while the loss of his long-term trainer, Kevin Rooney, and his former manager, Bill Cayton, with whom a contract dispute continues, will diminish the forces of responsibility that served to keep an impulsive, emotional and aggressive boxer on the rails at least some of the time.

I fear that Tyson, who is almost unchallengeable in the ring, yet clearly from Saturday's evidence against even a moderate opponent needs tactical advice, may not be able to marshal the enormous pressures which bear down on someone as famous, rich and vulnerable as he is. His immature vulgarity, in pretending to expose himself insultingly to Bruno on stage in public at the weigh-in, is just one small illustration of his instability. His lewdness in public is already regrettably well-documented.

When Tyson says, at his victory Press conference, that 'challengers with primitive skills are as good as dead', we wonder how many of those words may ultimately turn to become true of him. For the moment, his consuming power, the quickness of his hands, the variety of his hooks and the stunning ferocity of his uppercuts were an arsenal which overwhelmed Bruno, who never had any objective beyond survival without serious injury, in order that he may enjoy his rewards.

The injuries that may yet befall Tyson, outside the ring, are far more alarming in potential. Last week he told Johnny Tocco, father-confessor to so many fighters at his downtown gymnasium, that he had no friends he could trust. We have too often seen the mortality of heroes without friends. The fate of heroes without respect for the public is even more in doubt. Tyson was reminded last week of the words of Jack Dempsey: 'A champion owes everybody something. He can never pay back for all the help he got for making him an idol.'

AFTERWORD

The twentieth anniversary of Open Tennis in 1988 was a reminder that ever-escalating, big-money sports sponsorship had also become a fact of life in this same time-frame. In these decades, tennis, for instance, has seen its annual *chiffre d'affaires* rocket from one million to one-hundred million dollars; and any company seeking high-profile exposure for its product at an America's Cup series must these days be prepared to bid in a billion, instead of a million, dollar market. Besides the obvious advantages to both parties, the marriage of sports arenas to board rooms inevitably brings intense public interest.

The business of sports is examined in more detail year by year. Editors' demands for 'background' no longer focus essentially on the performers. Major features are now more likely to highlight the policies and positions of heads of state, ministers and national associations, down to managers, agents and coaches: a far cry from what was expected in earlier times. A top feature-writer must now have automatic access to the secret corridors where influence is brokered, and beyond his journalistic skills also be erudite enough to analyse the complex interlocking of sports with world markets and politics.

David Miller has proved to a succession of editors that in these respects he is the unquestioned leader. I have had the pleasure of knowing David as a friend since he was first featured in *The Times* (1956-59), then by the *Daily* and *Sunday Telegraph* (1959-73) and by the *Daily Express* (1973-82), before being re-called by *The Times* to his current post of chief sports correspondent. In these years, millions of readers have learned from him the idiosyncracies and implications of the world's major fixtures. He has made clearer the impact of sports business on our daily lives, whether from the latest pronouncements at Lord's, the International Athletics Federation, FIFA, or on-site drug controversies in the Olympics; even to the IOC President attending a small-town mass in the South Pacific. David is on record as saying he has never worried about being neither a Gallico nor a Hemingway. To everyday sports section readers this is immaterial. What we most welcome from him is his capacity to pinpoint sport's recurring iniquities, while balancing these against those deepfelt human emotions that are ultimately at the heart of every performer's performance.

The citation that accompanied David's much coveted Granada TV Award made a point of his attempt always 'to be fair' in his writings. This selection of David's columns illustrates the point very clearly. It also shows the ease with which he can switch his observations from Wembley to Augusta, Georgia, or from the Oxford and Cambridge boat race to Wimbledon or the West Indies. I cannot imagine anyone, however remotely interested in today's sporting scene, its personalities and its stormy cross-currents, not having enjoyed this anthology. If there was ever a read for all seasons, this is it.

Ted Tinling
Director International Liaison
Virginia Slims Series
Philadelphia